Imperial Russia 1801–1905

D0783306

Imperial Russia was at the height of its power and influence in the nineteenth century, and seemed set to dominate Europe after the defeat of Napoleon at Waterloo in 1815. However this threat came to nothing. Despite the efforts of successive Tsars, the country remained backward and bureaucratic. When at last change occurred, it was through the work of the revolutionaries during the 1917 Revolution.

Imperial Russia 1801–1905 traces the development of the Russian Empire from the murder of 'mad Tsar Paul' to the reforms of the 1890s that were an attempt to modernise the autocratic state. Each Tsar's reign is analysed in turn:

- Alexander I (1801–25)
- Nicholas I (1825–55)
- Alexander II (1855–81)
- Alexander III (1881–94).

The political, economic and foreign policy of the Tsars is discussed, as well as Russia's cultural developments, particularly in literature. The fascinating events of the Crimean War and the emancipation of the serfs are set in the context of the main themes of the period. The reign of Nicholas II is also introduced with the background to the Russian Revolution.

Imperial Russia 1801–1905 is essential reading for all students of the topic and provides a clear and concise introduction to the contentious historical debates of nineteenth-century Russia.

Tim Chapman teaches History at Wisbech Grammar School in Cambridgeshire. He is author of *The Congress of Vienna* (Routledge, 1998).

Imperial Russia 1801–1905

Tim Chapman

London and New York

HOUSTON PUBLIC LIBRARY

R01255 52491

First published 2001
by Routledge
11 New Fetter Lane, London EC4P 4EE

Simultaneously published in the USA and Canada
by Routledge
29 West 35th Street, New York, NY 10001

Routledge is an imprint of the Taylor & Francis Group

© 2001 Tim Chapman

Typeset in Sabon by
HWA Text and Data Management, Tunbridge Wells
Printed and bound in Great Britain by
TJ International Ltd, Padstow, Cornwall

All rights reserved. No part of this book may be reprinted or reproduced or utilised in
any form or by any electronic, mechanical, or other means, now known or hereafter
invented, including photocopying and recording, or in any information storage or
retrieval system, without permission in writing from the publishers.

British Library Cataloguing in Publication Data
A catalogue record for this book is available from the British Library

Library of Congress Cataloging in Publication Data
Chapman, Tim, 1964–
    Imperial Russia : 1801–1905 / Tim Chapman.
    p. cm.
    Includes bibliographical references and index.
    1. Russia–History–1801–1917. I. Title.

DK189 .C446 2001
947'.07–dc21   00–054368

ISBN 0–415–23109–4 (hbk)
ISBN 0–415–23110–8 (pbk)

Contents

Tables

Figures

Illustrations

Preface

This book is not based on primary research but tries to synthesise the work of other scholars who have unravelled the history of Russia. I am therefore indebted to countless historians on whose work I have relied. Any errors regarding the evidence or the arguments put forward, however, remain my responsibility alone.

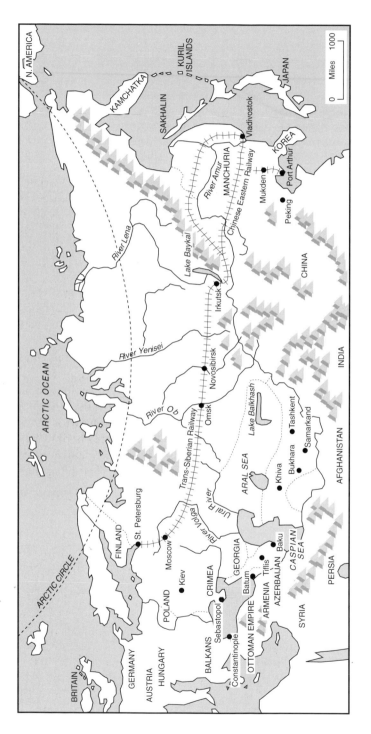

Map of Imperial Russia

Chapter 1

Russia in 1800

Russia has not been like other European states in modern history. On the political edges of Europe until the eighteenth century, it experienced neither the Renaissance nor the Reformation, and developed eastwards towards the Pacific across barbarous and desolate territory to make it an Asiatic power as well as a European one. It consisted of a country that conquered an empire in which its colonies bordered each other and so relied on a vast military-strength to keep control rather than on sea power as west European empires had. Its sheer size, in terms of land mass and population, separated it from other states too as it faced different problems in communications and in mobilising resources. And, until the twentieth century, this slow moving giant used a different calendar and even today it uses the Syrillic alphabet rather than the Arabic letters used in western Europe.

All of this has made Russian history more difficult to understand. In the mid twentieth century, Winston Churchill remarked that '[Russia] is a riddle wrapped up in a mystery inside an enigma'.[1] Even without the complications of Marxist ideology to make Russia more complex, there remain major problems for the historian of the nineteenth century. First, the legacy of Marxist writings in Russian history remains with its exaggerated emphasis on economic progress and class conflict. Second, there continue to be difficulties in finding good sources of information from a nation that remained mostly illiterate until the late nineteenth century. Thus, from a historiographical perspective as well, Russia has remained quite different.

Political structure

In 1800 Russia was an autocracy and as such was governed by an autocrat who took the title of 'tsar' meaning emperor. His power to rule was absolute as there was no parliament, no critical press and very little by way of public opinion. His status was confirmed by the Orthodox Church which assured the people of his divine right to rule on behalf of God, and Article I of the fundamental laws stated 'The Emperor of all the Russias is an autocratic and unlimited monarch. God commands that his supreme power be obeyed out of conscience as well as fear'. Thus, there was little need to issue laws other than by decree and the tsar was the final judge of all policies. His main tasks were to defend Russia from foreign attack and to maintain order within the frontiers and this was something that the Romanov dynasty had been doing since 1613.

In practice, however, the tsar was not entirely free to do as he chose. He was akin to the chief noble whose power was limited by that class and during times of crisis or misrule he could be extremely vulnerable. The Russian system of absolutism was tempered by assassination. Usually, it was the nobles that carried out the task (in their own self-interest) but not always. Thus, Catherine deposed Peter III and then consented to his murder in 1762. Tsar Paul was strangled by army officers acting on nobles' instructions in 1801 and Tsar Alexander I was blown up by a section of the educated élite that claimed to be acting on behalf of the ordinary people in 1881. The nobles expected privileged treatment for their support of the tsar and they got this in the form of exemption from personal taxes and ownership of serfs. The reluctance of nineteenth-century tsars to free the serfs reflected their fear of provoking the nobles' wrath.

The concentration of power in the hands of the tsar was designed to assert Russian control over a vast and unwieldy empire which he did not have the economic or techno-logical resources to enforce by means other than fear and deterrence. Only by demanding total obedience to himself, endorsed by the Church and backed up by a brutal army, could the tsar hope to keep together an empire that stretched from Poland to the Pacific, from the Arctic Circle to China. It was Russia's enormous size that gave it strength in the nineteenth century but it was also this basic fact that was its main weakness. It was never easy to control a large, sometimes restless and often remote population. And the nobility were only committed to the tsarist system while it func-tioned successfully since it upheld their rights as lords of their own estates and gave them considerable local power.

To help him in his rule, the tsar usually enlisted the support of a small number of advisers drawn from the nobility. One of these might emerge as a chief minister periodically, as Speransky or Arakcheyev did under Alexander I, but their hold on power was always precarious and entirely in the gift of the tsar; just as they were responsible to him so they were dependent on him. As many as ten to fifteen further advisers might be used, possibly as the heads of government departments, but equally there could be as few as four or five – as at the start of Alexander I's reign or during that of Nicholas I. Even the structure and organisation of the highest level of government was decided by the tsar and, since so much hinged on his character and preferences, changes could be rapid.

More consistent features of the autocracy were the chief institutions of the state which carried out its policies. The three elements here were the church, army and bureaucracy. The first of these was the Russian Orthodox Church which had split away from the Greek Orthodox in the fifteenth century. It had been rendered powerless in the 1760s when its lands were nationalised, or confiscated, by the state so as to secure a cash income. By 1800 it had become part of the government system, funded by it and used by it, to disseminate information into every village as well as to instruct the inhabitants to remain obedient to the tsar. Indeed the insistence on divine right included special claims for 'holy Russia' as the tsar was seen as a 'little father' who cared for his people in a God-like way. Similarly, Moscow was seen as a "Third Rome' or holy city after the failure of Rome and then Constantinople to provide a haven for Christianity from hostile armies. The leader of the Church was the Over Procurator of the Holy Synod, a layman appointed by the tsar from the early eighteenth century, which ensured effective state supervision.

The army numbered 3–400 000 men in 1800 but from 1812 and for much of the century stood at about one million. It was composed primarily of serfs who were often drafted into it as a punishment. Its military capability lay in part in its size since it could use attrition; Russia's manpower reserves were unlikely to be depleted before those of an enemy. However, it could also fight with skill under the command of officers drawn from the nobility. Tactical retreats were used to finally defeat Napoleon in 1812 and they could attack very successfully too as the succession of victories against Turkey and neighbouring states in Asia demonstrated during the nineteenth century. It was a huge drain on the government's limited finances, though; in 1815 it accounted for about one-third of all revenue.

The bureaucracy was an alternative career for those members of the nobility who did not enter the armed forces or whose estates could not support them. Russia's civil service numbered up to 20 000 in 1800 and it was based mostly in the two main towns, Moscow and Saint Petersburg. Its efficiency might be doubted, though, as in the 1810s the Minister of Justice, Troshchinskii, observed that for most everyday needs 'the greater part of the population of the state depend almost exclusively on local institutions'. It was the task of the tsar's provincial governors to keep him informed and, above all, to maintain order in each of Russia's fifty or so provinces. Compared to western Europe the bureaucracy was under-manned too.

Social structure

The social hierarchy in Russia closely reflected the political order, with the tsar and his court at its pinnacle and then a series of tiers of successively greater numbers of people reaching down to the serfs and peasants. The intermediate groups included the nobility, Church, army officers, merchants and bureaucrats each of which could overlap in terms of wealth and status, but despite this Russian society was not complex. Its most complicating feature was the diversity of nationalities within the empire.

The nobles amounted to just one per cent of the population. They were composed of an élite aristocracy with large estates and access to high government positions, and a lesser gentry class with smaller landholdings and fewer serfs. The aristocrats could typically trace their ancestors back almost a millennium to the foundation of Russia and they often took the title of 'Prince' (as did members of the royal family) although this might be translated as Grand Duke. Titles were inherited by all children. The nobles had effective control of their large estates since they enforced order and obedience among the serfs and in practice they were the most powerful individuals in the Russian Empire's provinces. The provincial governors were, of course, drawn from this class too.

The gentry were a lesser class but often lent their name to include the nobles. They held land which might be worked by a few dozen serfs but was very unlikely to exceed one hundred; about one-third owned fewer than ten serfs. Like the nobles, their social status was diverse, but it was the wish of many to advance up into the higher echelons of the hierarchy and the usual routes of advancement were the armed forces and bureaucracy. Although service to the state was not compulsory in 1800, many still spent some time working in this way. Thus, the social strata were woven into the framework of the state's institutions. The gentry (and nobles) were the political nation of Russia since they wielded considerable influence over the tsars despite not formally having any right to vote for either central or local parliaments. Their power was that much greater because of the absence of any significant middle-class too. Russian economic development was based on expanding traditional agricultural and manufacturing practices rather than innovating and changing the way they were organised. There were therefore almost no factory owners and the commercial middle class was composed of traders; among these were many Jews based primarily in Poland.

The clergy belonged mostly to the Russian Orthodox Church although there were some Lutheran (German Protestant) groups along the Baltic coast. Each village had a priest who remained with it all his life. He was allowed to marry (but not to re-marry) and his main function was to perform religious ceremonies – baptisms, marriages, burials – rather like a clerk or administrator. There was little by way of Biblical teaching since the level of education most priests achieved was quite low, but many of the sacred texts were related and even recited to the village. The clergy's income was made up of fees for the religious ceremonies and from their own farming practices since each priest had some land of his own. Above the village priests was a hierarchy of bishops as well as a tier of monks from whom the prelates were selected and this was the main distinction in the personnel of the church; between the 'black clergy' at the village level and the 'white clergy' or monks. The church as a whole received about four million roubles a year from the state (one per cent of its revenue) and this supplemented the priests' incomes too, albeit in a rather meagre way.

By far the largest group in the population was the peasantry which was composed of two main groups; the serfs and the state peasants. As with the nobles and gentry, the terms serf and peasant are often used interchangeably, but this is misleading. The serfs were privately owned labourers who could be bought and sold like livestock and amounted to almost half of the entire population. The state peasants belonged to the state (rather then to the royal family) but were in the gift of the tsar and they were often given away to nobles as a reward for services rendered; they accounted for 40 per cent of all rural workers. The Romanov family and the Church also owned a number of peasants amounting to some 10 per cent of the workforce. Altogether, the peasants and serfs made up 90–95 per cent of the population and it was therefore their labour that generated Russia's wealth.

Not all of the empire operated a servile economy, though. It was concentrated in European Russia, west of the Urals, and new territory that was acquired through conquest was by no means certain to be subjected to the system. Even within the areas in which it operated there was diversity since in the far north as few as six per cent of some villages were populated by serfs but in the provinces around Moscow the proportion was 70 per cent. The reasons for such differences were mostly strategic; in areas where Russia did not fear attack, there was little need to tie labourers to a particular estate but in the heart-lands of Russia the tsars had been keen to a hold on potential recruits to the army.

Conditions for the serfs were grim. Their masters had the right to sell them, flog them, exile them to Siberia or send them to the army for a typical twenty-five year period. Most serfs worked the land for their landlord (sometimes for six days out of seven) under a system called 'barschina'. It was most common in the black earth belt in the southern part of European Russia where the soil was fertile since lords wanted to maximise their own harvests. It could also extend to serfs who had to work in the lord's household as a domestic servant, and 200 000 were in this situation. Alternatively, serfs might work under the 'obrok' system in which they paid their lord cash (or goods) instead. This method allowed serfs to work in industrial jobs either on the lord's own estate or in a nearby town.

Working conditions were very difficult in either situation since the bulk of the landowners did not run their estates efficiently; the money that the state lent to them on the strength of their assets was often squandered on luxury goods rather than invested in new equipment or better farming practices. The workers themselves had little incentive to increase production beyond their own immediate needs – even if they had the ability to improve their land – since any surpluses were likely to be taken from them. However, there was little scope for them to improve their lot since there were desperately few schools. In 1800 there were no more than 70 000 children receiving primary education and most of those were in towns, so the level of rural literacy was extremely low – well below five per cent even in European Russia.

Taxation fell especially hard on this group, the poorest of all Russia's people, since it had to pay a poll tax (from which the nobles were exempt) and it paid again through taxes on alcohol, where the state operated a monopoly on vodka production. Over half the government's revenue was raised through these two taxes. The plight of peasants and serfs often became desperate and it was not surprising therefore that they could become restless and unruly in times of particular hardship; riots and violent protests were endemic to the Russian countryside.

Finally, it is important to bear in mind that Russia's population was not just made up of those of Russian extraction. By 1800, it included many ethnic and national groups such as the Germans living along the Baltic coast, Poles, Jews and Finns in Europe; and in Asia there were tribal groups that stretched across Siberia and about which Russia knew little. Nor were all Russians quite the same. There were 'Great Russians' whose focus was Moscow, 'Little Russians' based in the Ukraine and Kiev, and 'White Russians' who lived in Belarus. Cultural tensions between these groups remained from their medieval past. A further group that considered itself at least semi-independent was the Cossacks who lived in the southern lands of Russia and who had a reputation as excellent cavalrymen. By 1800, their autonomy was much reduced as they were obliged to fight for the tsar, and their skills on horseback were probably exaggerated. Still, they added to the diverse nature of society under the tsar's control.

The Russian economy

If the great size of Russia was its main weakness politically, then conversely this was its great strength economically. The vast expanses of territory were difficult to control but they were inhabited by huge numbers of people. With a population close to forty million in 1800, Russia was by far the largest of the European states. Its closest rival was France with just 27 and then Austria with 25. However, estimates do vary as to how large Russia's population was because it is difficult to find any statistical sources that are reliable. The first census was taken as late as 1897 and, despite the large bureaucracy, even this missed out entire provinces. Consequently, surveys of the Russian economy at this time tend to focus on characteristics rather than on ratios or figures; they tend to be qualitative rather than quantitative. Approximately 95 per cent of Russia's people lived in the countryside and even the main towns were quite small by western European standards.

The Russian economy was overwhelmingly agricultural. The system of farming for both serfs and peasants was based on the village community or 'mir' which operated

Table 1.1 Comparison of Russian and west European urban centres, *c.*1800

Town	Population	Town	Population
Saint Petersburg	300 000	London	960 000
Moscow	250 000	Manchester	75 000
Kiev	20 000	Birmingham	71 000
Odessa	11 000		
		Paris	600 000
		Rome	150 000

an inefficient three field rotation of crops that had been developed in the middle ages. This meant that many areas of Russia were unable to manage anything more than subsistence farming and that they were vulnerable to periodic famines. The worst problems of this kind occurred in 1891–2 and 1898. By contrast, there were some quite fertile areas such as the black earth belt of Great Russia and the steppes of the Ukraine which produced grain surpluses that were then transported to areas of shortage, but the size of the empire and the difficulty in moving goods of any kind through it meant that shortages persisted.

Transport links were poor. Roads were merely earth tracks of varying widths that were adequate in the warm summer months but became muddy or impassable in winter. Water-borne transport was difficult too since Russia's coastline was not continuous and its northern reaches (both in the White Sea and the Baltic) froze in winter. This same problem applied to many of its rivers which prevented barges distributing goods efficiently. Moreover, the warm water ports that Russia acquired on the Black Sea during the eighteenth century were very far distant from the main population centres. The route from Azov to Moscow was over 400 miles for instance. There were no railways, of course, until the 1830s and Russia was among the slowest of the European states to adopt them.

The severity of the Russian winters also left large tracts of its land unusable and the inhabitants impoverished. Parts of Siberia were subject to perma-frost that never melted and anyway access was difficult through dense forests. Moreover, in the outlying regions of the empire Russian control was not complete and local disputes with frontier tribesmen or hostile local populations meant that economic development of newly acquired areas could be very slow. This was true of Poland and especially the Caucasus.

Russia's most obvious economic asset was a mixed blessing. The system of serfdom was enshrined in law by Tsar Alexis in 1649 to ensure the security of the nobles' estates while they were away from home. Their absence had been required of them by the state so that they could carry out official business either in the army or the civil service. The guarantee of a compliant workforce might have offered advantages to enterprising nobles who could innovate on their estates either agriculturally or commercially, but this rarely happened. Economic specialisation remained minimal as each estate continued to produce the same crops primarily for its own needs and the labourers, who were tied to one estate, were also poorly educated. In practice, this meant an inflexible workforce of great size but little skill. In 1800, for example, 600 000 men were employed simply hauling barges along rivers.

Yet Russia did have some economic advantages. It had huge natural mineral resources which, in time, it was able to exploit. From the 1630s there had been an iron-working industry based in the Urals and this continued to expand in the eighteenth century so that by c.1750 it was the world's largest producer with a total of two million poods of pig iron (33 000 tonnes). By 1800 it was producing nearly ten million poods (160 000 tonnes). Russia also developed its textile industries (linen, silk, wool and cotton), tanneries, paper mills, mining (copper as well as iron) and candle manufacture. By the start of the nineteenth century there were 95 000 industrial workers.

The state had played a part in this process too. Tsar Peter the Great (1689–1725) had imported some western ideas and techniques in the early eighteenth century so as to modernise Russia. He set up a number of factories to serve the needs of the state (especially its army and navy) around his new capital, Saint Petersburg. Thus, the priorities were armaments, metallurgy, timber and cloth. Some of the two hundred factories he set up survived into the late eighteenth century.

Most of the units of production were small with only a handful of workers, often using traditional methods of production in their workshops. Rather than the emergence of large-scale enterprises using significant sums of capital to make use of modern technology, Russian industrial activity at this time saw the concentration of handicraft techniques in some areas. The 323 metal-fabricating workshops in the village of Pavlov in Nizhni-Novgorod province were an exception to the usual absence of specialisation. It was not quite unique as the textile works around Moscow, Saratov and Pavlov demonstrated.

The overall pattern of the Russian economy remained agrarian at the start of the nineteenth century and the few examples of industrial activity there were did not amount to industrialisation. Most people still worked on estates either as the property of the state or as serfs. While most of the population lived to the east of the Urals in the wide lowland plain of European Russia, this was again something that had more potential for the future than for the immediate enrichment of Russia in 1800.

Tsarist policies in Russia

The political and social systems in Russia that have been outlined so far provide only a static view of the situation by 1800. Change, of course, was also part of the process as each aspect of the Russian state adapted to new circumstances. The core population grew steadily for instance, but jumped forward when new lands were added and society tended to become more complex as a result; the autocracy and political culture could become more or less severe according to the character of each new tsar; and the economy lurched forwards or backwards according to war-time or peace-time needs. It is therefore useful to survey briefly the main developments of the eighteenth century to set out the direction in which problems and policies were flowing by 1800.

Political struggle at the very top of the autocracy was a constant feature. The assassinations of several tsars have already been highlighted but they were only part of the process as the succession was vulnerable to dynastic upheaval and threats from the noble class. The Romanov ruling family had come to power in 1613 after what was called the 'Time of Troubles' during the previous fifteen years and this had been caused when the Muscovite dynasty died out. Towards the end of the century, Peter the Great came to power as a joint tsar with his older half-brother Ivan V and his half-sister Sophia who reigned as regent 1682–89; the end of Peter's reign was no easier either as his only male heir, Alexis, was completely opposed to his father's reforms and this so incensed Peter that Alexis was sentenced to death. However, before this could be carried out, Alexis died during torture. More complicated still, Peter then issued a Law of Succession in 1722 in which the hereditary principle was ignored and the sitting ruler was empowered to nominate his or her successor. Unfortunately, Peter failed to nominate anyone before his death in 1725 with the result that over the next thirty-seven years Russia was subject to endless court intrigues between the six prospective heirs – whether direct or indirect descendants.

The situation only resolved itself in 1762 when Catherine II ('the Great') emerged as a strong tsarina capable of asserting effective control over the court and over Russia itself. In-fighting was banished during her reign following the murder of her husband, but the succession of more than twenty lovers meant that there was probably no royal Romanov blood in any of her offspring. And finally, Catherine herself set up another situation liable to cause confusion after her death. She was on bad terms with her first-born son, Paul, because she feared that her enemies might use him in an attempt to overthrow her. Paul had been taken away from her care by the previous tsarina and this made Catherine more suspicious; but she in turn raised Paul's two oldest sons, Alexander and Constantine, and prepared them for when they might become tsar. There was even the possibility that the succession would by-pass Paul altogether. In the event, Paul did become the ruler of Russia when his mother died in 1796 but he was disliked by many of the nobles and was murdered in a plot that included Alexander after just five years, in 1801. This was by no means the end of the dynastic troubles of the succession. Problems resurfaced again in 1825 when the throne passed from Alexander to his unsuspecting younger brother Nicholas and missed out Constantine altogether.

The threat from the nobles was a second long-term consideration in the struggle for supreme power in Russia. In any period of weak leadership, the nobles tended to become more independent and to try to assert more influence over the policies of the tsars or to secure more local autonomy. A clear example of the nobles' independence from the tsars can be found in the Time of Troubles in the early seventeenth century, but the problem can be traced back into Russia's medieval past as political control from Moscow (or, earlier, from Kiev) had to be wrested from an unruly and violent land. This was why the system of autocracy had developed to such an extent by 1800.

During the eighteenth century, the nobles' assault on tsarist power came in two ways. First, at the political centre, a group of nobles emerged in the late 1720s after Peter the Great's death who seemed ready to take control of Russia's government on behalf of the twelve-year-old Tsar Peter II. They formed a Privy Council and tried to impose a constitution on the Tsarina Anna in the 1730s, only to be beaten by a lack of support

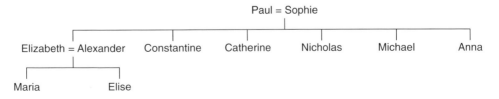

Figure 1.1 The Romanov family tree

from the rest of their class. This, though, allowed a second provincially based attack to be made. The nobles were granted a series of new rights and powers from the 1730s onwards which enhanced their control of local government and their own estates. The law of primogeniture was abolished, they were given greater police and judicial powers over the serfs and they were also made responsible for the collection of taxes from them. By 1760 they additionally had the power to exile serfs to hard labour in Siberia. Thus, the system of serfdom was gradually extended in the course of the eighteenth century partly as a means of keeping the support of the nobles.

From 1762 the nobles were no longer compelled to enter the service of the state and, lastly, in 1785 Catherine the Great formalised the status of the nobles as a privileged class in the Charter of the Nobility, which affirmed their exemption from taxes and absolute property rights. This left the nobility as a powerful political and social class with which all nineteenth century tsars had to work closely. In particular it meant that any attempt to abolish serfdom was going to be extremely difficult and this accounts for why Tsars Alexander I and Nicholas I only dared to tinker with the system. Not until the reign of Alexander II was serfdom finally abolished, in 1861.

The rebelliousness of the serfs was a further issue that tsars had to address. The vast numbers of serfs made them a considerable threat to the autocracy especially if there was any co-ordinated rebellion. The sparsely populated terrain made this unlikely since communication between peasant communities was difficult and they were always encouraged to be loyal to their lord and to the tsar. Despite this, peasant revolts were frequent and could be substantial as those led by Razin (1667–71), Bulavin (1707–08) and Pugachev (1773–75) demonstrated. This last example involved various disaffected groups along the River Volga who rallied behind a Cossack deserter who claimed to be Tsar Peter III and who promised an end to serfdom, taxation and military service. Over 1500 nobles were killed and the total number of victims approached 3000. This served as a warning to the tsar and nobles alike that even their hold on power could be precarious and that the mismanagement of issues such as the emancipation of the serfs could ignite spontaneous rebellions. This was why the committees that considered the issue of emancipation in the nineteenth century were always held in secret.

Tsarist policies abroad

Just as the tsars encountered regular threats to their position from within Russia, so there were dangers from abroad. By 1800, the pursuit of security, which was the primary aim of foreign policy, had come to focus on western and southern Europe. The northern frontier was safe since the Arctic Circle froze out any danger of attack from there and Sweden had been effectively defeated as a rival power in the Baltic as far back as 1721. The frontier to the east across the vast expanses of Siberia (reaching as far as the Pacific Ocean) was safe as it had been conquered in the early seventeenth century. The huge distance involved also afforded its own protection.

In western Europe, the key concern was Poland. This was subject to strong Russian influence not least because it was the Russian-backed candidate, Augustus, who emerged as the king after the War of the Polish Succession 1733–35. Poland acted as a buffer state for Russia and, as a weak neighbour, represented no threat to Russia itself. However, Poland was partitioned between 1772 and 1795 and thereafter ceased to exist as a sovereign state until 1919. In 1815 Russia took the bulk of Poland's territory in the form of 'Congress Poland' which left Prussia to take Posen and Thorn, and Austria with Galicia.

In southern Europe, it was Turkey that posed the problem. It was Russia's long term ambition to have naval access to the west not only through the Baltic but also through the Black Sea since the advantages it stood to gain were economic as well as naval. A further reason for Russia's conflict with the Ottoman Empire was the ambition of Catherine the Great (1762–96) to expel the Turks from Europe and create a Greek empire under her grandson Constantine. This was her so-called 'Greek Project'. Russia fought a series of wars against Turkey and through these extended its territory across the whole length of the northern shore of the Black Sea, including the Crimean peninsula. This area was then fortified and a Black Sea fleet constructed. The Russian impact on Turkey was the deeper because from 1774 it claimed the right to protect Christian subjects within the largely Moslem Turkish Empire. This right was asserted from the Treaty of Kutchuk-Kainardji.

One last feature of Russian foreign policy in the eighteenth century was the adoption of western technology which was used by the state to kick-start the economy's industrialisation and to modernise the armed forces. The key phase of this was under Peter the Great in the early eighteenth century but there were other times when foreign help was injected into Russia. It tended to discourage entrepreneurial activity by nobles as they looked to the tsars for initiative.

The reign of Tsar Paul 1796–1801

Catherine the Great died in 1796 having devoted the last years of her life to the final partition of Poland which took place in 1795. While she detested the ideas that lay behind the French Revolution of 1789 she did not fight against the French (managing instead to persuade Prussia and Austria to do so). But Russia could not ignore the threat indefinitely and in 1799 Tsar Paul joined the Second Coalition with Britain, Austria and Turkey against France. His generals met with some success – especially Suvorov in Italy – but the coalition fell apart due to a lack of trust and co-operation and by 1800 Tsar Paul was hoping to reach an agreement with Napoleon and was becoming more hostile to Britain. The policies he pursued against Britain were unpopular with some sections of the nobility as they had little coherence. This was plain from his proposed attack on India with just 20 000 Cossacks and also in his revival of the Armed Neutrality of the North; this had been devised originally by Catherine with the purpose of uniting the northern states around the Baltic Sea against British maritime supremacy. The attack on India was unlikely to succeed and the Armed Neutrality risked Russia's trade with Britain. 'In several months, Russia will be the laughing stock of Europe' complained Panin, one of the future conspirators against Paul.

Paul did little to endear himself to the nobles as he brought down a climate of fear in Russia during his reign. Despite freeing 12 000 people from prison in 1796, in the course of his reign Paul authorised the arrest of over 3 000 army officers, including 333 generals. He revoked part of the Charter to the Nobility which had enshrined the nobles' privileges and he imposed new regulations on the army that were so unpopular that 3 500 officers resigned. He even interfered with the nobles' private property by passing laws concerning the serfs. To some observers at the time, his policies and even he himself were described as mad. In more recent times, historians have accounted for his behaviour by pointing to the number of years he had to wait until he became tsar, at the age of forty-two. This may have made him determined to make an immediate impact as shown by the huge number of laws and decrees he passed; estimates vary but some of them reach as high as 48 000.

Paul's position soon became vulnerable to criticism and, by 1800, there were rumours of a conspiracy forming against him. They were well founded. A group of nobles began to plot Paul's fall from late 1800 and the matter became urgent in March 1801 when he confronted one of them about the possibility of his assassination. The five leading figures were Panin, Pahlen, Bennigsen and the Zubov brothers. On 21 March, Alexander (Paul's oldest son and the heir to the throne) was persuaded by Pahlen to join the conspiracy, although he did so on the understanding that his father was to be removed from power but not killed. Thus, on the night of the 23 March 1801, a group of Guards officers led by Bennigsen and Pahlen entered Tsar Paul's bedroom in the Mikhailovsky Palace. The events that followed are not entirely clear, but after a brief exchange of words there was certainly a struggle between Paul and some of the officers. In the course of this, he was struck first with a snuffbox and then strangled to death with a sash. Murder may not have been the intention of the conspirators as they had already drafted a decree for Paul to sign in which he was to announce his abdication, but they had hurried to write another document that proclaimed Alexander as the new tsar. He reacted very badly to the news of his father's death, having believed – perhaps naïvely – that no harm would come to him. 'I cannot go on with it', he said 'I have no strength to reign. Let someone else take over from me.'[2]

Despite this remorse and reluctance, Alexander did assume the leadership of Russia in March 1801. His position as tsar may have seemed precarious at first but within a matter of weeks he had become accustomed to the responsibilities of his position and after a few months was able to dismiss the coup's conspirators from the court. In this way, the government of Russia remained firmly in the hands of one man who ruled as an autocrat. As such, his views and personality, and those of each successive ruler, remained the crucial element in the direction of policies both at home and abroad throughout the nineteenth century. What may seem to be an undue preoccupation with personalities among historians is in fact the key to understanding the major developments. It is for this reason that Russian history in the nineteenth century is best organised in terms of the Romanov tsars who reigned: Alexander I 1801–25, Nicholas I 1825–55, Alexander II 1855–81, Alexander III 1881–94 and finally Nicholas II whose reign straddled two centuries 1894–1917.

Notes

1 W. Churchill, *Into Battle*, radio broadcast, 1941.
2 A. Palmer, *Alexander I: Tsar of War and Peace*, London, 1974.

Chapter 2

The reign of Alexander I

The enigmatic Tsar

Tsar Alexander I reigned 1801–25 but was reluctant to rule at all. His reasons for this were complicated and were bound up in his complex, sometimes unfathomable, character; he was impulsive, hesitant, secretive, sometimes confused and prone to contradictions. He wanted to be liberal but by the end of the reign he had reinforced the autocracy around himself and built up the obstacles to reform. He cared about Russia and considered reforms to its legal and political systems but in practice managed to change very little; in fact, the second half of his reign was marked by severe repression under his first minister Arakcheyev. By contrast he achieved a great deal abroad on behalf of other states, first by freeing some of them of French rule and then by supporting, in some cases, the start of constitutional government. Alexander, then, was an enigmatic tsar.

Alexander I: biography and background

Alexander was born on 24 December 1777, the first son of Tsar Paul but both he and Constantine, his younger brother by two years, were taken away from their parents in early childhood by their grandmother, Catherine the Great. She did this so that she personally could tutor and prepare them for ruling Russia in the future. While she was progressive in her thinking on education, she was also a committed autocrat and so she combined a desire to make the boys aware of the modern ideas of the enlightenment with a firm view on the importance of keeping an absolute grip on power. Recent commentators such as Janet Hartley in her biography 'Alexander I' have emphasised the liberal aspects of this education, but it all took place emphatically within an autocratic framework.[1] The splendid court surroundings, the absolute right of the tsar or tsarina to rule and the subservience of the state bureaucracy were all accepted features. Thus, while Alexander had one very liberal tutor called La Harpe, he also had several others who were conservative or reactionary; in particular, General Saltykov was a staunch believer in autocratic rule. Catherine was therefore the first, and probably foremost, influence on Alexander. Her plans for him went beyond his education and onto his marriage as she enjoyed the role of royal matchmaker. At just fifteen he was married to the fourteen-year-old Princess Louise of Baden (renamed Elizabeth when she was accepted into the Orthodox Church). By contrast, Alexander's wife seems to have had no impact in his formative years.

Nevertheless, the role of Frédéric César de La Harpe as Alexander's primary teacher cannot be overlooked. He was a republican and a democrat whose tuition helped to form many of Alexander's ideas from the mid-1780s. He made him consider liberal ideas such as the rights of citizens and the relationship between a ruler and society, but he also reinforced Alexander's tendency to be introspective and to be given to self-doubt. La Harpe encouraged him to reflect on his own failings and to admit to them, even to commit them to paper. As Alexander passed through adolescence this undermined his self-esteem and began to make him want to escape from his future responsibilities. This became a recurrent theme in Alexander's thinking throughout his adult life and was expressed most clearly in his Christian mysticism in which he later yearned, it seems, to become a monk.

A third influence on Alexander was, of course, his own father. Relations between them were not particularly affectionate but Paul did instil into Alexander a regard and even a liking for military matters. This meant attention was paid to parade ground discipline at his father's estate at Gatchina where Paul loved to practise marching and drilling his small guards unit and where he exposed Alexander to the regimentation and order of the army in the early 1790s. When Alexander reached Paris at the end of his campaigns against Napoleon in 1814 he ensured that some 150 000 Russian troops took part in a victory parade. This seems to suggest that his father's passion for military matters at least partly rubbed off on Alexander.

Paul did not have as much success in keeping the support of his oldest son during his short five-year reign 1796–1801. A study of Alexander's correspondence during these years shows that he had some misgivings about his father's rule and that his loyalty was not always certain. Two key letters stand out. The first was written in May 1796 to Victor Kochubei in which he expressed his desire to escape from the burden of political decision making and to live quietly as a private individual in Germany instead. The second letter dates from September 1797 and was written to La Harpe. He repeated his desire to be free of the Russian autocracy but he also criticised his father for the 'unfortunate situation of my country' and described Russia as being 'the play thing of a mad man'. Alexander had to be careful of what he said and especially of what he wrote in case his father discovered his views; the climate of fear in Paul's reign had an effect upon every level of society. Alexander was also deeply affected by the death of his father. His complicity in the plot that led to Paul's murder left him remorseful and wracked with guilt; perhaps he was naïve to think that Paul's life could have been spared but the act of patricide left him feeling even less keen on the idea of becoming tsar. This was reinforced by his mystical sense of Christianity and his longing to live a simple life. These feelings became stronger a decade or so later and surfaced in his ideas for a Christian Europe after the defeat of Napoleon; for the time being, they remained concealed.

He found some support from a group of friends who had gathered around him in the late 1790s. It became known as the 'Unofficial Committee' because of its informal status at a time when Alexander was not even tsar. As well as being a social group, its function was to serve as a forum for Alexander to discuss and exchange ideas on the problems and possible solutions that existed in Russia at the time. Obviously, one of these problems was Tsar Paul himself and he tried to break up the group by sending some of its members abroad on foreign postings. Adam Czartoryski for instance was despatched to Sardinia as its ambassador in 1798. He was a member of Poland's most aristocratic family and, having toured England and France, favoured constitutional government. Paul Stroganov had spent time in Paris at the time of the French Revolution

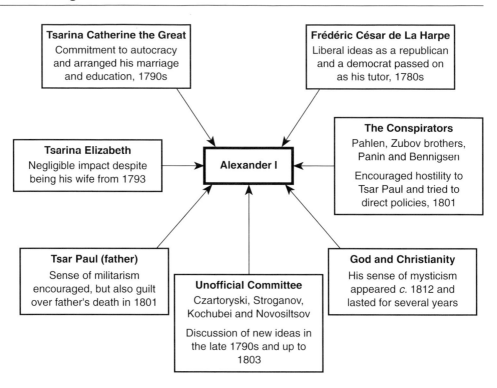

Figure 2.1 Summary of the influences on Tsar Alexander I, to 1801

and went to Jacobin meetings whereas another member of the group, Victor Kochubei, was much more conservative and believed in autocratic rule. The fourth and final member of the group was Nicholas Novosiltsov whose contribution focused on the practicalities of efficient administration, an area in which he excelled. This group's discussions earned it the nickname the 'Jacobin Gang' from Alexander but its attitudes were never as extreme as the French Republicans. It debated the usefulness of a constitution, the need for legal and bureaucratic reform, the scope for extending education in Russia and even the possibility of ending serfdom.

A last group of people was to have an influence on Alexander at the start of his reign. The small group of conspirators who had overthrown Tsar Paul affected the direction of his policies for a few months in 1801. Pahlen and the Zubov brothers in particular held sway from their positions in the Permanent Council as they encouraged Alexander to grant a constitution which would give more power to those in the social élite such as themselves. He resisted their calls for change and during the summer of 1801 felt sufficiently established as tsar to send them away from the court one at a time.

The diverse groups and individuals who had previously affected his attitudes were not so easily dismissed from his mind, however. Alexander grew up to be a very complex character whose approach to any given matter could be made up of several different attitudes or whose view changed quickly within a short space of time. This was to be borne out by the way he tried to introduce reforms in the early years of his reign. Contemporaries remarked on the difficulty of knowing the tsar's mind, from Napoleon who called him 'the Sphinx of the North' and 'a real Byzantine' to La Harpe who referred to him as 'the Russian Trajan'.

Reforms in Russia 1801–05

Alexander was crowned as the new tsar on 27 September 1801 but his work as tsar had begun on 23 March, as soon as his father was dead. He had begun by navigating not only the rapids of his own mind but also the rival political groups at the court. His first acts were among the easiest to make as it was customary for new tsars to make some gestures of goodwill at the start of the reign and, given that Paul had been unusually harsh, these were the more urgent. He reinstated about 12 000 army officers and civil servants who had been imprisoned by his father and allowed west European luxury goods to be imported once more – a small measure that affected very few people but one that pleased society in Saint Petersburg and Moscow.

In his accession manifesto, he promised a return to the ways of Catherine the Great. While he may not have been whole-hearted in his admiration for her, the start of his reign saw him adopt several of her policies. The 1785 Charter to the Nobility that she had granted but which Paul had revoked was accepted which meant that the nobles' exclusive right to the ownership of serfs, exemption from the poll tax and freedom to travel abroad were confirmed. Likewise, Alexander allowed Catherine's 1785 Charter to the Towns to operate which allowed representative bodies to meet in towns. And the Secret Expedition, or secret police, which Paul had used extensively was abolished in April 1801. Again, these measures benefited Russia's social élite above all and it was this group that Alexander was anxious to reassure.

These reforms raised little controversy but Alexander had weightier matters to deal with. He was under pressure from the conspirators to pass some kind of constitutional reform, an initiative that was likely to undermine his powers. The Unofficial Committee agreed with the idea of a constitution but saw it in much more limited terms and anyway opposed the influence that the conspirators might try to have on the tsar. A third group that tried to have an impact on Alexander was based in the Senate, one of the bureaucracy's chief institutions; it has become known simply as the 'Senatorial Party'. It was led by Alexander and Semen Vorontsov who had the support of many court nobles who had survived since the reign of Catherine. They too supported the notion of a constitution and Alexander Vorontsov drafted a 'Charter to the Russian People' which listed a series of rights for all Russian subjects.

Each group, however, was self-seeking and concerned not just to see political changes in Russia but also their own importance and powers increase. The rivalries that existed between each group served to strengthen Alexander's position, though, rather than weaken it, even on a matter where there seemed to be some consensus such as the constitution. Consequently, there was a great deal of discussion as well as a number of reforms 1801–02 within the highest echelons of Russian government. These deliberations led to a reorganisation of existing administrative organisations supplemented or even superseded by some new administrative tiers. None of the changes materially affected the status of the tsar who, as an autocrat, remained in an unassailable position. Thus it has become one of the frustrations for those studying Russian history at this time that so much seemed to be done but so little seemed to happen.

While the issue of a constitution dominated the first few months of the reign, none was ever introduced; Alexander himself remained deeply interested in the idea and it surfaced again in 1809 and in 1819 – but with no result. Instead, the main changes to government brought about at this time affected the status of the Senate and the structure of the bureaucracy. The Senate had been created in 1711 by Peter the Great as a body that could temporarily supervise the running of the Russian government while he was away fighting wars abroad. Its authority was soon extended into areas such as justice and trade, and this led in turn to a formal structure of nine administrative colleges in 1718 over which a Procurator-General presided as head of the Senate from 1722. It was through this system that the Russian civil service bureaucracy operated and it was the power base of the Senatorial Party of the Vorontsovs.

After discussions with the Unofficial Committee, Alexander asked the Senate to review its own status and powers in June 1801 and this process was led by Count Zavadovsky during the summer. The result was a decree of September 1802 which largely confirmed the Senate's existing powers which amounted to the maintenance of Russian laws and the supervision of other government institutions. This appeared to elevate the Senate to a new position of importance as a council of senior advisers between the tsar and the rest of the government organisations. However, its lack of independence from the tsar was made plain when it tried to block a new law in 1803. Alexander simply overruled and rejected its verdict. As the American historian George L. Yaney has observed, 'the Senate did not lose its institutional position in 1803, because it never had one'.[2] Yet again, the status of the tsar as an autocrat was clear.

This was reinforced by Alexander's creation of eight new government ministries in 1802. Some of these took over the work of colleges that already existed (such as those for the Navy and War) but others operated alongside the colleges. So, what appeared to be an attempt at rationalising the structure of government organisations in fact complicated and confused the situation. Both the colleges and the new ministries were directly responsible to Tsar Alexander and so his importance was, if possible, elevated further. The eight ministries were each headed by one individual who belonged to a new Committee of Ministers, but in no way was this a cabinet or a team and the ministers were, predictably, responsible only to the tsar. However, during the wars against Napoleon, it was this group that was appointed to supervise the government while Alexander was away, thereby taking over the traditional role of the Senate.

Finally, Alexander also set up a Permanent Council in April 1801 the purpose of which was not entirely clear – since Alexander's own instructions on the matter varied – but which seemed to be responsible for state affairs and decrees. Its membership included some of the conspirators such as Pahlen so, given Alexander's desire to free himself of their influence even in 1801, its importance was likely to be in doubt. Indeed, the Permanent Council was meant to be only a temporary body and it was simply a mark of the inefficiency of Russian government that it lasted until 1810.

Economic and social reforms were also passed by Alexander during these early years of his reign. The impetus for this came from his discussions with the Unofficial Committee in the 1790s and it continued to have direct access to Alexander until 1803. The view of this group was that Russia was in need of some modernisation; as has been seen, the political system changed little and only served to reinforce Alexander's own authority, but in areas where his power was not directly threatened it seemed that there was more chance of success.

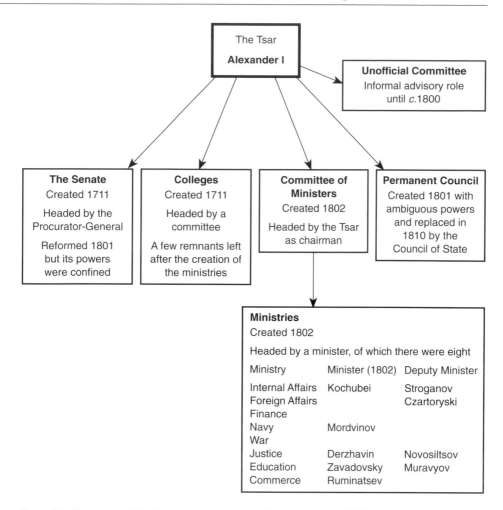

Figure 2.2 Structure of the Russian government and bureaucracy, *c.*1803

A law commission was set up in August 1801 with a view to codifying Russia's laws. This had last occurred in 1649 and, despite some periodic reforms such as Peter the Great's military law code of 1716, Russian law was confused, complicated and sometimes contradictory. The man appointed to lead the commission was Alexander Radischev, a known radical and thinker who had been exiled under Catherine in the 1790s for his dangerous views. Radischev laboured under a superior who showed little enthusiasm for the work involved and, in despair, he committed suicide in 1802. Alexander, too, was prepared to let the work of the commission languish and, when it finally reported and made recommendations in 1812, he ignored it. Not until the 1830s was the overdue reform of the law code achieved. Alexander was beginning to show his impulsive nature.

Education was another area that Alexander had identified as being in need of reform and, in this case, expansion. By 1800, the innovations of Peter the Great and Catherine the Great had given Russia the structure of an education system but not the content as there were too few pupils in too few schools. Education remained the preserve of the élite as there were barely 20 000 pupils attending the 300 or more schools in a population approaching forty million. By the end of Catherine's reign in the 1790s, the educational hierarchy consisted of three tiers; the universities, the provincial (major) schools and then the district (minor) schools. The 1804 Statute of Schools doubled the number of universities from three to six by adding universities at Saint Petersburg, Kharkov and Kazan to those at Moscow, Dorpat and Vilna. Each one became the centre of an educational district from which the schools were to provide students, but a fourth lower tier of school was created at the community or parish level. This meant that in theory education was available to all children who could attend the parish school for a year, followed by two years at a district school and four years at a provincial school. In practice, schooling was not widely available and the vast majority of Russians received no education at all because the resources and funding for such an ambitious scheme did not exist. The improvement was significant, though; the number of district and provincial schools rose to almost 1200 by the end of the reign in 1825 and 69 000 pupils were receiving instruction. There were also a great many children who received education outside of this state system, either through military schools (100 000), church schools (50 000) or specialised schools based in factories or intended for girls (40 000). The social élite also continued to educate their children at home (5000) which meant a total of some 265 000 pupils received some form of tuition by 1825. Alexander could not overhaul the entire system overnight, though, and his hopes of reviving Russia through education had to be tempered by what was practical.

The serfs also benefited from some small scale reforms. The key change was the Free Cultivator's Law of March 1803 which allowed landowners to free their serfs voluntarily if they chose to do so. Some 47 000 serfs were freed in this way by 1825, although 13 000 of these were released from their bondage by just one noble, Alexander Golitsyn. An earlier reform of December 1801 broke the nobles' monopoly of land ownership as it allowed other classes such as merchants and artisans to buy land – but this had to be without serfs. Alexander wanted to do something about the system of serf labour and recognised it as slavery. However, the nobles were hostile to any significant threat to what they considered to be their property and so the tsar was able only to tinker with the system. Moreover, he was guilty of sending many of the state peasants into serfdom by making more than 250 gifts of groups of peasants to nobles whom he wanted to reward. He also refused to consider any changes in the conditions for household serfs, those who worked as domestic labour in nobles' houses, despite the suggestion being made by Zubov in 1801. The influence of La Harpe, as an egalitarian, was still with Alexander but he could do little more than suffer with his conscience.

Foreign policy 1801–07

On his accession, Alexander became leader of a country at war. This course of action had been adopted by Tsar Paul in 1799 when he joined the Second Coalition with Britain, Turkey and Austria so as to fight against Napoleon. His military successes had begun to threaten Russia – even though the two states were at opposite ends of Europe – because in 1798, France had taken control of the Ionian Islands in the Adriatic Sea. This in turn meant that France could launch an attack on the Balkans and seriously jeopardise Russian interests there. In this indirect way, Tsar Paul had felt that Russia's security was at risk. This was a grave matter since the defence of Russia was and always had been the primary aim of foreign policy.

However, security could also be pursued through peaceful means. This had been Catherine's policy during the mid-1790s when she avoided war with France so as to concentrate on the partition of Poland. In 1800, Paul had begun trying to extricate Russia from the war partly because he was so disillusioned with his allies in the coalition and he wanted to reach some form of agreement with France. This presented risks. Not only did he want to ally Russia with the country that had begun the war in Europe – and one that was spreading a message of revolution – he was also set to challenge Britain's naval supremacy. It was this perverse combination of aims that helped to galvanise the conspirators' efforts against him.

Alexander continued with his father's pursuit of peace but was wise enough to extend it to both Britain and France. In fact, he began very well indeed given that he had not really considered foreign affairs in the 1790s, preferring instead to concentrate his thoughts on Russia. He was a little naïve at first as he declared idealistically that 'I only want to contribute to peace in Europe' and he genuinely seemed to think that this was something that was in his gift. However, he worked quickly and effectively to make peace where he could.

In October 1801 Russia and France agreed peace terms such that the Ionian Islands were recognised by both sides as being independent and France agreed to withdraw from Egypt (an area that could also threaten the Balkans). He smoothed over the dispute with Britain concerning maritime rights (just in time, as a British fleet was sailing up the Baltic in an attempt to crush the Armed Neutrality of the North) and the Cossack force that was advancing on India was recalled. Better relations with Prussia were also ensured through a personal visit to Frederick William III and Louise, the king and queen, with whom Alexander struck up a very good relationship almost straight away. Interestingly, Russia's foreign secretary at the time knew nothing of the visit, which demonstrated that Alexander was as much an autocrat in foreign policy-making as he was with domestic issues.

Franco-Russian relations quickly became strained, though, as Napoleon continued to advance his armies into central Europe. In particular, his occupation of several German states (including Hanover in May 1803) meant that he could threaten the Baltic Sea and its trade routes which were important to Russia. Moreover, Alexander strongly disliked the French kidnapping and execution of le Duc d'Enghien in March 1804 and so refused to recognise Napoleon as Emperor when he crowned himself as such in May of the same year. Russian and French foreign policy aims were soon becoming incompatible. The lack of trust between them was shown by Russia maintaining a force of 11 000 men in what were supposed to be the neutral Ionian Islands and from 1804 Vorontsov, one of Alexander's senior aides, was advising war.

A stronger relationship with Britain developed during 1804 which was based on their common concern about France. Britain had been almost permanently at war against France since 1793 having had only a few months respite between the Treaty of Amiens (March 1802) and the renewal of the war in May 1803. Britain was therefore keen to persuade Russia to join another coalition against Napoleon and this was something Alexander agreed to do after a lengthy exchange of views with Britain's Prime Minister, Pitt the Younger. Their un-named proposals from 1804 included wide ranging ideas on the future shape of Europe's frontiers and were to be a useful reference point when eventually Napoleon was defeated some years later. More immediately, in April 1805 Russia and Britain agreed to attack France without waiting for any further provocation from Napoleon. Their agreement was the basis of the Third Coalition.

While Britain continued its naval warfare against France, Russia committed 115 000 men to an army. This was augmented by 235 000 Austrian troops in August 1805 and a further 180 000 from Prussia in November. Britain bankrolled the armies by agreeing to pay £1.25 million each year for every 100 000 troops in the field. With this much brute force from four great powers directed against him, Napoleon seemed to have become quite vulnerable. Russia by contrast seemed to be in an unusually strong position because it had also secured its borders with Turkey and Sweden by signing alliances with each of them in 1805. However, the course of the War of the Third Coalition went badly for all of the allies' land forces and only Britain made any progress.

The Battle of Trafalgar on 21 October 1805 left Britain in command of the seas after sinking almost all of the French and Spanish fleets. But, two days earlier France had beaten Austria at the Battle of Ulm partly because the 40 000 Russian troops that were meant to have also been fighting were some 170 miles away. As a result, Napoleon entered Vienna in mid November. Worse was to come. At the Battle of Austerlitz in December Napoleon defeated a combined Austro-Russian force under the command of Alexander himself. Russia lost 25–30 000 troops compared to France's 8–9 000. It was an abject failure and one that could be blamed squarely on the tsar since he had deliberately ignored the advice of his own commander, Kutuzov, and rushed into battle without waiting for the 30 000 reinforcements Bennigsen was marching towards him. In fact, Alexander had put more faith in the Austrian generals than his own.

The Third Coalition began to fall apart. Austria was forced to make peace, at Pressburg, since Russia could offer it no immediate help. At this, Prussia began to lose courage and signed an alliance with France without having played any active part in the war. However, when Napoleon abolished the Holy Roman Empire in July 1806 and threatened to overwhelm all of Germany, Prussia was provoked into war against France. Prussia lost in October 1806 at the Battle of Jena and suffered the same fate as Austria in that Napoleon entered its capital city, Berlin, in triumph the same month.

Alexander continued the war with much more determination than his allies had done. In Russia itself Alexander ordered the formation of a militia of 612 000 men to defend the homeland in case of invasion. While this was intended to bolster Russia's defences against foreign attack, many nobles in Russia now felt that they themselves were vulnerable to attacks from armed peasants. In November 1806 Russian troops entered east Prussia en route to Warsaw where Bennigsen's force won a minor victory over the French in the small Battle of Pultusk. This was only a preliminary exchange, though, and the two decisive battles were at Eylau in February and then at Friedland in June. The first of these saw both Russia and France suffer casualties of 25–26 000 men although it was Russia that was forced to retreat. The Battle of Friedland proved France's superiority as Russia was forced to march east again and Alexander felt he had to secure a new peace treaty.

By 1807 he had good reasons for wanting peace. First of all, Russia was in retreat and was isolated apart from its alliance with Britain – an ally with whom Alexander was becoming increasingly disillusioned. The financial subsidies that Britain had paid amounted to £500 000 but seemed to be a small price paid compared to the loss of

Russian lives. The British also gave the impression of caring more about renewing a commercial treaty with Russia than with fighting the war. The opening exchanges between Alexander and Napoleon were therefore very amicable as they swapped insults about what they thought of the British. A further concern for Alexander was the situation in the Balkans where Turkey was shifting its allegiance from Russia to France as it saw how the battles ran in Europe. After Ulm and Austerlitz, the Sultan began to think that France offered Turkey better security than did Russia and so closed the Straits of the Dardanelles to Russian warships in April 1806 – denying them access to the Mediterranean. This was followed up by Turkey deposing the rulers of the Danubian principalities of Moladavia and Wallachia who were pro-Russian. At this, Russia declared war on Turkey in 1806 and the conflict lasted until 1812. It was, however, also to Napoleon's advantage to stop the war since the French forces were too small to pursue the Russians much further – and it was actually Napoleon who took the initiative in suggesting a peace treaty. It allowed Napoleon to consolidate his gains in central Europe and to focus on the war against Britain.

The Peace of Tilsit which was agreed between Alexander and Napoleon in July 1807 followed a very amicable exchange of views on many European matters that took place on a raft in the middle of the River Niemen since this was the only neutral territory that could be found. First, they agreed on a series of territorial changes in Europe. Russia lost no land and acquired part of Poland, Bialystok, from Prussia. Napoleon also promised to try to make peace between Russia and Turkey, and Russia agreed to leave the Ionian Islands. The chief beneficiary, though, was undoubtedly France as Napoleon was able to create a new client state, the Grand Duchy of Warsaw, from the lands lost by Prussia. This could pose a serious threat to Russia in the long term since it gave France a direct route of attack; however, in the short term France and Russia signed offensive and defensive treaties to preserve their own security. The defensive treaty meant that they could rely on each other for help in fending off any aggressor (such as Britain), while the offensive agreement was based on Napoleon's Continental System. This was an attempt to defeat Britain by commercial means, by setting up an economic blockade of mainland Europe's entire coastline such that Britain could buy goods from the continent but could not sell any. The effect of this was

Table 2.1 Summary of Russian foreign policy, 1799–1807

1799 War	This was the legacy of Tsar Paul who took Russia into the second Coalition of countries against France, which also included Britain, Turkey and Austria.
1801 Peace	With France but tension continued as Napoleon advanced further into central Europe. Alexander I became Tsar in March and peace was established in October.
1805 War	Against France in alliance with Britain. When they were joined by Austria (August) and Prussia (November) it became the Third Coalition. Britain was successful at sea with the Battle of Trafalgar (October 1805) but there were defeats on land for Austria at Ulm and Austerlitz (1805), Prussia at Jena (1806), and for Russia at Eylau and Friedland (1807).
1807 Peace	Was made with France in the Treaty of Tilsit. This agreement lasted until 1812 but relations were never easy due to rivalries in the Near East and over the Continental System.
1806–12	Russia was also at war with Turkey.

expected to be the bankruptcy of Britain. Clauses in the treaty made provision for Denmark, Sweden, Portugal and Turkey to be forced to join this pact, and for Austria to join the alliance against Britain too.

The War of the Third Coalition was quite short-lived. Russia's allies were either defeated by France or proved, in Alexander's view, to be of too little help. The result was that Alexander sued for peace as an equal partner at Tilsit but in the event was left with very little to show for the war. He was criticised for accepting such terms by members of his family at the court as well as by the diverse members of the Unofficial Committee. The problem was that the threat of France had been in no way lessened and it had committed Russia to a trade war with Britain which was set to be very damaging. The strain that it put on the Russian economy became intense over the next five years. However, this same period of peace that followed Tilsit enabled Alexander to return to his reforms within Russia, since the war had suspended all such efforts.

Speransky and reform

During wartime, there was no internal reform in Russia. The absolute priority was the conflict with France and all other government activity was suspended. However, the return of peace in July 1807 allowed Alexander to turn his attention to the modernisation of Russia once more and for this he enlisted the help of a new chief adviser, Mikhail Speransky. He dominated government business until 1812 and, although Alexander remained in control of policy decisions, it was Speransky who drove along the proposed reforms.

Speransky's background was unusual for such a senior political figure because he was born in 1772 to the son of a village priest whereas most of the tsar's advisers came from noble families. His rise to power was therefore due to his enormous intellectual ability. He was conspicuously successful at school in his home district of Vladimir and at the seminaries in Suzdal and Saint Petersburg. By the 1790s he was teaching Maths and his civil service career began in 1797 when he became the private secretary of Prince Kurakin, the Procurator-General. In 1801 he was transferred to the chancery of the Permanent Council and then to the Ministry of the Interior the following year. It was not until 1806 that he met Alexander but his talent was quickly recognised and in 1807 he accompanied the tsar on army manoeuvres and then went with him to Erfurt in 1808 where he encountered Napoleon. From this point on, he was Alexander's closest adviser.

He was not a popular man. His humble origin did not give him any humility and many at court despised his cool and even arrogant manner. He was accused of behaving as if he was in touch with 'superior beings' whose intelligence those around him could not appreciate. His personal life also picked him out as being different as he married an English woman, Elizabeth Stevens, who bore him a daughter but who died within a year of their marriage. He was left to bring up his child alone and he chose to do so in an unfashionable part of Saint Petersburg near the Tauride Gardens. He had, then, a lonely existence partly through choice but partly through circumstance. He spent his life devoted to his daughter and, above all, to his work.

His ideas have been the centre of some debate among political historians since there are numerous documents that have survived that detail his attitudes on the problems facing Russia at the time.[3] He was, by Russian standards, very radical in his ideas as he was heavily influenced by French writers and he hoped to use them so as to transform Russian society. He advocated a constitution and a role for public opinion in law making, an independent judiciary and a free press, and he hoped to extend public education throughout the empire. These borrowed ideas were given more credibility by his own insights on Russian life. For instance, he appreciated the contradictory nature of tsarist policies in the recent past as they lurched from the grip of Catherine, to that of Paul and then on to Alexander in the space of just six years. He argued that the instability that this created was more significant in the minds of the Russian people than any specific policy and so Alexander needed to provide some measure of continuity. He also made unfavourable comparisons between the dependency of the nobles on the tsar and the serfs' utter slavery in the service of the nobles. Shrewd though these observations were, they were not always welcome in polite society! Speransky's solution was to direct Russia to what he called 'monarchical government' which amounted to an autocracy with rules – rules by which even the tsar was bound. The model of a west European constitutional monarchy of the time was a close equivalent.

To this end, Speransky readily devised a draft constitution for Alexander, at his request, in 1809. In it, he tried to preserve the status of the tsar while also satisfying the conflicting views held at court regarding the best way in which to govern Russia. The traditional view was that the tsar needed an advisory council, while the Unofficial Committee had pressed for an efficient bureaucracy and Speransky himself hoped for some representative bodies to play a part in government. Inevitably, the result was a compromise.

The town, district and provincial dumas met once every three years and each of them elected representatives to the next tier up. The state duma was to meet once a year and was to be composed of representatives chosen by the tsar from a list drawn up by the provincial dumas. It was not to have the power to begin legislation but all taxes and laws were to be put before it. Although it was going to be able to reject legislation, the tsar would have the right to dissolve it.

This is where the most intense debate has occurred among historians since, if the constitution had been adopted, it would have radically altered the way in which Russia was governed and could have led to a liberal path of reform and toleration during the nineteenth century. The possibilities for change in Russia that this constitution could have allowed are speculative, but potentially they were enormous. The chief biographer of Speransky, Marc Raeff, claimed that the proposed state duma had no right of veto but this view has been overturned by the research of John Gooding which emphasises again how far-reaching the results of the plan could have been.[4] Raeff's interpretation is that Speransky was trying only to make the Russian government run more smoothly but David Christian has argued that the constitution was set to move Russia away from an autocracy.[5] The fact that Alexander did not enact any of the constitution in 1809 and only accepted a small part of it in 1810 suggests that he fully realised the scope for change and backed away from it.

One of Speransky's reforms that did succeed was the reorganisation of government ministries in 1810. Some of the existing ministries that had only been set up as recently as 1802 were abolished, such as the Ministry of Commerce, while the Ministries for the Army and for the Navy were combined. The Ministry of the Interior was reformed so that it lost control of the police and this became a department in its own right under Balashov. Two further ministries were created for Communications (including transport)

upset by what happened, commenting soon afterwards 'Last night they took Speransky away from me' which reads like a vain attempt to blame someone else for what was definitely his decision. Speransky was exiled to the town of Perm near the Urals.

The uneasy peace 1807–12

The alliance between Russia and France that had been set up by the Peace of Tilsit in July 1807 was not based on firm foundations; rather, it was based on convenience. Both Alexander and Napoleon wanted a respite from fighting each other so as to pursue interests elsewhere. In the case of France it meant concentrating on the war against Britain, while for Russia it allowed time for the internal reforms that Speransky organised as well as the chance to fight weaker enemies to the north and south. In the short run, co-operation was possible. However, the tensions caused by France's control of central Europe and the toll taken by the economic blockade of Britain (the Continental System) meant that by 1811 France and Russia were preparing for war once more.

Napoleon had largely given up hope of invading Britain after the defeat of the combined French and Spanish fleets at Trafalgar (October 1805). The British fleet was simply too strong. But by 1807 France controlled virtually the entire coastline of the European mainland either directly or through its allies. Thus, he decided to try to bankrupt Britain by mounting an economic blockade of the island and to replace British goods in Europe with those made in France. The ploy failed since France itself needed many of the things that Britain manufactured, such as shoes, and continued to import these using neutral ships. Moreover, Britain did its utmost to defeat this strategy, by finding new markets outside Europe (especially in South America) and by direct action such as destroying the Danish fleet in Copenhagen, September 1807, so as to prevent it from joining.

It was Russia, though, that suffered as much as any state in the Continental System. Hitherto, it had exported large amounts of naval supplies to Britain – hemp, flax, wood, tallow and such like – and imported above all textiles such as cotton, either as yarn or as finished cloth. In short, Britain was Russia's major trading partner. The impact on Russia was that the value of its foreign trade (imports and exports added together) carried by ship fell by two-thirds during 1807–08 and the entire population suffered from the tsar down. Government revenues crashed from 9.1 million to 2.9 million silver roubles, 1805–08, and the value of paper roubles slid from 50 to 23 silver copecks, 1808–11, as money was printed to meet government spending. Landowners were unable to sell their wood and grain, merchants could not secure credit on such good terms and the working population at large produced increasingly for local markets as the economy experienced a dramatic fall in demand. Agricultural specialisation declined. Even the nobles were affected as they had to pay highly inflated prices for luxuries such as sugar. Each group had reason to criticise the tsar.

By 1810, Alexander was becoming anxious about the situation. Some neutral ships, especially from the USA, had delivered cargoes of manufactured goods to Russian ports and even some British ships had got through the blockade, but this was not enough. France had failed to make up the difference partly because it could not transport goods effectively and Russian industry was by no means capable of producing enough. Thus, in December 1810 the tsar issued a decree that effectively took Russia out of the Continental System. It imposed heavy duties on goods arriving in Russia by land (such as from France) and set up much lighter rates for goods arriving by sea. The state of the Russian economy, though, was not enough for the tsar to break an agreement with Napoleon so dramatically. The change in his commercial policy was a reflection of how the political and military aspects of the Franco-Russian alliance were weakening.

Poland was the main source of friction between the two leaders. Alexander was always uneasy about it emerging as the Grand Duchy of Warsaw as it was a client state of France and so gave Napoleon an easy route through which to attack Russia if the need arose. In 1807, it was made up of land taken only from Prussia but in 1809 it was enlarged by western Galicia being added. Alexander tried to compensate for this by taking land for Russia in the Polish hinterlands but neither Bialystok in 1807 nor eastern Galicia (Tarnopol) in 1809 amounted to much. Furthermore, the Poles were keen on what Napoleon had done for them since he had granted a constitution, allowed the formation of a Polish army and ended serfdom. This all gave rise to a renewal of Polish nationalism which Alexander did not want to encourage; Napoleon himself commented that 'It is difficult to convey a proper idea of the national movement in this country ... Priests, nobles, peasants – they are all of one mind'. It also made it harder for Russia to win support among the Poles both at the time and in the future. In 1810 Alexander did enquire, via Czartoryski, how the Poles might react to the possibility of returning to a Russian-dominated Poland similar to the situation at the end of the eighteenth century. The price of their support for any such change was far too high; further territory, revival of the 1791 constitution and access to the sea. Alexander remained concerned about the situation in Poland but could do nothing about it.

Sweden, by contrast, was a country on which both leaders could agree a policy. France was hostile towards Sweden because its king, Gustav IV, refused to join the Continental System. Russia was hostile because it hoped to take Finland from Sweden and thereby make its own Baltic coastline safer from attack. Russia had few difficulties in the war that followed, only encountering serious resistance at the fortress of Sveaborg which guarded the sea route to Finland's capital, Helsinki. A guerrilla war soon followed as the Finnish population resisted Russian occupation, and it was this problem that persuaded Alexander to recall the Finnish parliament and promise, in person, to maintain Finland's laws and institutions. This paved the way to a peace treaty in March 1809 in which it did not become part of Russia but, as a Grand Duchy, was ruled by the tsar as its Grand Duke. Sweden made peace in September 1809 by relinquishing Finland, joining the Continental System and declaring war on Britain. Russia therefore achieved its own aim of territorial expansion, but was forced to widen the French economic blockade which was doing it so much harm.

The war with Turkey, which Russia had been fighting since 1806, was also a contentious matter since both France and Russia had designs on the Near East. Russia hoped to be able to annex the principalities of Moldavia and Wallachia and so advance towards Constantinople; France wanted to extend its influence in the Levant beyond the Ionian Islands to Egypt and possibly beyond. Under the terms agreed at Tilsit, Napoleon was to try to broker a peace deal for Russia and Turkey but this did not happen in 1807 and had no chance of being achieved after the outbreak of a rebellion in Spain in 1808, as it was under French occupation. Hence, the war continued with Russia taking control of Moldavia and Wallachia, and reaching the River Danube by 1810 – including the stronghold fortresses of Rustchuk and Giurgevo. Little further progress was made in the months that followed as Russia began to look for a peace settlement that would free its troops to muster back in Russia proper. A peace agreement was eventually reached in the Treaty of Bucharest, May 1812, which meant Russia had to give up Moldavia and Wallachia but it held on to Bessarabia and so its frontier did move forward a few dozen miles.

Relations with France had deteriorated so much by the middle of 1811 that an attack was anticipated within months and this was why Russia needed to pull troops out of the war against Turkey. This situation had been reached partly because of the problems in Poland, Sweden and Turkey, but also because of the wider European context in which the other three great powers were involved. The backdrop for all of this period, of course, was the war being fought between France and Britain which had been going on continuously from 1793 with only a brief respite during 1802–03. Britain was always keen to find allies in Europe to join the war against France and so Alexander was aware that an alternative alliance was possible at any stage. Napoleon knew this too and as a result had to ensure that Alexander was either persuaded or coerced into thinking that his alliance with France was more advantageous.

Persuasion was used when Russia was given territory as part of the spoils of war. Russian gains included Bialystok and eastern Galicia for which it did no fighting itself, as well as Finland and Bessarabia which were secured effectively with French consent. Napoleon also tried hard to charm Alexander at their two face-to-face meetings at Tilsit and Erfurt. The second meeting occurred in September 1808 and was called by Napoleon in order to get some reassurance from Alexander that their alliance was still operational and to make arrangements for the coming year. In the summer of 1808 a rebellion had broken out in Spain and this was something that tied down French troops. It also encouraged Austria to launch a war against France in April 1809 as it thought that France was weak. In fact, Napoleon scored two major victories over Austria at the battles of Aspern and Wagram, in May and July, and was able to impose a harsh peace treaty on Austria at Schönbrunn in October of the same year. Austria had to join the Continental System, pay a fine of eighty-five million French francs and cede territory. It lost land to the Grand Duchy of Warsaw and the Dalmatian coast to Italy. It was at this point that Russia gained eastern Galicia.

Coercion also had to be used in order to keep Russia as an ally for as long as possible. The ultimate threat was a renewal of war against Russia but Napoleon also tried to extract promises and commitments from Alexander when they met; their meeting at Erfurt was therefore a mixture of compliments and veiled threats. Napoleon wanted Alexander to promise support for France in the approaching war against Austria but Alexander would only do this verbally and committed himself to nothing in writing. When the war was in progress, Russian troops did advance towards Austria but they dragged their feet and in practice took no part in the fighting. Napoleon was livid at this tactic which he saw as a betrayal and he became much more aggressive in his own policies towards Russia. Late in 1810 he occupied the German free cities of Bremen, Hamburg and Lübeck and then in January 1811 he annexed the Grand Duchy of Oldenberg in Germany. This was more than a demonstration or even a warning of France's strength in central Europe. Given that the tsar's favourite sister, Catherine, was married to the heir to the Oldenberg throne, it was also a personal snub to Alexander. It could also be seen as a small gesture of revenge on Napoleon's part since he himself had hoped to marry Catherine. Whether the prospect of becoming wedded to Napoleon was intended as a form of persuasion, or of coercion, is not clear.

The relationship between Alexander and Napoleon was therefore always uneasy. Even as he negotiated with Napoleon, Alexander was in communication with the other great powers and considered his options at each point. On his way to Erfurt, he was asked by one of Prussia's leading ministers, Stein, to join an alliance against France. Likewise, he promised Austria not to help France any more than he could help in the war of 1809, as he was in communication with its foreign minister, Stadion. Only while the alliance with France offered more advantages than disadvantages did he keep to it and, by 1811, it no longer did so. Britain was a ready ally with which Russia was beginning to trade more freely after withdrawing from the Continental System in 1810. The war with Turkey was effectively over and a peace treaty was imminent; and Russia was better organised and prepared for any conflict than it had been in 1807 due to the efforts of Speransky. All that remained was the final preparation for war, which began in the spring of 1811 – on both sides. The outbreak of hostilities was only a question of time.

War and the fall of Napoleon, 1812–15

Russia's preparation for war took different forms. Diplomatically, it sealed its northern and southern frontiers through a treaty of mutual defence with Sweden in April 1812 and with Turkey through the Treaty of Bucharest. Agreements were made with Prussia and Austria, too, unknown to Napoleon, by which the former promised to do as little as possible to help the French despite being forced to provide 20 000 troops, while the latter told Alexander that it would take no active part in the fight against Russia. Strangely, there was no agreement made between Russia and Britain, but Britain was sure to continue its war regardless.

Alexander joined his army's headquarters at Vilna on the Baltic coast in May 1812. He was persuaded by his sister Catherine and one of his senior advisers, Arakcheyev, not to lead the army (after the disaster at Austerlitz for which he was responsible). Instead, overall command was given to the army generals, Kutuzov, Barclay de Tolly and Bagration. Their armies amounted to less than 200 000 men in the spring of 1812 and they were separated by hundreds of miles. Napoleon's 'Grande Armée' numbered 400–500 000. It was a multinational force of Poles, Prussians, Germans and French which did not have the motivation and patriotism of his previous forces. Communication, too, was a difficulty between so many national groups.

After a final and rather futile gesture at peace made by Alexander in April 1812, Napoleon invaded Russian territory in June by crossing the River Niemen. No formal declaration of war was made. Napoleon's strategy was to force Russia into an early and decisive battle – possibly before its disparate armies could unite – and secure a victory before the year was out. The Russian strategy was the opposite of this. First devised by Barclay de Tolly in 1807, the Russian policy was to retreat for as long as possible before squaring up for a full scale battle. There was a vast area of Russian plain into which the army could march away from the enemy and in the meantime that same enemy's supply lines could become stretched and its forces could be harassed by small-scale attacks.

The Russian policy succeeded. Thus, the Grande Armée quickly reached and captured successive towns; Minsk, Vilna, Vitebsk and then Smolensk by August 1812. Napoleon had hoped to have his battle at Smolensk after the long advance eastwards because the city was the first one situated in Russia proper – rather than White Russia – but he was again disappointed. There was a battle which lasted for two days in the middle of August but it was inconclusive and the Russians soon began to retreat again. As they left, they set the city alight (the inhabitants having already fled) which deprived Napoleon of vital supplies. By this stage, his supply lines were already becoming stretched and it might have been wiser to winter in Smolensk, but Napoleon decided to pursue his quarry further into Russia, still convinced that he would force it into one mighty battle.

Further small battles occurred in August to the north and south of the main French attack. The battle of Polotsk to the north and the minor clashes around Gorodechno to the south saw no overall victory for either side. Napoleon continued to advance through the centre. The time that the Grande Armée took to march this far was used by Russia to good effect. Government loans were raised and a large amount of revenue to finance the war was secured through voluntary private contributions. Eight million roubles, for example, was given by the merchants of Moscow. A 'scorched earth' policy was also employed, in which water was poisoned with rotten horse meat or human flesh and local crops were destroyed or concealed. And the Orthodox Church played its patriotic part by branding Napoleon as the anti-Christ so as to reinforce the peasants' hostility to the foreigners. At length, in September 1812, he reached the hinterlands of Moscow which the Russian public would not let Alexander abandon without a fight. While all Russian territory was seen as precious, the historic capital itself and the 'Third Rome' could not be handed over as if it was just another stretch of dirt. Thus, the major battle of the campaign was fought seventy miles west of Moscow outside a little village called Borodino.

The battle of Borodino was fought on 7 September 1812 between 135 000 men in the Grande Armée and 120 000 Russian troops. The advancing French force was already seriously depleted from its initial 400–500 000 soldiers. The losses were enormous on both sides, with French casualties estimated at 40 000 and Russian at 50 000. It is possible that Napoleon might have won the decisive victory he wanted if he had committed his Imperial Guard towards the end of the conflict, but he chose not to do so as he was mindful of the need to make good a retreat later if necessary. This was not the first time that the French allowed a good opportunity to elude them. In June, there had been the chance to drive a wedge between Russia's two main armies to stop them uniting; and after the battle at Smolensk, more decisive action by Junot in support of Marshal Ney might have seen the defeat of Barclay's army. The Grande Armée was commanded well, but it still made mistakes.

The most serious mistake was Napoleon's belief that the capture of Moscow, which the battle of Borodino permitted, would lead to Tsar Alexander I agreeing peace terms. The scorched earth policy was intensified when the Russians themselves set fire to Moscow and retreated further east. Responsibility for the fire, which destroyed three quarters of the wooden town, lay with its governor, Rostopchin. It meant that Napoleon had nowhere to spend the winter which was now coming down on Russia. He remained in the smoking ruins for thirty-three days while there seemed to be the possibility of making peace but then in mid-October was forced to begin the long retreat back to France.

The contemporary French accounts of the retreat have found good reasons for the defeat. 'General Winter' rather than General Kutuzov or General Bagration was blamed in particular but it is clear that most of the damage was done to the Grande Armée

The French Retreat over the River Berezina, 26 November 1812 (Anonymous watercolour, photo copyright Musée de l'Armée, Paris)

during its advance to Moscow, not its retreat. The return journey was, though, by far the more wretched and humiliating. Stranded in a desolate city and angry at Alexander's obstinacy, Napoleon tried to blow up the Kremlin but the fuses were too damp and the buildings survived. His men were emaciated and fell to scavenging in villages or seizing on the meat of dead horses. Discipline was difficult to maintain, especially among the non-French troops; when food supplies were reached at Smolensk and later at Vilna the meagre rations were scoffed and plundered. Reaching these destinations was a desperate affair since the Grande Armée was forced to retrace its steps by Kutuzov. He blocked the southerly return route by fighting the battle of Maloiaroslavets in October 1812 and this meant that the same impoverished ground was marched over once more and there were no new sources of fresh supplies. The peasants looked out for stragglers and in some cases clubbed them to death or buried them alive. Guerrilla tactics were used by Davydov and Figner so as to harry or ambush small groups of the French force while the main Russian armies were all the time converging on it. Kutuzov was in pursuit from the east, Chichagov from the south (having set off in August after the peace with Turkey) and Wittgenstein was descending from the north as the French general Victor had not protected Napoleon's flank adequately. Natural obstacles caused problems too. The first snow fell in early November, but the climate was not as harsh as expected and so the River Berezina had not frozen over when it was reached in late November 1812. This led to the terrible forced crossing of its icy waters recorded in contemporary accounts and paintings. Some 15 000 members of the Grande Armée crossed the river, but at least as many again were abandoned on the east bank and were massacred by Cossacks. The retreat from Moscow can be couched in polite historical language. It might be called a terrible débâcle or merely Napoleon's lowest point; but in practice it was miserable, hellish and cruel.

The Grande Armée that had marched away to Russia in the spring of 1812 staggered back out of it. When all of the soldiers who returned were counted up, they amounted to barely one tenth of its original size. From this point, there seemed to be no hope of return for Napoleon. He did succeed in raising new forces back in France and managed to inflict some military defeats on his opponents, but the coalition of forces that emerged to fight him in the months that followed was too much. Perhaps the key moment in this was Alexander's decision to pursue Napoleon beyond the Russian frontiers and, if necessary, to follow him all the way to Paris so as to guarantee a complete victory. This decision was by no means certain and Alexander received conflicting advice. The peasants were generally hostile to any continuation of the war and predictably took a parochial view of what was important for Russia. However, they were suffering the results of the war as much as any group due to their casualties and the shortages of food. Kutuzov also felt that Russia should protect only its own territory. Alexander disagreed and followed the advice of foreign aides such as Stein and Yorck from Prussia and Sir Robert Wilson from Britain. The significance of his decision cannot be underestimated since it ensured the complete defeat of Napoleon and the liberation of the continent from French rule or domination. It also committed Alexander to an ongoing commitment to European affairs after the war had finished as he felt a moral obligation (quite apart from any strategic advantages) to remain involved.

The course of military events that followed can be outlined simply. Alexander strengthened his position in February 1813 by allying with Prussia in the Treaty of Kalisch which added a further 80 000 Prussian troops to the war. It also included an agreement for Russia to annex Poland and Prussia to take over Saxony in any future peace settlement by way of reward for their sacrifices and risks in attacking Napoleon from this stage onwards. In March, Prussia declared war, and in April Britain agreed once more to bankroll their armies by donating two million pounds. Napoleon achieved two minor victories at the battles of Lützen and Bautzen and engineered an armistice in June during which both sides regrouped and diplomatic negotiations focused on where Austria's support was going to lie. Eventually, in the Treaty of Reichenbach, Austria joined with Russia and Prussia and the war restarted. The decisive battle was at Leipzig in mid-October 1813 – the so-called 'Battle of the Nations' – in which half a million men fought for control of Germany. France was forced to retreat again, this time back inside its traditional frontiers.

At this point, the war could have ended as both Austria and Prussia were prepared to make peace with Napoleon. Alexander, by contrast, was determined to press on so as to ensure not only the defeat of France but also the capitulation of Napoleon himself. In this, he had the support of Britain which was still fighting a simultaneous war against France without any formal alliance with the eastern great powers. The situation was changed in March 1814 by the signing of the Treaty of Chaumont. Largely devised by Britain's foreign secretary Castlereagh, it set out in general terms the territorial pattern of a postwar Europe. Germany was to become a confederation of small states and independence was agreed for the Netherlands, Spain, Italy (as several states) and Switzerland. The means to ensure this were also agreed, with Britain paying out a further five million pounds to its allies and an agreement to remain in alliance until France was totally defeated. Significantly, Poland was left out completely. Perhaps the tsar did not see its future as being in any doubt and assumed that the Treaty of Kalisch would be adopted by Austria and Britain. Perhaps he thought that he could persuade them at a later date. In either case he was wrong. When the final settlement of Europe was made at the Congress of Vienna a major dispute occurred and the tsar lost out.

The Congress of Vienna 1814–15

The Congress of Vienna was meant to be a short meeting of the four victorious great powers to tie up the loose ends from their earlier agreements. In fact, it became a lengthy and protracted series of talks that lasted from October 1814 until June 1815. By this stage, Napoleon had been defeated since the allies had entered French territory in January 1814 and marched into Paris in March. Napoleon had abdicated in April and the peace terms that applied to France had also been agreed.

The First Treaty of Paris in May 1814 treated France very leniently. This was very much in keeping with Alexander's views since he had always claimed that his war was against Napoleon and not the French people. Thus, France was limited to its 1792 frontiers and was given a constitution which in theory limited the rights of the restored Bourbon king, Louis XVIII. The 'Charter' as it was called was the chief means by which the absolute rule of the *ancien régime* was to be fused with the liberal ideas of the revolution. Again, Alexander was pleased to see this as he supported the idea of constitutions wherever he thought they were appropriate. Napoleon was exiled to Elba in the first instance but his dramatic return to France in March 1815 and the subsequent defeat of his army at Waterloo meant that he was sent away to the remote South Atlantic island of Saint Helena and France was punished more harshly. The Second Treaty of Paris pushed the frontiers a little further back to those of 1790, an indemnity of 700 million French francs had to be paid and an army of occupation was imposed for three to five years. The latter included a contingent of Russian troops.

The balance of power in Europe that was created at Vienna integrated the Paris treaties into its terms very successfully. It was a territorial settlement that was intended to keep the peace in Europe by ensuring, in so far as it was possible, that each great power felt safe from attack by any other single state. Thus, it was an agreement founded on the great powers' most basic need: security. This axiom has recently been emphasised by Chapman.[6] The arrangement included France and this was why it was treated leniently since any feelings of revenge felt by the defeated state could destabilise Europe in the long term. Alexander accepted the need for France being dealt with in this way. What he could barely tolerate, though, was the balance of power as it applied to Russia since he expected to annex all of Poland in line with the Treaty of Kalisch. It was the view of the British and Austrian representatives, Castlereagh and Metternich, that this would leave Russia in a menacing position in which it could attack central Europe far too easily. Talleyrand, the French delegate, endorsed this view and in January 1815 these three states allied against Russia (and against Prussia which was holding out for its own annexation of Saxony). The result was a tense few days in January 1815 during which there seemed to be the chance of a war between the four victorious great powers. Details of the alliance were leaked to Russia and Prussia and as a result a compromise was reached in which Russia took the bulk of Poland – 'Congress Poland' as it was called – and Prussia got approximately half of Saxony. The other areas of Poland were taken by Prussia (Posen and Thorn) and Austria (Galicia).

What Castlereagh and Metternich in particular feared was that the domination of Europe by France was going to be replaced by the domination of Europe by Russia. Certainly, Alexander was at the peak of his power at this time and was widely heralded as the 'saviour' or 'liberator' of Europe. But the balance of power meant that Russia's strength had to be limited and in a military sense cancelled out by the potential counter-weight of France. This east-west balance was matched by a north-south balance in central Europe between Austria and Prussia, which were separated by the power vacuum of the German Confederation. France was penned in behind a cordon sanitaire of buffer states such as the Netherlands or Piedmont, and Britain, in the meantime, took no interest in taking mainland territory and so acted as arbiter in any disputes while quietly acquiring overseas colonies for itself.

Russia fared reasonably well at the Congress of Vienna but really it should have done better given the position of strength that it had. Congress Poland was still a major gain and Castlereagh felt that it was too much; he feared that it left an imbalance in Europe and that Russia might well use its new window on the west to advance further very soon. Russia's earlier wartime gains to the north and south were also confirmed as it kept Finland and Bessarabia. One possible reason for Russia not making even greater gains has already been highlighted in the Treaty of Chaumont. Another is that Alexander was not confident of his diplomatic skill and overestimated the sophistication and subtlety of western diplomats. He took with him to Vienna a huge international entourage whom he hoped would outmanoevre his opponents. His advisers included Czartoryski (Polish), Stein (Prussian), Capo d'Istria (Greek), Pozzo Di Borgo (Corsican) as well as his Russian foreign secretary Nesselrode but he relied on none of them and they were often as unsure of his foreign policy aims as were their counterparts from Britain, Austria or Prussia. A great deal of unnecessary confusion followed. It might well have been the case that if he had made plain his desire to annex all of Poland sooner, then it would have happened.

The mystery of Alexander's mind was made deeper by the mysticism of his Christian faith which became very obvious at this stage. He had always held Christian values but after the profound shock of his homeland's invasion and the razing of Moscow he had turned to God in his time of greatest need. His views were informed by regular reading of the Bible but also by letters and visits to Baroness Krüdener, the wife of a nobleman in the Russian diplomatic service. In this way, his policy towards Europe after the Napoleonic Wars also became his mission and it was in this light that he devised the Holy Alliance in September 1815. It was intended that he and his fellow Christian rulers would 'take for their sole guide the precepts of that Holy Religion ... Justice, Christian Charity and Peace' in their foreign policies. He tried to persuade his peers to sign up to it and was largely successful as all of Europe's rulers agreed to it with a mere handful of exceptions. The Sultan refused as he was Moslem; the Pope refused as he disliked an Orthodox initiative that made Catholicism seem less important; and Britain's Prince Regent refused on the advice of his Cabinet that wanted to avoid any 'European entanglements' as they were called. Even those that did sign up seemed to do so only to humour the tsar. Metternich, for example, dismissed it as 'a loud sounding nothing'. To contemporaries it was an optimistic aspiration without much substance since it was so vague.

Nevertheless, Alexander was sincere in his ideas at the time and if his ideals matched up with what was in Russia's interests then so be it; such was the will of God. Russia had, after all, claimed a right of protection over Orthodox Christians in the Turkish Empire since the Treaty of Kutchuk-Kainardji so there was a tradition of Russian compassion, it could be argued. While it seemed to have little diplomatic value in the eyes of foreign diplomats, the Holy Alliance did make a difference to Alexander. He applied its principles to Poland almost as a pet project and set about the task immediately. The Polish army that had fought against him was given safe passage back to Poland and a new army of 35 000 was organised from Warsaw by a military commission headed by his brother Constantine. This was begun even while the Congress of Vienna was still in session, something that was possible since Poland was under Russian occupation at the time. He also introduced a new constitution against the advice of those around him. It included a bicameral parliament composed of a Senate of 83 nobles and bishops and an elected lower house (the Sejm) made up of 100 members elected by over 100 000 voters. Rights were granted to ordinary citizens too – freedom of the press, of religion and from arbitrary arrest. The freedom granted to Poles (and earlier to the Finns) was in stark contrast to the political conditions in Russia itself but Alexander justified this on grounds of suitability; the two states that Russia had annexed were ready to operate such a system whereas Russia was not. And it is important to be clear that Russia had indeed annexed these states; their freedom was in the context of overall Russian control. Thus, the Finnish Diet met in 1809 but did not do so again until 1863 and the Polish state remained only semi-independent while it was loyal. Russian troops crushed the nationalist rebellions there in 1831 and again in 1863 so as to maintain effective control from Saint Petersburg.

Russia and the congress system

The Holy Alliance that Alexander had devised in 1815 was something that he pursued for several years afterwards and in that time, not surprisingly, it evolved. What began as an apparently meaningless document, 'a piece of sublime mysticism and nonsense' according to Castlereagh, became a means by which the three eastern great powers of Russia, Prussia and Austria could crush rebellions and preserve the status quo. They hoped to maintain the rulers and frontiers of Europe precisely as they had been laid down at Vienna. This was the complete opposite of Britain's view of how best to sustain the balance of power. Such a situation was reached by 1820 but the divergence of views and aims was evident from the beginning.

What had united Russia with Prussia, Austria and finally Britain in 1813–14 was an overwhelming need to defeat France. Once that necessity was removed, they began to disagree. It had taken the extreme threat of invasion and even total destruction to overcome the rulers' deep-seated suspicion of each other and finally force them to unite together in the Treaty of Chaumont. Once the war was over the suspicions resurfaced quickly and one of the main areas of concern was the slow pace of Russian demobilisation. Alexander decided to maintain the Russian army at its wartime level of one million men even though the conflict was over. While this was designed to be a defensive move against foreign attack it was of course seen by the other states as highly aggressive. Having seen French troops in Moscow in 1812 and Russian troops in Paris in 1814, observers at the time felt Europe was still in flux and that the balance of power might very well not last. There was therefore a genuine fear that Russia would use Poland as a springboard for an attack on central Europe. In practice, Alexander's intentions were not as offensive as this. He felt a moral obligation to try to defend the Vienna settlement and the maintenance of so many troops was in part a sign of his own weakness since he feared what could happen if so many ex-soldiers were returned to civilian life in Russia too quickly. The forces that he could use to defend law and order might not be adequate if a general peasant uprising occurred.

One interpretation of the evidence available has suggested, though, that Alexander's ambitions were much larger than even the European theatre of activity. The Belgian historian Pirenne has argued that Alexander had a global strategy and hoped to extend Russian influence into the Americas.[7] He offered Russian troops to Spain in order to end the rebellions in South America, for instance, which fuelled contemporary west European fears. Russia also expanded its influence in north America by setting up a Russian settlement at Fort Ross on the Pacific east coast in 1812 and by sending a naval vessel to explore the Hawaiian islands. He tried to co-operate with the USA in the 1820s by agreeing an Alaskan frontier in 1824. However, Pirenne's view is reminiscent of twentieth-century fears of Russian expansion typical of the cold war rather than of the early nineteenth century. Back in Europe, Britain and Austria remained on good terms as they still feared Russia (and to a lesser degree France) as a potential threat to the balance of power after 1815. Prussia gave up its working relationship with Russia and relied instead on Austria as the senior partner in its defence policy. This meant that almost straight away, Russia felt isolated from its former allies. In order to remedy this, Alexander was keen on the speedy return of France to the concert of Europe. The very threat that Britain and Austria feared most, an alliance of the continent's military heavyweights, seemed to be about to happen because of their own actions.

When the five great powers met at a second congress at Aix-la-Chapelle in 1818, there was already some tension between them. They met in order to complete the business left over from Vienna regarding France's punishment. It had managed to pay off the indemnity promptly and this meant that the army of occupation could be withdrawn since in 1815 it was agreed that the army would stay for between three and five years. The four victorious states agreed that the army should now leave and that France should be admitted to the European concert again. The French representative, Talleyrand, knew who to thank for this, commenting 'It is owing to the Emperor of Russia … that we have attained this end', and it was noticeable that Russia was keen to court French friendship. France was duly accepted back into the concert of Europe but the other four great powers renewed their alliances with each other. While there was agreement over the return of France, there was no consensus over a series of secondary issues that were raised. These ranged from the policing of the Mediterranean against pirates to the immorality of the slave trade and to the future of the Spanish colonies in South America.

The most contentious matter at Aix-la-Chapelle was one that the tsar brought forward involving the Holy Alliance. He tried to resurrect it in a new form as an 'Alliance Solidaire' or universal union. This time, he wanted more than a union of Christian monarchs and proposed that the great powers guarantee the existing rulers their thrones while also granting their subjects rights through the introduction of constitutions. Both Castlereagh for Britain and Metternich for Austria were opposed to this idea, but for quite different reasons. The former disliked the idea of committing Britain to any long-term alliance based on abstract principles such as legitimacy, while the latter feared a ploy by the tsar to extend Russian influence further across Europe. The matter was dropped but it was significant that the tsar was still keen on Christian ideals and on liberal ideas. He continued to believe in his own mission.

The turning point was 1820. In the years 1815 to 1819 the great powers had set their own agenda but from 1820 they had to respond to events. A series of rebellions broke out which threatened the rulers of several minor states and the great powers had to take some decisions as to how they were to react. In Spain, a group of army officers rebelled against King Ferdinand VII's attempt to send a naval force from Cadiz to reconquer the South American colonies in January 1820. This was followed by an uprising in Naples in July 1820 in which another group of officers tried to impose a constitution on King Ferdinand I. Castlereagh was first to respond. In May 1820 he issued a famous State Paper that defined the British attitude to unrest abroad and how Britain viewed the maintenance of the balance of power. He was quite happy to see small changes to the map of Europe and even to see rulers rise and fall. He did not see the wartime coalition as having any lasting significance in peacetime and it was certainly not intended to be 'for the superintendence of the internal affairs of other states'. By contrast, the three eastern great powers did see it as their role to intervene as necessary with armed force so as to keep the 1815 settlement intact in its entirety. A congress was called in late 1820 and between October and December these three met at Troppau, eventually producing a document that came to be known as the Troppau Protocol. This asserted that Russia, Prussia and Austria had the right to restore deposed rulers in 'States that have undergone a change of government due to revolution'. This seemed to be a curious twist of events since Alexander had claimed to support liberalism and constitutions and the rebellions in Cadiz and Naples were above all liberal in their intent. They did not mean to remove the existing rulers but merely to secure guarantees of each ruler's political behaviour.

The tsar's change of mind about liberalism can be explained, in part, by events in Russia. In December 1820 the Semenovskii Guards mutinied. This was one of the units on which the tsar thought he could always rely and he never anticipated any disloyalty from it. In practice, the incident amounted to little more than a temporary breakdown in discipline on the parade ground but it had an impact on the tsar. It was a tiny concern but just enough to tip the tsar over to Metternich's line of thought. He had niggled away at the tsar, warning him of revolutionary conspiracies emanating from Paris and the importance of defending monarchs and their authority to the last drop of blood. The result was that the tsar's concerns about revolution were magnified and he became determined to see any rebellions crushed. While he was prepared to experiment with liberalism, he was not prepared to risk revolution. It was he that was most nervous when the rebellion in Cadiz occurred and he asked for a congress immediately; Metternich, more cool and much more calculating, refused the request but was then in a strong position when the Neapolitan uprising occurred in Italy, an area of Austrian influence. The language that Tsar Alexander used to Metternich to describe his change of heart reveals an anxious man. 'Between 1813 and 1820, seven years have elapsed but they seem to me like a century. Under no circumstances would I do in 1820 what I did in 1812. You have not changed but I. You have nothing to regret but I.' He readily offered the use of Russian troops to crush the Italian rebellion. In the event, it was Austrian troops that marched into Italy to crush the uprising in Naples and did so with the full authority of the three Holy Alliance powers which they gave at the third congress to be held, at Laibach between January and May 1821. The same army also ended the unrest in Piedmont that had erupted in March 1821. This took place much to the relief and satisfaction of the tsar.

The rebellions that occurred in Europe in 1820–21 were not confined to Italy and Spain. Portugal also experienced an uprising in Lisbon in August 1820 but it was beyond the control or influence of the Holy Alliance since British naval vessels could provide protection against it by mooring in the deep River Tagus that ran through the capital. In fact, Spain too was beyond the range of Russian or Holy Alliance influence as well and it was France that intervened on its own account in April 1823. However, the rebellion that broke out in Greece in April 1821 was very much in an area of Russian interest since it was an uprising within and against the Turkish Empire.

Alexander's first reaction to the Greek rebellion seemed to revert to the hesitancy of his earliest weeks in power. He was caught between two basic but conflicting aims. He wanted to intervene to crush a rebellion against a legitimate ruler (the Sultan) even though the Turkish Empire had not been part of the Vienna settlement and so was hardly under the jurisdiction of the Holy Alliance. But he was also concerned to act in the defence of the Greek revolutionaries since they were Christian and his belief in his own divine mission to help Europe at large had not completely disappeared. There was also the more down to earth possibility of any war against Turkey allowing Russia to take more land from it. As Metternich shrewdly commented, 'He wriggles like a devil in holy water'! Because of these contradictory aims, Alexander did not manage to make a decision one way or the other during the remaining years of his reign. This was despite 25 000 Greek Orthodox Christians being massacred on the island of Chios in 1822. Alexander had to wrestle with his conscience, but the best that he managed was further discussion. He tried to organise a congress on the issue in Saint Petersburg in January 1825 but there was no consensus among the participants. And in August he issued the Nesselrode Memorandum which announced a more strident attitude, asserting 'Russia will follow her own views exclusively and will be governed by her own interests'. However, it fell to Alexander's successor, Tsar Nicholas I, to commit Russia to definite action when he came to power in December 1825.

The Arakcheyevschina: Russia 1815–25

The primacy of foreign policy over domestic affairs continued after 1815. During the war, Russia's very existence seemed to have been under threat as Napoleon penetrated so far east and so Alexander was compelled to make it his priority. In the years of peace that followed he chose to give it most of his personal attention because of his conviction that Russia had a new role to play. While he was abroad at congresses and conferences, therefore, he left the everyday government of Russia to a subordinate, Aleksei Arakcheyev, after whom the period is named. The discernible aims of Alexander's domestic policies revolved around the maintenance of internal security and the promotion of church influence – which was itself another way of keeping the population under control. His liberal idealism showed some signs of continuing until about 1820 after which his policies resembled a more traditional and autocratic approach.

Arakcheyev was no liberal. His background was a military one that stretched as far back as the reign of Tsar Paul. Under Alexander, he took charge of organising the Russian army's artillery section from 1803 and then became Minister of War in 1806 before being made responsible for the military department of the Council of State when it was set up in 1810. In the war against Napoleon, Arakcheyev worked closely with Alexander and the successes that he achieved in this role explain the tsar's decision to appoint him to a position of pre-eminence in Russia by late 1814. His power was second only to that of the tsar; he himself commented that 'I am the friend of the Tsar, and complaints about me can be made only to God'. The machinery of government co-existed with him. The Committee of Ministers headed by Saltykov and of course the different ministries themselves were merely administrative tools which were subordinated to his power. His position made others vulnerable to his whim and his personal reputation did little to reassure anyone. Rumours circulated that his appetite for absolute order led to him biting off a soldier's ear on the parade ground, and that he had all the cats on his estate hanged so that they could not catch the nightingales which he loved to hear sing.

The Arakcheyevschina lasted for ten years, from the return of peace until the death of Alexander. Its most distinctive characteristic was the introduction of military colonies, an idea revived and then pioneered by Arakcheyev himself, and which were to last until 1857. They were military villages inhabited by soldiers and peasants alike and which were run with harsh discipline. Their main activity, however, was farming. Thus, they were reviled by the soldiers who had to work in the fields and by the civilian peasants who were strictly regimented. Similar projects had been experimented with in Russia in previous centuries but they had never been pursued in any systematic way. The first colony of Alexander's reign was set up by Arakcheyev on his own estate at Gruzino in 1810. Alexander visited it and was so impressed that he ordered a major scheme under state control in Mogilev province the same year. Further progress was held up by the war against Napoleon but the tsar returned to the idea in 1816 and put Arakcheyev in charge.

Despite their unpopularity, Alexander was determined to expand the scheme. This reason on its own was enough to ensure the military colonies were built. He explained that 'There will be military colonies whatever the cost, even if one has to line the road from Saint Petersburg to Chudovo with corpses'. But there were other advantages too. Alexander was aware of the threat to law and order within Russia that mass demobilisation could cause. By 1815, the army numbered one million men so to return to earlier peacetime levels would mean that hundreds of thousands of trained men would be released into civilian life once more and this was extremely dangerous. Rather than risk this, he decided that their physical presence on the borders of Russia, where many of the colonies came to be sited, would serve as a useful bulwark to Russian security. This strategic argument was a strong one so soon after Napoleon's invasion, although most colonies were on the southern and northern frontiers rather than in Poland through which any western attack was likely to come. Estimates vary, but by 1825 up to 375 000 troops were posted in the colonies and perhaps 200 000 of them along Russia's borders. This amounted to one third of the entire army.

There were also economic and social advantages. Maintaining the army in peacetime cost the state one-third of its annual income. By forcing the soldiers and their families (many of whom were ex-peasants and serfs) to work the land the state was becoming more productive, not least because the colonies were encouraged to use modern farming techniques. They were also paid very little for their work – barely 10–20 per cent of the usual day labourers' rates – which meant that that by 1826 the colonies had accumulated a profit of twenty million roubles for the state. Since the peasants were given land and because they were educated in the colonies' own schools, it has been suggested that Alexander was attempting some form of social engineering. Even though he contemplated emancipating the serfs, this interpretation is unlikely. The advantages included clean living conditions, brick houses and paved streets but the disadvantages more than offset this. The farmers disliked the severe discipline which included being given orders and having to wear a uniform. Their children were sent away to settlements elsewhere in order to be educated from age seven and family life was damaged further by women being expected to bear a child once a year and for daughters to marry bachelor soldiers. These latter measures were designed to increase the population and so strengthen the military reserve.

The irony of the situation was that while the military colonies were designed to preserve law and order they were the cause of some of the worst unrest in Alexander's reign. They were universally detested by those who lived in them and riots began to break out almost straightaway. The most serious episode was in 1819 when 9 000 peasants rebelled in Chuguev. The army was used to quell it and to carry out the punishments; over 300 were sentenced to flogging and knouting and as a result 25 died. The conditions of slavery under which colonists lived in some settlements was shown in 1824 when a rebellion on Arakcheyev's estate left Nastasya Minkin, his mistress, dead. A further major rebellion occurred in Novgorod in 1831 during the reign of Nicholas I and this effectively ended the programme of military colonies. Arakcheyev himself had told Alexander that 'I weary of all this' in 1819 but Alexander had been determined to press on.

Education and religion were combined with the military colonies to ensure that Russia's internal security was maintained while the tsar was away. True, Alexander had genuine religious convictions, but it was no coincidence that the Church served the state as a tool for keeping order among so many million souls, either in its church buildings or in its schools. Both institutions taught obedience to the tsar. The Ministry of Spiritual Affairs and Education (or Dual Ministry), which was set up in 1817, therefore combined the two aspects and allowed a more coherent policy. The man put in charge of this government body was Golitsyn. He was ideally suited to the job since, as the Over Procurator of the Holy Synod from 1803, he was the layman in charge of the Church. He was also a long-standing personal friend of the tsar. The policies that he pursued were a mixture of evangelism and repression; the first of these was for the Church and the second was for education.

The Russian Orthodox Church had to accept a number of evangelical efforts that were in the tradition of its Protestant rivals. A British-backed Bible Society began work in Russia from December 1812 and by 1820 it had in excess of two hundred branches that were busy issuing mostly New Testament texts in 25 languages and dialects. The number of copies printed approached 400 000 after the first decade. This was quite a novel approach since, traditionally, the Orthodox priests were among the few Russians who could read and it had been left up to them to explain the scriptures to their congregations. The aim of making the Gospel more widely available could obviously be carried out in conjunction with the education programmes that taught basic literacy. However, Alexander hoped that the result of these changes would be the rejection of contemporary western views such as liberalism by the new readership. This motive was hardly progressive since it aimed to strengthen his own autocratic position. More tolerance was shown, though, towards Protestant sects in Russia such as the German

Lutherans, the small number of Quakers and the Catholics. The status of the Orthodox Church was therefore eroded as the Bible Society's activities by-passed it and the privileged status it had enjoyed with respect to other sects was undermined. Even so, the Catholic priesthood's intellectual élite – the Jesuits – were expelled from Russia despite having only just been revived by Pope Pius VII in 1814.

The education policies were harsh and earned the Ministry of Spiritual Affairs and Education the sobriquet the 'Ministry of Darkness' or 'Ministry of the Eclipse'. Golitsyn was helped in this respect by several very conservative subordinates, among them Magnitsky, Sturdza and Runich. They were hostile towards liberalism and discouraged any influence from the ideas of the French Revolution. Thus, neither students nor their teachers were allowed to spend any more time studying at foreign – especially German – universities (which had already been contaminated by the Enlightenment) and there were purges of suspect Russian professors. Censorship increased to such an extent that even scientific books were removed from university libraries and students' notes were checked. Stress was placed on Bible study courses and theology; the basis for Philosophy was to be the New Testament Letters to the Colossians; and politics courses had the Old Testament prophets of Moses and David as their starting point. These measures were in stark contrast to those of the late eighteenth century when Catherine the Great had tried to separate education and religion. The most severe restrictions on universities were brought in by Magnitsky in 1819 after his cursory inspection of Kazan University. He reported that it was so irreligious that it should be closed down; Alexander was not prepared to see something so drastic occur but consented to Magnitsky taking over at the university and purging it of all its non-Russian lecturers. Nor did the local school system escape the changes. Here, more emphasis was placed on religion rather than on technology or the natural world.

Major liberal ideas featured for one last time in Alexander's thinking in 1819 when he instructed Novosiltsov to draft a constitution. The situation was similar to what had happened in 1809 when he told Speransky to submit a plan. The inspiration for this move seems to have been the Polish constitution and Alexander's opening of the Sejm. Novosiltsov's scheme was simpler than Speransky's but – just as before – had to preserve the tsar at the very pinnacle of government and organise a new hierarchy of administration beneath. The 1819 draft incorporated a representative and elected assembly directly beneath the tsar rather than allowing any advisory body such as the Council of State to interpose between royalty and the electors. There were, however, to be regional assemblies as before and ordinary citizens were to have a role in electing them. Despite the thought and consideration that went into Novosiltsov's draft constitution, which preserved more power for the tsar than had Speransky's, Alexander rejected the idea in 1820. By this time he was reverting to traditional tsarist ways in the light of the European rebellions and the supposed mutiny among his own Guards units. No further plans for constitutional reforms were contemplated but greater efficiency was sought in some areas and for this reason Speransky was recalled from retirement to become governor of Siberia in 1819 after the poor administration of the area under Ivan Pestel. Siberia was a vast area and the return of such an able governor was significant, especially because it was at the same time as the appointment of Balashev to the governorship of six provinces south of Moscow. It suggested a more general change in the pattern of regional rule towards a tier of unusually powerful governors but, if this was the intention, it was not developed any further in the 1820s.

Minor reforms were made to the system of serfdom but the vast bulk of it remained intact. The serfs in the Baltic provinces were freed after 1815, the last of which was Livonia in 1819, but while they were granted their freedom, they received no land. This was perhaps an experiment that – if successful – could be repeated elsewhere in the empire and in 1818 Alexander told Arakcheyev to come up with a scheme for the emancipation of all serfs. What he proposed was for the government to buy land and serfs from landowners at the rate of five million roubles per year. This was a small sum given the number of serfs involved but also highlighted the huge expense that complete emancipation could entail. It was clearly beyond the means of the state to fund any such method and the idea was dropped. Emancipation was in any case a dangerous proposition even to consider since it risked the wrath of the nobles and the unruliness of the serfs. Any suggestion that they might soon be freed was likely to lead to a spontaneous uprising unless the process was managed very carefully. In the years 1816–20, there were 66 occasions when troops had to be called out to stop peasant unrest and Alexander had no wish to make the situation worse. He took some steps to improve the condition of the poorer classes through semi-independent charities to which he made donations. Their work concentrated on education, poor relief and prisons and may have made a difference to a small number of people. The best work on this has been done by Janet Hartley.

The Arakcheyevschina was a period dominated by familiar tsarist aims. Because Alexander was primarily concerned with foreign affairs, he wanted minimal risks to be taken back in his homeland. Internal security was ensured by the maintenance of a large army which itself was kept in check by the use of military colonies. Education was censored and retarded so as to forestall the spread of dangerous western ideas. Where Alexander was more permissive, in his church policies, it was with a view to keeping the reading public obedient as the Orthodox Church could continue to stress the Bible's message of obedience to authority. And when Alexander did consider genuinely liberal measures, he was hesitant. He shrank away from the constitutional changes put forward by Novosiltsov and he limited the emancipation of the serfs to the Baltic provinces. In the second half of his reign, Alexander had more aspirations than achievements.

The death of Alexander and review of his reign

Tsar Alexander I of Russia died on 1 December 1825 at Taganrog, a remote town on the Sea of Azov. He had fallen ill three weeks before but had refused any treatment until the later stages of his illness. Exactly what caused his death is unclear but the town was located near areas infected with malaria. His body was transported back to Saint Petersburg by February of the following year and his wife, Elizabeth, followed behind in April. She, too, however died in the middle of the journey home. Rumours have circulated since that Alexander faked his death and disappeared into the countryside to live out the life of a monk. What evidence there is to support this rests on the early age at which he died – he was only 48 – and that when his coffin was opened later in the century no remains were found. Moreover, Alexander had frequently commented on his reluctance to rule and the period of his accession exposed this most obviously. However, the likelihood is that he did indeed die at Taganrog in December 1825 and that the rumours have continued simply because the circumstances of his death were unusual rather than suspicious.

His reign can be readily divided into two halves, the turning point of which was 1815. During the first phase, he alternated between reforms at home and wars abroad while in the second he gave over the day-to-day running of the country to a subordinate so that he could concentrate his efforts abroad. His reputation as a liberal during the first period is based more on his hesitancy at becoming tsar and his intentions than on what he actually achieved. There was always more bureaucratic planning than definite legislation. He investigated the idea of a constitution twice, most seriously in 1809, for instance but then dropped the idea; he seemed to be interested in expanding educational opportunities but created a framework in 1804 rather than an operational system. And he behaved impulsively in his efforts to modernise the legal system under Radischev and the system of serfdom through the Free Cultivator's Law. Speransky's rise and fall served as a measure of the regime's flirtation with reform. Those reforms that did have a significant effect tended to be of an administrative nature and they tended to reinforce his own powers such as the creation of successive advisory bodies and new ministries in the early years. Alexander was concerned to maintain the strength of his own position, even if he did have doubts about becoming tsar initially. Little wonder, then, that the draft constitutions were abandoned; Alexander I was not a risk taker.

His greatest achievement was in the defence of Russia. There were few occasions when the status and integrity of the Russian state was threatened as severely as when Napoleon led France. The periods of peace between Russia and France were always tense times, 1801–05 and especially 1807–12, as there was little doubt that in the long term the two states posed a serious threat to each other. The war of the Third Coalition 1805–07 exposed the problems of co-operating with other great powers in the struggle against Napoleon and it suggested that conventional pitched battles against a man of such military genius would prove futile. Thus, the tactics employed in 1812, of retreating indefinitely and harrying the Grande Armée, were the right way to proceed. Unlike the Crimean War of the 1850s or the succession of wars fought against the Turkish Empire, the campaign of 1812 was a matter of the very survival of Russia; it was fundamental. Even the burning of Moscow was a small price to pay for the successful defence of the state as a whole.

If the risks were big, the rewards were huge. In view of the defeat of Napoleon by 1814, Alexander I was in an enormously powerful position in Europe and stood to make considerable gains at the peace settlement. However, he won the war but lost the peace. He enjoyed the prestige of the moment as he commanded the attention of the western diplomats and rulers, but he was not able to translate this into sufficient territorial gains for Russia. 'Congress Poland' and the confirmation of his acquisition of Finland and Turkish land did not match the sacrifices of Russian blood and resources in the preceding war. He was outmanoeuvred by Castlereagh and Metternich in the Vienna talks and made an early mistake in agreeing to the terms of the Treaty of Chaumont that made no mention of Poland. Nevertheless, the British view was that Russia was already overbearing and a threat to the balance of power.

This fear was not justified in practice because of the skilful diplomacy of Metternich who was able to play upon the tsar's conservatism in the face of revolution. Instead of Alexander I introducing his league of Christian rulers, or using his by now massive standing army of one million men to intervene at will in Europe, he was persuaded to adopt the rules laid down by Metternich in the Troppau Protocol. This effectively shored up Austrian security while giving Russia little in return; so the revolts in Italy were crushed by the Holy Alliance as Austria wished but those of Spain and its colonies were left. Alexander did not feel comfortable with the situation and had to grapple with his conscience in particular over the Greek uprising but never managed to break free of Metternich's diplomacy. Foreign policy in the ten years after the Congress of Vienna was a missed opportunity for Russia.

In Russia itself, the second half of the reign was more reactionary than the first. The Arakcheyevschina was hallmarked by the widespread use of military colonies that seemed to be universally reviled by peasants and soldiers alike. Unrest was crushed with little regard to the Christian concerns that Alexander expressed in private and he passed no serious reforms for Russia proper. The Baltic provinces by contrast witnessed the freeing of their serfs 1816–19 and Poland enjoyed the freedom of a constitution. The autocracy was reinforced by the merging of the church and education departments to form the Dual Ministry or 'Ministry of Darkness' in 1817. After the exposure of many of his officers to liberal western the ideas, Alexander was vulnerable to criticism and even attack from the army after 1815. The disgruntled Semenovskii Guard made a minor protest in 1820 but it was the Decembrists, again drawn form the army, who were to present the most serious threat to the Russian rulers.

Alexander therefore carved out for himself a unique position in Europe in the course of his desperate defence of Russia 1812–15 but he was unable to capitalise on it. Russia had undoubtedly emerged from the political edges of Europe by 1815 but its potential to dominate remained unfulfilled. Its backward economy and autocratic system were not out of place during the first quarter of the nineteenth century but, if it was to continue to develop its strength over the coming decades, it needed to reform itself. In this respect Alexander I did desperately little in his twenty-four-year reign and he gave no guidance to his successor as to how to proceed.

Notes

1 J. Hartley, *Alexander I*, London, Longman, 1994.
2 G. Yaney, *The Systematization of Russian Government*, London, 1973.
3 M. Raeff, *Michael Speransky: Statesman of Imperial Russia 1772–1839*, The Hague, 1959.
4 J. Gooding, *The Liberalism of Michael Speransky*, Slavonic and East European Review 64, 1986.
5 D. Christian, *The Political Ideas of Michael Speransky*, Slavonic and East European Review 54, 1976.
6 T. Chapman, *The Congress of Vienna*, London, Routledge, 1998.
7 J.-H. Pirenne, *La Saint Alliance*, Neuchâtel, 1946.

Chapter 3

The reign of Nicholas I
Orthodoxy, autocracy, nationality

Tsar Nicholas I reigned for thirty years but it was as if time stood still. There were desperately few reforms in this period and what there were tended to be bureaucratic so as to reinforce the system of autocratic control. As in previous reigns, the policies reflected the personality of the tsar very closely since without his consent to any changes they were not going to happen. Nicholas was a hard-headed military man who had not expected to rule and whose life before 1825 had therefore been devoted to the army. What he brought to the Russian government was a strong sense of duty and a desire for order but very little by way of innovation. More than previous tsars, he saw himself as a steward of the dynastic position and, for three decades, seemed to be preparing merely to pass on what he had inherited. To do this, he stepped up the scale of repression in three successive stages – some feat after the Arakcheyevschina – and fought a series of wars abroad.

Nicholas I: biography and background

As the third son of Tsar Paul, Nicholas had never expected to have to rule and he was never encouraged to think in these terms by the family. Thus, he was groomed for a military career. Born in 1796, he was cared for by Jane Lyon, a Scottish nurse, until he was seven when he was passed to General Matthew Lamsdorff for further instruction. Lamsdorff was a keen disciplinarian and it was probably he who was responsible for instilling in Nicholas a preoccupation with neatness and regularity. His interests revolved around the army and included horsemanship. Nicholas completed his education under Lamsdorff in 1811 and moved straight on to become an officer in the Russian army. He was not allowed to join Alexander in the 1812 campaign against Napoleon but he did go to Paris after the defeat of France and from 1814 to 1817 he was able to tour parts of western Europe. He went to England at the age of twenty and, while he was unimpressed with the British parliament, the Duke of Wellington – himself a military man – did have an impact.

Nicholas was obedient and direct in his approach to his life and work and expressed none of the complexities of Alexander's character. He followed the route mapped out for him and, in keeping with this, married a German princess, Charlotte of Prussia, in 1817 partly to strengthen relations between Prussia and Russia in the postwar years. His character was charged with the traditional military features; discipline, detail and drill. He so liked the culture of the army that he typically dressed in uniform even when not on duty and he used its language to express himself. When he became tsar he explained that 'I am a sentry at an outpost on guard, to see all and observe all. I must stay there until relieved'. This almost sacrificial sentiment pointed to the loneliness of the task that lay ahead of him and how he felt that he could trust almost no one as he carried it out. This distrust was heightened by the circumstances in which he came to the throne. Just as Alexander I's reign was coloured by the way that it began with the murder of Tsar Paul, so the reign of Nicholas was overshadowed by the revolt that he had to deal with in December 1825.

The Decembrist Revolt

Tsar Alexander I died on 19 November 1825 but Nicholas did not accept the throne until four weeks later, on 14 December. The reason for the delay was that the line of succession had been changed by Alexander and the heir, Constantine, in 1823 without Nicholas being fully informed. Some discussion had taken place between himself and Alexander as early as 1819 but this had not gone very far and so in 1825 Nicholas was very unsure of his claim. He was, of course, told of the arrangement as soon as Alexander died but the news was nevertheless a shock. Confusion inevitably followed. Letters were exchanged between Nicholas (in Saint Petersburg) and Constantine (in Warsaw) for a period of days while couriers made the seven day journey to and from each capital. Neither brother seemed ready to take over or, as *The Times* observed, Russia was 'in the strange predicament of having two self-denying Emperors and no active

The Insurrection of the Decembrists at Senate Square, Saint Petersburg on 14 December 1825 (Russian School, 19th century. Source: Novosti/Bridgeman Art Library)

ruler'. At length, Nicholas accepted that he was to become tsar and was proclaimed as such on 14 December 1825.

In the meantime, the absence of government allowed a rebellion to take place. It had been planned for 1826 but was brought forward to take advantage of the opportunity. Despite his love of army life, Nicholas was not popular with the officer corps and this made him nervous of accepting the throne prematurely. He knew that the army might mutiny if it appeared that he was seizing the throne and he only needed to recall the fate of his father to realise that the position of a tsar was vulnerable. It was indeed the army that formed the basis of the rebellion in 1825 but only part of it was involved and enough troops remained loyal for it to be crushed within a day. Some 3 000 troops from the Moscow Regiment and from two Guards units were persuaded by their commanding officers to assemble in Senate Square in the centre of Saint Petersburg where they refused to take the oath of loyalty to the new tsar on the very day of his accession. Nicholas did not want to begin the reign with unnecessary bloodshed, especially within the army, and so tried at first to negotiate a solution. As the rebels waited in the ice and cold, Miloradovich, the Governor of Saint Petersburg, crossed the square to talk to them. He failed in his mission and paid with his life as one of the rebels, Kakhovsky, shot him dead. Two more peacemakers were sent; the chief Orthodox priest of Moscow, Metropolitan Serafim, and Nicholas' younger brother Grand Duke Michael. These too failed. As the darkness closed in on the winter day, Nicholas became anxious to end the rebellion quickly and decided to use the troops who had remained loyal to him. There were 9000 of these and he ordered that they fire their artillery pieces across the square at the rebels immediately. The cannons were loaded, levelled at the troops and fired three times. Seventy or eighty men were killed or wounded. The Decembrist Revolt was over.

The origins of the revolt lay in the reign of Alexander and have been the subject of considerable research.[1] They can be traced back to the defeat of Napoleon since the Russian army that pursued him to Paris was composed of a literate officer class which was receptive to new ideas and which learnt from its exposure to the west. Many officers who compared the British and French political systems with their own became frustrated by the limited nature of Russian government under Arakcheyev when they returned home and some of them began to form secret political groups dedicated to the reform – or overthrow – of the tsarist system. One of these was the Union of Welfare, set up in 1817 to campaign for a constitution and the end of serfdom, but which also encouraged its members to pursue charitable work with prisons, hospitals and the poor as well. Originally based in Moscow, it split into two groups in 1820 when it feared that it had been infiltrated by tsarist agents.

One half became known as the Northern Society and began to operate from Saint Petersburg. Among its leaders was Nikita Muravyov who drew up a set of plans aimed primarily at political changes through a constitution. The tsar was to continue but was to be salaried and to fulfil a function similar to that of the President of the United States. Local government was also to be reorganised. The other half became known as the Southern Society and was based in the town of Tulchin hundreds of miles to the south. It was led by Colonel Paul Pestel whose aims were more extreme than those of Muravyov. Pestel wanted radical social changes that could only be engineered by a revolution. He elaborated the rules under which serfs were to be freed and how all peasants were to have rights to farmland. Political change was sought through a single parliamentary chamber and a committee of five acting as a State Council. The tsar and the ruling family were to be executed. The Northern and Southern Societies co-operated with difficulty in the early 1820s as Pestel pushed for action as often as he could while Muravyov, Obolensky and Trubetskoy, the northern leaders, were more cautious. Pestel consequently enlisted the support of other secret societies such as the Polish Patriotic Society and the United Slavs. He also spear-headed a plan to assassinate the tsar in 1826. The death of Alexander in 1825 precipitated a crisis for which neither Society was ready but they reacted as best they could and it was the northern group, despite its less radical approach, that organised the army mutiny on 14 December 1825.

The research has been so extensive because the Decembrist Revolt marks a turning point in the history of unrest in Russia. It cannot easily be categorised as either a popular uprising of peasants (despite the large number of ordinary soldiers), or an army coup typical of the eighteenth century (which its leadership might suggest). It marks a transition from the latter to a new form of rebellion based on an intellectual élite with political aims of its own. The army officers involved were educated and were informed by the ideas of western Europe, the Enlightenment and of the French Revolution. They did not simply want to replace one tsar with another (as had happened in the previous century) but wanted to alter the nature of Russian government by introducing a constitution so that it became more open. In short, they wanted an end to autocracy. They also acted on behalf of others rather than as a self-seeking group that wanted to protect its own interests. And this was to be the pattern in future uprisings; those in the early 1880s against Alexander II and by the Bolsheviks of the twentieth century tried to transform Russian society through violence. The army itself never led another rising.

The results of the rebellion were widespread and long lasting. In the short term, Nicholas ordered the capture of as many rebels as could be found. Some were apprehended the day before, such as Pestel himself, as he was betrayed by an informant. Others, belonging to the Chernigov regiment, surrendered to loyal troops in the Ukraine on 3 January 1826 after having roved around the countryside as a maverick army contemplating an attack on Kiev. In the medium term, most of the conspirators were caught and interrogated as part of a commission of enquiry set up by Nicholas. In all, about six hundred individuals were brought before it and were subsequently punished. The ringleaders were executed: Pestel, Ryelev, Muravyov, Bestuzhev and Kakhovsky. Their immediate subordinates, more than one hundred of them, were exiled to hard labour in Siberia for various periods of time, including life. Many more of the ordinary soldiers who were caught up in events were simply flogged.

But it was perhaps the long-term implications that were the most significant. Nicholas had not felt secure about becoming tsar because of his older brother's prior claim; the Decembrist Revolt made him extremely and permanently distrustful of the nobility. This meant that he tried to rely on as few advisers and bureaucrats as possible. He began to create his own alternative system of government administration based on Sections rather than on the existing ministries so as to bypass them. The first of these was the Imperial Chancery (or first Section) which was set up in 1825. Five further Sections followed. One of the effects of these Sections was to refocus all decision-making on the tsar himself in what was already an autocratic system. Inevitably, this led to bottlenecks in the process as he could not manage the volume of work. It also made for more confusion in the administration due to overlapping, and even rival, government bodies. Their roles were often repressive so, when Nicholas became alarmed by the European rebellions of 1830–31 and 1848–49, their activities were stepped up. There was little relief from Nicholas' determined attempt to control Russian society.

Obstacles to reform in 1825

In this environment, it is hardly surprising that there was little reform. What changes there were tended to be aimed at tighter control rather than any more freedom since this was the will of the tsar. Yet Russia needed to reform if it was to maintain its presence in Europe as a great power because the western states were beginning to develop economically as well as politically in ways that could threaten Russia. The liberal ideas expressed in Britain's unwritten constitution and, since 1814, in the Charter in France gave legitimacy to political activists throughout Europe, including Russia. The industrial revolution that was accelerating most quickly in Britain was making obsolete the Russian reliance on sheer size in order to preserve its strength. New weapons were being developed, ranging from iron-clad ships to more efficient light arms; and more trade was being conducted which meant that tax revenues could enrich the western governments. War could be financed more readily, as the coalitions that Britain had bankrolled to fight against Napoleon had demonstrated. In the mid nineteenth century, great power status began to depend on the quality of a state's resources as well as its quantity. Russia could not risk or afford to stand still.

But this is what it did. Against the revolutionary slogan of 'Liberty, Equality, Fraternity' Nicholas I adopted Uvarov's phrase 'Orthodoxy, Autocracy, Nationality' so as to champion the traditional Russian ways. As an autocrat, responsibility for the security of the state and its internal strength rested with him and he chose to concentrate the state's efforts on the suppression of dissent. He was entirely straightforward and direct about this, in keeping with the military tradition that he knew. 'Revolution is at the gates of Russia' he explained 'but I swear that it shall not enter as long as I have a breath of life within me'. He was convinced that this was the right way forward and duly set up a new secret police in 1826 which took the name of the Third Section. The work of the Second Section was to codify the laws so as to make the legal system operate more efficiently. Punishments were made no more lenient and for this contribution Nicholas earnt the accolade 'Nicholas Flogger' or more plainly 'Nick the Stick'. The clamp-down on the Decembrists turned out to be the shape of things to come. A Fourth Section dealt with education but this involved a great deal of censorship work in conjunction with the secret police and in many respects the quality and availability of education declined. Abroad, Nicholas was headstrong and acted decisively to end rebellions whenever he could. For this, he was nicknamed the 'gendarme of Europe'. In almost every area of Russian policy during his thirty-year reign, Nicholas was distrustful and pursued harsh policies. Clearly, the single most important obstacle to reform in Russia was the tsar himself.

Nicholas was not solely to blame, though; had he wanted to modernise instead of simply maintain his state, he was set to face fundamental problems. With the exception of the small group of Decembrists themselves, no other group in society had any inclination to see change occur. The nobles amounted to one hundred thousand families with hereditary titles (in a population of up to fifty million) and so represented the élite of the social hierarchy. They were educated and provided the personnel needed for the army and navy officers, civil service and political advisers as well as being the vast majority of the landowners. Without the support of this class, the Russian state could not function and its relationship with the tsar was crucial. In some respects, the tsar was nothing more than the chief noble who could be removed if he failed in his primary governmental tasks. As a group, it was intensely conservative as it enjoyed sufficient wealth from its estates to live well and it could govern these same estates with a fair degree of autonomy since the serfs who worked on them were treated as property rather than as citizens. There were also tax exemptions, for instance from the poll tax, and privileges that came with noble status such as education and access to careers in the bureaucracy. Any changes to this system were therefore strongly resisted as they had most to lose. The most obvious case of where serious change was considered by Nicholas (and by Alexander) but where nothing was done was with the issue of the emancipation of the serfs. Both tsars preferred to tinker with the system rather than change it significantly for fear of the wrath of the nobles who might decide that assassination was their only defence against the tsar. Changes to landowning, the armed forces, the government departments and the legal system could hardly leave them in a better situation than they already enjoyed; they therefore opposed any reform and advised against it.

The serfs and peasants were by far the largest class of people in the Russian Empire and they too provided no pressure for change. This was because they were incapable of applying any co-ordinated pressure and because they had no real political aspirations. The sheer size of Russia meant that communities were isolated and poor transport links such as earth (or mud) roads limited the degree of communication. The harsh winters also restricted movement over long distances and so it was only the rich, the landowners, who could afford to travel. In these circumstances, there was no prospect of any mass conspiracy, although it was something that tsars still feared after the experiences of the Pugachev Rebellion of the 1770s. The non-political and parochial outlook of the serfs and peasants was not only due to the geographical dispersal of the population. The system of social organisation, based on the home village, also tied them to the soil. As rural labourers, they were born into their class and had almost no opportunities to leave it since they were the property of the landlord. If they went to work in one of the new factories, and there were some that were in operation by the 1820s and 1830s, it was still as serfs. Most of them remained on large estates where landlords were keen to take profits from year to year rather than invest in long-term land improvements. This meant that the farming techniques they employed were unlikely to improve. The medieval three-field rotation continued to be employed and so a great deal of land was left fallow and under used each year. Given that the soil in Russia, outside the black earth belt, was quite poor and considering that the harsh climate made good harvests quite rare, Russia was trapped in a low yield, low tax economy. There were some exceptions to this pattern, but the net effect of low tax revenues for the state coffers obviously limited the amount of money the tsar could spend on reforms, whether in education, agriculture or industry. This was especially true during wartime but since 1815 Russia had kept a standing army of one million men and this was a constant drain on finances.

To compensate for the lack of investment in their farms, the nobles tended to rely on the exploitation of their workforce, the serfs. As a class, it was desperately poor and was left uneducated for generation after generation. The absence of schooling meant that the serfs (and the peasants on the tsar's estates) could do little to improve farming practices. Just how dire their life experiences were is hard to describe since, being illiterate, they have left no written records. Even their villages have been destroyed since the houses and hovels were made from wood and so have either been burnt down or rotted. The existence of a serf was one of abject poverty and subsistence. Yet despite this, the loyalty of the serfs still seems to have been with their local communities, including their landlords. They had no discernible aspirations of a political kind and were preoccupied with securing good harvests above all else. They necessarily had a limited world view. When rebellions did occur, it was in defence of the established order rather than as a way to bring about change. Examples of this kind of behaviour are clear in the protests and riots that the new military colonies provoked such as at Novgorod in 1831. Later in Nicholas' reign, there were riots over the introduction of a new crop, the potato, especially in the early 1840s. The combined strength of the serfs and peasants was a massive force for inertia.

Between the nobles and the serfs there were few intermediate groups in Russian society. The army operated as the armed wing of the nobility and the church was entirely subordinate to the tsar – and had been so for centuries. The middle class was too small for much since it was confined to the towns and ports and tended to focus on commercial matters rather than on political or constitutional ones. Industrialisation in Russia was slow to occur. Between 1804 and 1858, the number of factories increased from 2 400 to 14 000 and there was a corresponding rise in the industrial workforce. But there was no working-class movement and even if there had been, the industrial sites were so remote that unrest was never likely to threaten the tsar. The large concentration of iron works in the Urals, for example, was hundreds of miles from Moscow on the extreme edge of European Russia. The cotton industry was developing at this time but it relied on foreign technicians and machinery to operate it as there was so little indigenous expertise. Manufacturing counted for only a tiny part of Russia's economy and did not generate the profits (and tax revenues) to fund reform elsewhere. There was a small class of intellectuals based in Russia's six universities but these were such an obvious source of opposition that successive tsars monitored their activities very closely and were quite prepared to censor the books or articles that were written. Likewise, the students were watched carefully and could be held in check either by reducing their numbers or fixing the courses that were available to them. Nicholas did all of these things.

Groups outside Europe were also an obstacle to reform because of the way that the tsar and other senior political figures reacted against them. The problem was not so much the foreign rulers since Nicholas was fairly confident of the friendship of Austria and Prussia and did not fear any immediate threat to Russia's security. The problem lay instead with the rebellions that occurred in Europe 1820–21, 1830–31 and especially in 1848–49. The tendency of foreign urban populations to rebel meant that Nicholas feared that Russia might become vulnerable to the same disorder if the corrupting influence of liberal and nationalistic ideas was to spread. Poland was affected in 1830–31 which was effectively part of Russia itself and, it seemed, all of Europe except Britain and Russia were rocked by revolution in 1848–49. If this was the result of reform, toleration and freedom, even in the limited forms that Europe accepted at this time, then Tsar Nicholas I wanted no part of it and saw the solution as even firmer government. The influence of these foreign nationals at long distance was indirect and only served to emphasise once again the pivotal position that the tsar had in directing Russian policies.

Finally, for advice and confirmation of his views, Nicholas could turn to his own conservative advisers like Uvarov and Kankrin or he could turn to the policies of the past and trust in those. Previous tsars had created the system of autocracy and it seemed to have served them well. Alexander I had wanted to reform but in the course of twenty-five years had actually done little and eventually relied on Arakcheyev. Tsar Paul was hardly a liberal, having persecuted, imprisoned and tortured his enemies. And Catherine the Great had succeeded by being single-minded and strong in her plundering of the church, elevation of the nobles and extension of the frontiers. As far as Nicholas could see, the Romanovs were all in it together and he was not about to change course unnecessarily. Reform was too risky.

The six Sections

The main change that Nicholas made to the autocratic government was the formation of six new Sections, beginning with a personal Imperial Chancery of close advisers in 1825, to which the others were subordinate. His aim was to circumvent the existing ministries and councils set up by Alexander because he did not trust them. In theory, the new Sections would enable Nicholas to implement decisions more quickly but, because he tried to make so many of the decisions himself, the process was often slowed down. At other times, he issued decrees without any consultation at all and the Section heads only learnt of his decision once it had been published. This unpredictable state of affairs was counter-productive and made the bureaucracy rather less efficient.

Within this system, Nicholas pursued quite traditional aims. His methods were repressive but he aimed like previous tsars to defend the security of Russia against foreign attack and against internal disorder. To do this, he wanted to strengthen the autocracy as far as possible. There were signs at the beginning of his reign that he intended to do this partly through liberal methods. He dismissed two of Alexander's harshest ministers, Arakcheyev and Magnitsky, and he re-appointed Speransky, a known liberal. He also confirmed Catherine the Great's Charter to the Nobility. However, these symptoms were more a reflection of his desire, common to many new rulers, to make an impact as soon as he was in power and to create his own framework for government. With the benefit of hindsight, it also becomes clear that the years 1825–30 were the most tolerant of the reign, or what Westwood has called the 'honeymoon years'.[2]

The first Section was composed of a small number of men on whose loyalty he felt he could rely. Several of them were German – Benckendorff, Nesselrode and Kiselev

Table 3.1 Summary of the six Sections

	Short description	Date	Personnel	Task
First Section	Imperial Chancery	1825	Section heads and ministers	Advice
Second Section	Law reform	1826	Speransky	Codification
Third Section	Secret police	1826	Benckendorff, then Orlov	Surveillance
Fourth Section	Charities	1828	Uvarov, then Shikmatov	Education
Fifth Section	State peasants	1836	Kiselev	Modernisation
Sixth Section	Caucasus	1842	Vorontsov	Supervision

for example – and each was charged with a specific task that Nicholas thought was in need of attention. In other words, they were based on practical requirements rather than any carefully thought out plan, and the way in which new Sections were created in the 1830s also demonstrates this. It was a mark of the success that Nicholas felt the early Sections had achieved. Noticeably, there was no Section created to deal with the state finances which remained the responsibility of Kankrin in one of the old style ministries and the same was true of foreign affairs, entrusted to Nesselrode. There were other aspects of the existing senior councils that survived, too, but in a less important role. The Committee of Ministers, composed of the chief of each Ministry, continued to meet but it had less power and none of its members ever reached the status that Arakcheyev had enjoyed. It became more important during wartime but while the tsar was in Saint Petersburg he kept it under very close watch. Its chairman 1827–34 was Kochubey and from 1834–38 Novosiltsov. Likewise, the Senate and Council of State remained in place but with less influence. They were scrutinised by a committee set up on 6 December 1826 that met until 1832, and which made recommendations to the tsar about administrative reform. At the start of his reign, Nicholas was keen to catch up with developments with which he had not expected to become involved and this accounts for the flurry of activity.

The second Section was led by Speransky who in 1826 was recalled from his posting as governor of Siberia. He was a liberal and had been dismissed by Alexander I in 1812 under pressure from the nobles because of the imminent war against Napoleon. He was also a highly efficient administrator and it was probably this that affected Nicholas' choice. His task was to codify the Russian laws, something that he had begun to do 1808–12 after the slow progress of the 1801 Law Commission set up under Radischev. Despite his earlier intervention, the position was still confused. Borovkov complained that 'We have one edict after another. One stops something, the next restarts it … we have a multiplicity of mutually contradictory laws. As a result, the strong and slanderers profit whilst the poor and innocent suffer.' The second chance that Speransky now had to clarify the vast number of laws seemed to be a liberal and even compassionate move by Nicholas.

In fact, the prime motive for his action was to increase the efficiency of the state. By removing obsolete and/or contradictory laws from the list of statutes, the tsar could prosecute criminal subjects more effectively and the speed at which this could be done might also be increased. It was no coincidence that the start of the reign was dominated by the trials of the Decembrists. The work of codification was completed in a similarly incisive way. The Section began on 26 May 1828 and published its 'Complete Collection' of forty-five volumes of 30 000 laws on 1 April 1830. Despite its name, the Complete Collection was added to in 1832 with a fifteen volume 'Digest' which came into effect in 1835. If the speed was impressive, the quality of the Section's work was less so. Often, the easiest route to simplification was chosen, such that the most recent law was kept and any previous rulings were rejected; this meant that the greater wisdom of previous years was sometimes lost. Gaps were also left by, for instance, the omission of church laws and the absence of any edicts issued during periods of crisis over the last century.

The overall effect of the second Section was to scale down the volume of laws that had to be considered and this measure made for a clearer system of justice. This had an effect in particular on the relations between landlords and their serfs in favour of the latter. It highlighted above all something that had been widely acknowledged before – that the practice of serfdom was illegal. Nicholas did not act to correct this, though, since the position of the nobles was being weakened by the work of the second Section and he did not want to lose their support. Moreover, any change to the position of serfs would require massive readjustments to the organisation of society at large and Nicholas was not prepared to do this. In the 1830s, the second Section continued its efforts by assimilating laws of foreign origin into the system. Its work also led to the creation of a centre for formal legal training at the 'Imperial School for Jurisprudence' in 1835. Properly trained legal professionals were employed in ever greater numbers in the decades that followed.

The third Section was led by Benckendorff from its inception in 1826 until he was replaced by Orlov in 1844 and they both organised the secret police. The history of this group over the previous decades had been chequered. Under Catherine the Great the 'Secret Expedition' as it was called played only a minor role and concentrated on investigating major acts of treason such as the Pugachev Rebellion but under Paul its role was widened as his well-founded fear of plots against him grew. Alexander had abolished it early in 1801 and had specifically forbidden the use of torture. However, a secret police of a kind still operated under a different name. Now, Nicholas tried to make a new beginning after proposals put before him by Benckendorff. During the first five years of the reign, it won the support of what public opinion there was in Russia, among the nobles and gentry in Moscow and Saint Petersburg, because it promised to root out corrupt officials and landlords. But, with the passage of time and the alarm that foreign rebellions caused to the tsar, its functions changed and it became more concerned with censorship and surveillance. The biggest impact it had was on the urban and educated classes of society rather than on the poor or rural population, as was shown by the groups that it targeted and by its struggle to control the printing of the written word. This, and the mismanagement of one or two trials, added to its notoriety when in fact most Russians were unaffected by its work.

The duties of the third Section were listed as the collection of information on suspicious individuals and groups such as political opponents, foreign nationals and religious sects. It was responsible for their apprehension and punishment. It staffed some of the prisons and it collated statistics on the activities of those it watched, including its role as censor of all theatre productions. Regular reports were written on the state of public opinion. Its members were dressed in conspicuous uniforms of bright blue with white gloves in order to emphasise their purity, which led to their nickname of the 'blue archangels'. They watched over about two thousand people each year but had their attention drawn to many more. Petitions to the tsar, for instance, were always investigated by the third Section and informants were encouraged to come forward by being offered financial rewards. The use of bribes, of course, was open to abuse and led to many unfounded allegations and cases of people being detained wrongly. Another way in which the third Section actively tried to prevent conspiracies was by issuing propaganda of its own. Anonymous articles were placed in friendly newspapers in Russia and abroad in praise of the tsar's efforts. Censorship of critical views became widespread. A law of 1826 allowed the suppression of almost any publication but it was applied more in later years. Only three periodicals were ever banned outright but there were some bizarre examples of what was deleted from proposed texts, from descriptions of poverty in Russia, to corpses in medical books and even a reference to 'free air' in a cookery book! Further more, the third Section developed a kind of corruption of its own as it became steadily easier to punish than to investigate; consequently, by the 1840s, the trust placed in it by the public was dwindling.

The record of achievement left by the third Section certainly became tainted as it began to focus more on repression on behalf of the tsar than on suppressing corruption on behalf of ordinary people. Ironically, what was at the heart of the problem was the absence of any serious political threat to Nicholas which might have justified the Section's existence. It was brought into being primarily by the tsar's own fears of conspiracy which were begun by the circumstances of his own accession and reinforced by the foreign rebellions. The intensification of its surveillance after 1830 led to two infamous cases of prosecution in which the Section seemed to be trying too hard to find conspiracies since neither amounted to a threat to the regime. The first was in 1847 when a Ukrainian nationalist society was uncovered. This was used as a reason for stifling any expression of Ukrainian culture or identity such as the work of its leading poet, Shevchenko. Second, in April 1849, the Petrashevsky Circle was discovered. It might be seen as nothing more than a group of people who met to discuss Russian affairs, but the degree of criticism its members levelled against the political system led to 39 of them being arrested. They were taken to court, accused of being revolutionaries and some of them were sentenced to death, including the novelist Dostoyevsky. They received a reprieve from the tsar when they were almost at the gallows and he hoped that this act of clemency would win him public support. He was wrong. The use of these innocent people to demonstrate the tsar's power and arrogance won him no friends at all.

The fourth Section dealt mostly with education and was led by Uvarov when it began in 1828. It worked closely with the secret police as they had a common interest in suppressing dangerous ideas; put simply, one tended to focus on adults while the other targeted the young. Uvarov himself had a background in education, having been head of the Saint Petersburg education district until 1819 and he was an intellectual who had a love of the classics. Nevertheless, he was a conservative who was wary of educating too many people since he believed that education should befit a person's status. His control of the freedom of expression in Russia lasted from 1833 until 1849 when he was succeeded by Shikmatov. Uvarov inherited an education system that had become much larger under Alexander I but which still failed to reach the vast majority of the population – the peasants and serfs. It was based on four tiers, beginning with parish schools and district schools, and then moving to the higher echelons of provincial schools and finally the six universities for the nobles. Alexander and his Unofficial Committee of young friends had identified the lack of well qualified bureaucrats as a serious weakness in Russian society and had attempted to remedy it. No such ambition was shown in the reign of Nicholas: quite the opposite. He saw education as dangerous.

It was Uvarov who devised the maxim 'Orthodoxy, Autocracy, Nationality' in the early 1830s and which was adopted as a motto for the entire regime. It was sometimes known alternatively as the doctrine of 'Official Nationality'. Orthodoxy amounted to the support of the Orthodox Church, especially in Russia's border areas such as Poland, but the word was also used to imply support for conventional attitudes and behaviour, in keeping with Russia's own past. In this respect it supported the work of the third Section where critical (unorthodox) views were discouraged. It had an impact on the major cultural discussion of the period, that between westernisers and Slavophiles. Autocracy meant support for the established system of government and in particular for the tsar. His status as an absolute ruler was to be unchallenged. Nicholas' position was reaffirmed by reference to Russia's history and his position even began to attract a mild personality cult (on which Nicholas himself was not keen). One historian proposed, rather optimistically, that Russia be renamed 'Nicholaevia'. Nationality was a potentially dangerous idea to promote since the Russian Empire was composed of many different nationalities. But in this instance, it meant only Russian nationality and was a euphemism for the promotion of Russian ideas, language, culture and religion. It was made up of a synthesis of the two previous ideas, orthodoxy and autocracy. 'Orthodoxy, Autocracy, Nationality' amounted to an overlapping set of values rather than a coherent set of policies but as a snappy summary of what Nicholas liked it was quite effective.

Several groups within the empire suffered as a result of 'Nationality'. A group of intellectuals, led by Shevchenko, were jailed for trying to revive a sense of nationhood in the Ukraine. Jews were forced to join the army from the age of twelve in an attempt to make them lose their separate identity (from 1827), and in the 1840s a package of measures was devised to integrate them into Russian society, including their migration from the countryside to towns. In this sense, the concept of 'Nationality' was used as a punishment against resistant minorities. By contrast, in Siberia Speransky's reforms of the 1820s continued to operate and to benefit the population at large. The Finns retained their own laws, Lutheran Church and tariffs under Menshikov as a reward for remaining loyal. The groups to suffer most were those peoples who were still being conquered and subordinated by Russia, in Poland and the Caucasus, which are considered later.

The application of the doctrine of Official Nationality to universities meant a meaner and narrower view of the purpose of education than under Alexander and after 1848 the situation became grim. Uvarov reorganised the universities in 1835 by weakening their autonomy so as to make them more accountable to him. One way in which this became apparent was that new appointments to the post of professor had to be made by him. The teaching at universities was supervised more closely so that what the lecturers and the students wrote was subject to inspection. Despite this, significant progress was made with teaching natural sciences and, at Uvarov's instigation, Oriental Studies too. The study of History was encouraged (in line with the idea of autocracy) but, by contrast, Philosophy was cut back heavily. He was interested in restricting university education to the nobles and to discourage the middle-classes' access; thus, he raised the fees during the late 1840s. However, the number of students at university increased from 2150 to 3490 between 1832 and 1842. And Uvarov tried to raise the quality of teaching in universities by nurturing more Russian talent and becoming less dependent on west European staff.

A huge change occurred in the policy towards universities after 1848. Uvarov resigned when Nicholas began a clamp-down on universities after the 1848–49 revolutions in Europe. He was replaced by Shikmatov whose policies were extremely harsh and almost led to the closure of some universities. Student numbers fell by about a quarter in his first two years (down to 3000) as he carried out panic policies inspired by the tsar. 'I have no thought, no will of my own – I am the blind instrument of the will of my sovereign' he explained. Now, scientific and technical subjects were promoted at the expense of arts (and especially political) courses. Classics, the area that Uvarov had loved, was cut back in particular because it included a study of Greek civilisation which was considered much too liberal. Students had to wear uniforms and even conform to having the same haircut. Overall, the courses that were taught prepared graduates for entry to the bureaucracy as a practical use of their education, rather than as a means to discover new or radical ideas.

Under Uvarov, schools were expanded within the existing four-tier system. At the top level, the provincial schools (or 'gimnaziia') were increased from 64 to 76 between 1832 and 1842. Likewise, the district schools increased from 393 to 445 and the lowly parish schools doubled in number from 552 to 1067 during the same period. The total number of pupils rose in line with these figures by about a third, although precise statistics are hard to pin down because there were several alternative groups of schools run by the churches and the military colonies. While most children in the empire still received no education at all, the number was clearly rising and gaining momentum. One innovation of the period worthy of particular note was the foundation of some three hundred Sunday schools by Pirogov mostly in the Kiev education district which taught literacy (rather than knowledge of the scriptures).

The fifth Section was founded in 1836 and was led by Pavel Kiselev and its official name was the Ministry of State Properties (or Domains). Its function was to increase the economic efficiency of the state peasants so as to provide an example to the private landlords and thereby encourage them to make changes too. It had no jurisdiction over the serfs but became a rival to the Ministry of the Interior which was responsible for them. The fifth Section was comparable to the military colonies except that there were no soldiers involved. It compelled the state peasants to improve their farming techniques, for instance, and imposed on them new crops such as potatoes. Up to 200 000 peasants were forcibly resettled in new villages with better facilities such as schools, hospitals and churches. Loans were made available to the peasants so that they could buy their own land, possibly as a forerunner of a wider scheme for the emancipation of the serfs. The rights of peasants were confirmed, in line with Speransky's up-dated legal Digest of 1832, and legal advisers were appointed in order to defend them. This may be evidence of a more liberal side to Nicholas' otherwise repressive policies but it must be borne in mind that this was something that he inflicted on them. Many resented it because they were deeply attached to their existing villages – and they were so wary of the new farming methods that there was a wave of riots in the early 1840s. Nicholas' liberal motives may be doubted.

The more likely reason for the creation of this Section was that the state's land was poorly run but, if properly managed, could be turned into an important source of revenue. The state peasants amounted to about half of Russia's entire workforce and had a vast potential to boost exports and pay taxes. A survey of the early 1830s suggested that forestry yielded 600 000 roubles of revenue each year but incurred costs of 900 000 due to fires and illegal felling of trees. Investment in each mir was recognised as being desperately low, but there was little information on which to base any decisions for improvements. The fifth Section was divided into four departments which dealt either with a geographical area (Russia and the outlying regions) or a special interest (forests and land use). These then provided information on which long-term plans could be made. The policies that Kiselev implemented successfully raised government income, from 280 million roubles in the twelve years 1826–38 to 360 million roubles 1838–50. But how far the resettlement of even two hundred thousand people could change Russian society, which numbered close to sixty million by 1850, is debatable and Kiselev himself was left making admissions of the programme's limited scope.

The serfs and the Russian economy

The serfs accounted for the half of the population that was not living on land owned by the state. They were the property of their landlord and were usually treated as such. Their existence was likely to be miserable as they relied on subsistence farming for their own food while having to work the land of their lord. In theory, this kept him in sufficient funds to maintain an affluent lifestyle but the mismanagement of many private estates meant that a significant proportion of the nobles were in debt. This situation rarely prompted them to make any improvements to their land, though, as they tended to take a short-term view of their assets and frequently mortgaged them to the state so as to raise funds. This undermined the strength of Russia as a whole, something of which Nicholas was well aware.

The serfs were discontented with their situation. Most had aspirations of eventual emancipation – so far as their attitude can be gleaned from what records there are – but in Nicholas' reign there were no immediate prospects of this happening. The successful war against Napoleon in 1812–15 had raised their hopes of freedom but nothing had changed as Alexander had passed only minor reforms. The most significant of these was the 1803 Free Cultivator's Law which allowed landlords to free their serfs if they saw fit. Nicholas' view was that the situation needed investigation, not least because Speransky's second Section had shown serfdom to be illegal. There was a series of secret committees organised by Nicholas to look at the serf question but little was actually done. Some cruel punishments were banned, like knouting, and some humanitarian measures were introduced, such as banning the sale of serfs by auction and the splitting up of families. How far these laws were upheld, though, is doubtful. A law on obligated peasants of 1842 meant serfs and lords could draw up their own terms for employment, and the equalisation of the status of household and agricultural serfs was established with a law of 1844 allowing lords to free the former if they saw fit. The committees had to be kept secret for fear of news of them leaking out to the general population and causing unrest. Certainly, the serfs themselves were likely to react – possibly with rioting and widespread violence – but the nobles might become restless too and turn their anger against the tsar. A growing number of nobles were reinforcing the usefulness of the system of serfdom by sending them to work in factories and so were determined to maintain the system. By 1855 there were 500 000 serfs employed in this way. In common with the laws passed for agricultural communities, the laws passed to regulate industrial work places were not effective.

Exploitation was not unusual in the serf economy but in Nicholas' reign there emerged another way in which the serfs' conditions deteriorated. The population was outstripping the food supply and severe hunger was becoming a more common experience. The situation did not quite reach famine proportions and the problems could be localised, but the level of the problem was growing as the statistics for unrest demonstrate. Research by Jerome Blum has revealed that the number of serf (and peasant) rebellions that required troops to quell them more than doubled in the mid nineteenth century.[3] There were 148 such cases in the period 1826–34, compared to 216 for 1835–44 and 348 for 1845–54. Unrest peaked at times of general scarcity after poor harvests, such as in 1848–49, but could also be induced by an epidemic such as cholera breaking out, as it did 1830–31 and again in the dreadful period of 1848–49. Up to 150 000 people were exiled to Siberia as a result of rebellion during Nicholas' reign. The increase in unrest was not a short-term feature that was likely to disappear if the tsar rode out the storm; by the 1840s and 1850s the prospect was for a continual worsening of the situation unless something fundamental was changed. Nicholas, however, was not ready to make the change that was needed: the emancipation of the serfs.

Industrialisation remained sluggish and confined to a few manufacturing sectors. Iron output continued to be based around the Urals but large-scale investment in foundries did not take place. Pig-iron production doubled between 1800 and 1860 from 9.9 to 20.5 million poods, while the amount of cotton spun inside Russia meant that it was 90 per cent self-sufficient by 1860. This one activity accounted for as much as a third of the industrial workers yet it was dwarfed by the number of cotton workers who were employed in the domestic 'putting out' system (which totalled 350 000). The extent of textile production was confined to the areas around Moscow and Saint Petersburg. Accurate statistics are difficult to calculate on the basis of the limited evidence left by the tsarist regimes and the fact that many historians' surveys deal with several decades at a time indicates how little discernible change there was. However, one measure that might be used to gauge industrialisation is the proportion of the population living in towns; this is still a blunt instrument, though, since a lot of industrial activity was rural. The major towns grew significantly. Moscow increased from 270 000 in 1811 to 463 000 in 1863. For the same period, Saint Petersburg grew from 335 000 to 540 000, but the biggest growth was in Odessa, from 11 000 to 120 000. The last example reflected not industry so much as the increase in trade in grain. Russia remained an emphatically rural society with an agricultural economy throughout Nicholas' reign.

Russian commercial and financial policies were the responsibility of the Ministry of Finance, which was not superseded by any new Section. The man in charge from 1823 to 1844 was Kankrin, a German and former army quartermaster. He supported protective tariffs on foreign imports, which served as a way of raising additional government revenue from the otherwise untaxed nobility, and he ensured that exports of grain increased during Nicholas' reign. Russia's share of world trade remained stable at approximately 3.5 per cent at a time when world trade was expanding on a huge scale. His financial policies meant that the state budgets were made to balance and he stabilised the value of the currency which made for easier trading conditions for the merchant class – until the turmoil caused by the Crimean War. Intervention in the economy was difficult when revenues were limited but he tried to ignite change by providing technical training and supervisory bodies with specialist knowledge. The Council of Manufactures (1828) and the Forestry Institute (1829) fell into this category. What he neglected, though, was the development of railways. The first section of track, from Moscow to Tsarskoe Selo, was opened in 1838 but the twin capitals of Moscow and Saint Petersburg were not linked until 1851. By 1854, Russia still had only 700 kilometres of track. Kankrin believed that railways were unnecessary to economic growth, despite the remoteness of some of Russia's manufacturing bases such as the Urals, and he was aware that they could be misused to spread unwelcome literature and ideas. Thus, one of the key developments of the age was retarded by the one man who might have been expected to invigorate the Russian economy.

Westernisers and Slavophiles

It was in part the economic backwardness of Russia that provoked a debate during Nicholas' reign about the status of Russia compared to its west European great power neighbours. This period in English and French history was studied by contemporaries who were concerned about the living and working conditions of the labouring classes. On one side of the Channel it was called the 'condition of England' question and was debated in parliament, in the press and in working class circles; on the other it was more of a subject for left-wing activists but they had a broad following in the major cities. In both cases the arguments were over the unwanted effects of rapid and unplanned industrial expansion. In Russia, a debate emerged about the more fundamental issue of how best to preserve the country's status and strength as a great power, which included industrial growth but went much deeper. There were two groups involved and both were patriotic and concerned only for Russia's long term future. One of these was the Slavophiles, who looked to Russia's traditional practices based on the mir, the autocracy and the Church for inspiration. The other was the westernisers who looked abroad for their guidance and recruited Peter the Great as an example of a tsar who had used western expertise to inject new vitality into Russia. This kind of debate was itself new to Russia and reflected the arrival of something that had only recently emerged in western and central Europe. This was the expression of open debate, in newspapers and periodicals, or in coffee-houses and clubs that made governmental affairs part of the public domain. It had become a legitimate activity to scrutinise the state in such a way and had become, in a sense, a right. It was this that had concerned the third Section so much when it uncovered the so-called conspiracy of the Petrashevsky Circle in 1849 and which also explained the indignation of Russian public opinion when Nicholas only gave those involved a reprieve when they were about to be executed.

In all of this debate, the number of individuals involved was relatively small and they mostly belonged to an educated class of intellectuals, the intelligentsia. Some of them worked for the government. As a group, it was increasing in size as the readership of one leading journal *The Contemporary* demonstrates. Its circulation rose from 233 in 1846 to 3100 in 1848 and 6500 by 1861. Its characteristics have been summarised by Offord as being critical in outlook, largely outside the centres of power and being prepared to suffer penalties and punishments for standing up to the regime. However, the two opposing groups were not divorced from each other and their dialogue was not confined to the pages of learned periodicals since they were of much the same social class and frequently met face to face in each other's houses in the 1830s and early 1840s. Attitudes hardened in the later 1840s, though. The debate was triggered by the publication of a 'Philosophical Letter' by Peter Chaadayev in 1836. It took a very critical view of Russia's past and asserted that because it had been isolated from Europe for much of its history, including the Renaissance and Reformation, it was a quite different society and was therefore set to develop in future in different ways too. It was a pessimistic view as it seemed to condemn Russia to remaining economically backward and culturally unsophisticated. It was an attack not on an aspect of Russian life but on the whole of its existence, past and present. Caught up in this, of course, was the tsar himself. This kind of criticism was intolerable and *The Telescope*, the journal that carried the article, was closed down; its editor, Nadezhdin, was placed under internal exile and Chaadayev himself was put under house arrest and declared to be mad.

The 'Philosophical Letter' was a beacon for the westernisers who believed that radical changes were needed in Russia. It appealed to a number of educated men who had felt adrift from society after the failure of the Decembrist Revolt and it was thus a rallying point. The westernisers were led by Belinsky who was a literary critic, Herzen who was the editor of *The Bell* a radical periodical published in London from 1856 and smuggled into Russia, and by Granovsky who was a professor at Moscow University. Their views were diverse and prone to change in the light of events at home and abroad. Herzen, for example, was known as the 'first Russian Socialist' and was very much on the left-wing of the group. He initially believed that Russia first needed to transfer power away from the tsar and to communities of peasants and ex-serfs. His attitudes changed after witnessing the revolutions of 1848–49 towards more controls on the kind of leadership any new states might have so as not to replace one unaccountable ruler with many others at a local level. His influence was restricted by the exile that he had to endure but it suffered again after he backed the Poles' rebellion in 1863 as even Russia's intelligentsia did not care so much for the rights of Poles. However, he had a lasting impact in the legacy given to future revolutionaries who wanted to change Russia radically. It was Belinsky, however, who wrote the classic anti-church text of the westernisers in 1847 in his 'Letter to Gogol'. This was a damning diatribe about the role of the church as the 'handmaid of despotism'.

The Slavophiles were led by Khomyakov and Kireyevsky and they opposed the pessimism to be found among the westernisers. They remained much more confident of Russia's own virtues and, not surprisingly, tended to be more establishment figures. They defended the system which protected and supported them and they tended to be a more homogeneous group. They also displayed much more conviction about Christianity and Khomyakov in particular argued that the Orthodox faith was superior to the Catholicism of the west. Slavophiles championed the mir as a distinctively Russian institution and set great store by its preservation – something that westernisers adopted more as time passed. In contrast to Chaadayev's 'Philosophical Letter', the Slavophile view was that Russian history was something of which to be proud and they saw the westernising influence of Peter the Great as something of an aberration. Clearly, this group was the one that Nicholas was ready to embrace as it fitted in so obviously with his three watchwords of 'Orthodoxy, Autocracy, Nationality'. He tried to silence the westernisers by exiling or imprisoning some of their leaders but such an approach lacked understanding; both groups involved in the debate cared a great deal about Russia and its destiny.

One effect of Nicholas' intolerance of criticism and his use of censorship was that westernisers – and other groups or individuals like them – were forced to find less obvious outlets for their views. While newspapers and topical periodicals could easily be censored if their content was overtly political, it was more difficult to control or direct the work of literary figures. This may in part account for the rise of Russian literature during this period to new heights of achievement since it carried the burden of intellectual discussion more heavily than in other countries. It was no coincidence that Belinsky was a critic. The writers who published material at this time used novels, plays and poems to express themselves and did not feel confined to any one of the three literary forms. Novels were often serialised in periodicals or magazines which proliferated in the 1830s and 1840s as a result. Their circulation varied from a few hundred for the likes of the government-backed *Muscovite* to several thousand for

Table 3.2 Major works of Russian literature under Nicholas I, 1825–55

Writer		Major works	Date
Pushkin, Alexander (1799–1837)	poet	*Boris Godunov*	1825
		Eugene Onegin	1831
		The Bronze Horseman	1833
		The Captain's Daughter	1836
Lermontov, Michael (1814–41)	poet	*A Hero of Our Time*	1840
Gogol, Nikolai (1809–52)	novelist	*Dead Souls*	1842
		The Government Inspector	1836
Turgenev, Ivan (1818–83)	playwright/ novelist	*A Month in the Country*	1849
		Sportsman's Sketches	1852
Dostoevsky, Fyodor (1821–81)	novelist	*Poor Folk*	1846

Library of Reading. They could be closed down if they offended the censors and this was what happened to *The European* in 1832 and to the *Moscow Telegraph* in 1834. However, the system of censorship was not so efficient that it was able to stop an attack as blatant as the 'Philosophical Letter' getting through – even if *The Telescope* which ran it was subsequently suppressed. By 1848 there were twelve agencies that could censor work either before or after publication, and the period from 1848 to 1855 when Nicholas died, became known as the 'dismal seven years'. Despite this the reign of Nicholas could not prevent a fair measure of debate taking place.

The subjects for discussion varied but most writers took a negative view of the reign of Nicholas since it was so hostile to their art; thus, their legacy and criticisms have informed subsequent students' views of the period while those of people outside of the literate intelligentsia have not survived. The play *The Government Inspector* by Gogol was one of the most directly political and critical texts as it dwelt on the corruption of local officials. Pushkin was treated leniently by Nicholas given his bitter condemnation of Arakcheyev with which many could identify. Turgenev's *Sportsman's Sketches* tried to make the peasantry seem human, a novel concept to many of those in authority or who owned estates, and this was also a challenge to the autocratic system. Perhaps too many words were written lamenting the premature deaths of both Pushkin and Lermontov in duels since the literary world could also be a small one, but another significant theme in some of the literature of the age was the idea of the 'superfluous man'. He was first identified by Lermontov in *A Hero of Our Time* and the typical character who fell into this role was someone of education and talent whose abilities could not be fulfilled due to the nature of the Russian society in which he lived. The problem he faced was that there were too many people like him and he could not find appropriate employment. The fictional and eponymous figure at the centre of Pushkin's *Eugene Onegin* fell into this category. Just as there was a flow of informed literature being written, so there was a supply of critics who were ready to interpret the texts for the readership and in this way an intellectual debate took place under the noses of the censors. Moreover, the importance of the novel in Russian society was elevated as a result and went on to play an even greater part in society under the next tsar, Alexander

II, in the 1860s and 1870s. Despite the writers' gloomy despondency, they managed to achieve a great deal in the face of adversity.

The problem of Poland

Poland was presented by the tsar as being a free state. Nicholas I claimed it was not part of the Russian Empire as he was not its emperor but its king and he relied on his older brother, the Grand Duke Constantine, to govern it in his absence. From 1816, Poland had had its own parliament, with a Senate and an elected lower house or 'Sejm'; and it still had its own army of 35 000 men. However, this was a façade. Poland was under Russian rule and had been so since the Congress of Vienna had created 'Congress Poland' in 1815. It comprised the heartland of Poland with the capital, Warsaw, at its centre but it did not include many of the territories to which it might lay claim. Prussia had annexed the province of Posen (Poznan) and the city of Thorn (Torun) both of which lay to the west. Austria had taken a tract of land to the south known as Galicia. Kraków became a free city. And Russia had kept as its own sovereign territory a giant swathe of land first annexed in the 1772 Partition of Poland and which had never even featured in the talks at Vienna. From 1815, Poland was not even half the state it had been in the eighteenth century. It was perhaps the best candidate for some recognition of national independence to be granted at Vienna as its people had their own language, culture and history. Its political élite wanted to be governed not just separately but independently, preferably by their own Polish leaders. But Poland was subjected to the machinations of great power diplomacy because it was too weak to defend itself against them and after Napoleon had been expelled it was occupied by 600 000 Russian troops.

Under Tsar Alexander I, Poland was treated leniently in that it was able to develop its national life, using the constitution as a starting point. This was a deliberate policy since Alexander saw it as something of an experiment and he was pleased to open the first session of the Sejm in 1818. The rights of ordinary citizens were recognised such that Polish remained the official language and the Roman Catholic Church was free to minister to its followers – most of the Poles. The Napoleonic Code, which had been introduced to Poland under French occupation of the Grand Duchy of Warsaw, was maintained and the country was administered by Polish officials. In fact, there was a large degree of continuity between the Napoleonic state and the Russian equivalent. Educational expansion was impressive as the University of Warsaw was set up in 1816 and the number of primary schools exceeded one thousand by 1820. This did not satisfy significant numbers of the educated élite who, as army officers or as students, continued to hope for Polish independence. There were several secret societies set up during Alexander's reign each of which was nationalistic and they even hoped to recover lands that had historically belonged to Poland such as Lithuania. The main example of these was the Polish Patriotic Society, set up in May 1821, and which had links with the Russian Decembrists.

The early years of Tsar Nicholas I's reign also showed a large measure of continuity. He did not like so liberal a state within the territories he ruled but was prepared to tolerate it so long as it remained loyal. Good work was being done by Poland's finance minister, Drucki-Lubecki, who believed that co-operation with Russia would make for prosperity in Poland. His landmark achievement was the creation of a state bank in

1828. However, the links between the Polish Patriotic Society and the Decembrists left Nicholas very sceptical about the kingdom's future status and, symbolically, he delayed his coronation as king until 1829. He also extended the work of the third Section, the secret police, to Poland which was an ominous sign. The Sejm tried to assert as much independence as it could manage and defied the tsar over the trial of Krzyzanowski, a member of the Patriotic Society linked to the Decembrists, by insisting it was held in Poland rather than in Russia. This only served to irritate Nicholas further.

The Polish Revolt of 1830–31 changed the strained Russo–Polish relationship and changed Nicholas' attitude as he simply lost all patience and resolved on a demonstration of Russian power – a situation that had always existed in practice but which had not been forced to the surface until now. Whereas the Sejm could manoeuvre skilfully in technical legal cases, it could do nothing to stop the intervention of Russian troops to keep law and order and to reassert Russian control. The causes of the rebellion are not difficult to find. The deeply held dislike of Russian rule among the élite meant that outright hostility was only a question of time. When Paris rose in rebellion in February 1830, it served as a beacon to political activists all over Europe – Belgium, Italy, Germany and Poland – and encouraged another group of conspirators in Warsaw, led by a junior army officer called Wysocki, to mutiny. Some form of action was urgent because the group which he was leading was under investigation and was likely to be uncovered in the foreseeable future. It had planned an assassination attempt against Constantine. Moreover, Tsar Nicholas was set to increase the number of Russian troops stationed in Poland with a view to using them against the rebellion that had occurred in Belgium, and so any rebellion in Poland itself stood a better chance of success before their arrival. The difficult economic conditions prevalent in much of Europe at this time did not seem to have any bearing on the rebellion; the peasant population in Poland remained unmoved by the entire episode and took no part in it.

The course of the rebellion had as its starting point the young army officers' mobilisation of ten thousand troops in Warsaw on 29 November 1830. It began in the Military Academy but soon spread to the civilian population of the city when rifles and ammunition were given out. Grand Duke Constantine, as viceroy, fled from the danger but chose not to use any force himself in an attempt to encourage restraint among the rebels. The initial act of disobedience snow-balled in the Polish winter when troops from outside the city, under the command of General Szembek, joined the rising. During December the news of the Polish rising reached Nicholas and he quickly decided that there would be no compromises reached with the rebels and he called on them to surrender. The Poles themselves were unsure of the best course of action since Warsaw was in armed revolt but stood no chance against the Russian army which was about to be despatched. Two groups emerged from a chaotic situation; the moderates who urged caution and the radicals who were much more extreme and demanded war against Russia and a return of the lost territory of Lithuania. This was madness but the euphoria of rebellion was intoxicating. It was the radicals whose view prevailed and by January a state of war existed between Poland and Russia. The early exchanges favoured the Poles whose army numbered 70 000 and was initially larger than the Russian force under Dybicz. Minor battles were fought in eastern Poland from February to April 1831 but the decisive encounter was at Ostroleka in May. Although the casualties on each side were similar, Russia won the day and the Poles retreated towards their capital. Cholera began to decimate both armies but, lacking reinforcements, the Polish army was affected more. By September Warsaw was being besieged by the Russian General Paskevich and, after the Poles had failed to counter this move, their last troops surrendered to the Prussians in October 1831.

The rebellion failed because it lacked support. It had the backing of the Polish army which gave it an early advantage and it was quickly adopted by the middle class of Warsaw but it never made any impact on the rural population of peasants. The Polish landlords did not invite the support of their peasants by promising any kind of land reform that might have won them over. More important than the peasants, though, were the great powers. From the start, Nicholas was certain of his need to crush the rebellion, acidly stating that 'Russia or Poland must now perish'. He was supported by Prussia and Austria, both of which closed their borders to the Poles and moved troops to their frontier with Russian Poland so as to discourage any sympathy rising among their own Polish populations. In these circumstances, there was nothing that the western states of Britain or France could do. The Polish rebels called for assistance in April 1831 but the leadership had known from the start that this was unlikely. Poland was an area beyond the reach of western European states. They could watch and make speeches as gestures of support but there was nothing practical that could be done.

As a result of the uprising, Poland was brought under closer Russian control. An Organic Decree was issued by way of a surrogate constitution which preserved the rights of individuals but abolished the Sejm and meant Poland was subject to rule by military decree. General Paskevich became the new viceroy who ruled on Nicholas' behalf and his style of government soon earnt him the nickname 'Prince of Warsaw'. Constantine had died in the cholera epidemic of 1831 but his moderation towards the rebels had probably jeopardised his position anyway. The Polish army was disbanded and integrated into the Russian forces before being sent to fight in the Caucasus. Many of the landlords were punished by the confiscation of their estates and as much as one tenth of Poland's land was redistributed to Russians. Some 80 000 ordinary Poles were sentenced to exile in Siberia and were forced to march there in chains. The first stages

Table 3.3 Major events in Polish history, 1772–1863

1772–1795	*Partitions of Poland* between Russia, Austria and Prussia. Poland disappeared from the map as a separate state.
1807–1812	*Grand Duchy of Warsaw* created by Napoleon.
1815	*Congress Poland devised at the Congress of Vienna* which was under Russian control but left Austria to rule Galicia, and Prussia to rule Posen and Thorn. Russia kept the Lithuanian lands to the east but granted Congress Poland a constitution and allowed it an army.
1816	*University of Warsaw established.*
1818	*Sejm first met.*
1821	*Polish Patriotic Society, a nationalist group, was set up.*
1828	*Polish State Bank created.*
1830–1831	*Polish Revolt* began in November 1830 in Warsaw and was led by the army. It failed to win over the peasants. The decisive battle of Ostroleka in May 1831 led to Warsaw being besieged and surrendering in October. Russification began.
1848–1849	No rebellion in Poland, unlike elsewhere in Europe.
1863	*Polish Revolt* broke out once more.

of the Russification of Poland began – a policy that was to be intensified after the rebellion of 1863 – and this was entirely in keeping with Nicholas' policy of 'Nationality'. An Orthodox cathedral was built in the middle of Catholic Warsaw and a fortress constructed as a stronghold and prison. The Russian language was taught in schools and became the official form of communication in the civil service. The universities in Vilna and Warsaw were closed down. Many Poles fled the country and lived in exile, mostly in Paris but also in London. They included Czartoryski who had joined the rebel government and the pianist and composer Chopin and altogether numbered between 5 and 10 000. They formed pressure groups and secret societies abroad but the western great powers needed little persuading of their plight. The British government voted funds to the refugees in Britain, and the French parliament kept the issue alive by passing a motion of support for the Poles every year. But when much of Europe was in the throes or rebellion again in 1848–49, Poland did not rise; Nicholas had stifled the opposition.

The rebellions in France and Belgium also exercised Nicholas' mind. Before Poland rebelled, it had been his intention to send an army to Russia's most westerly frontier so as to threaten an invasion of these states that had been infected by revolution. The Holy Alliance, which had been divided over the Greek revolt, was set to return and try to maintain the Vienna settlement in its original form. The Troppau Protocol was to be invoked again. The rising in Paris was of particular concern because it meant that a great power had become affected and Louis-Philippe, its new king, felt quite vulnerable on the throne in the early months of his reign. He was acutely aware of the fact that he was not a legitimate ruler in the view of the three eastern great powers and so courted the friendship of Britain. Belgium was a more credible target for Russian intervention since it was only a minor state and its rebellion had altered the Vienna frontiers. In practice, the close co-operation of France and Britain rendered the ambitions of any other state pointless and Belgium was able to secure its independence in 1839. The anxiety that Nicholas felt towards west European unrest, though, was genuine and was set to return with the next series of rebellions in 1848–49. It was this preoccupation with order, or perhaps inertia, in other countries that earnt him the accolade of 'the gendarme of Europe'.

The Eastern Question: the Greek rebellion

Nicholas' foreign policy was dominated by the problems caused by the Eastern Question. What this issue amounted to was the future of the Turkish (Ottoman) Empire and what was to be done with it when it collapsed. Most informed observers at the time agreed that it was unstable and likely to break up. The most pressing problem that the empire faced when Nicholas came to power in 1825 was the Greek rebellion which had begun in 1821. Despite the Turkish massacres of Greek Christians on Chios, the rebels had fought well in the early years but began to weaken when the Sultan, Mahmud II, secured the help of Ibrahim Pasha of Egypt. He was the oldest son of Mehmet Ali Pasha, ruler of Egypt, and a local warlord who was subordinate to the sultan within the Turkish Empire. The use of the Egyptian fleet in the Greek islands from 1825 was highly effective and the rebellion looked to be doomed. After landing on Crete, his troops moved onto the Morea (Peloponnese) and began to force the rebels back. However, Tsar Alexander had been moving towards a policy of intervention 1824–25 as shown by the congress he tried to hold on the issue in January 1825 and the Nesslerode Memorandum of August the same year which warned the other great powers that he might intervene unilaterally. Alexander died in December and, from the start of the following year, Nicholas pursued his predecessor's policy in a much more vigorous way.

Russian relations with Turkey were deteriorating because of an entirely separate issue as well. The last war against Turkey had ended in 1812 with the Treaty of Bucharest. This had been concluded as speedily as possible by Russia because of the immediate threat of invasion by Napoleon. It had left Russia in control of Bessarabia (confirmed at the Congress of Vienna) but it had had to return the principalities of Moldavia and Wallachia (modern Romania) to Turkey. The Treaty had placed certain obligations on Turkey for the treatment and government of the principalities which would ensure their semi-independence. By 1824–25 Turkey was in breach of this because it had sent in troops. This animated Nicholas sufficiently to send an ultimatum to the Sultan in March 1826 demanding their withdrawal and threatening war if no action was taken. This caused alarm elsewhere. Neither Britain nor France were ready to see a renewal of war between Russia and Turkey, and so in April 1826 Britain persuaded the tsar to pursue a course of joint action the details of which they declared in the Protocol of Saint Petersburg. France also applied pressure to Turkey to give way to Russian demands and as a result Mahmud II agreed to negotiate. In the Convention of Akkerman, October 1826, the semi-independent status of the principalities (as well as of Serbia) was reaffirmed and Russia also got assurances of free passage for its merchant ships through the Straits of the Dardanelles. This meant its trading links were maintained between the Black Sea and the Mediterranean.

The Greek rebellion continued while this separate dispute was being settled. Ibrahim's progress against the rebels had been unabated and the Sultan had used the talks over the principalities as a way of gaining more time for his ally. By June 1827 Ibrahim had captured Athens. However, the great powers were by now galvanising their efforts. Keen to prevent Russia, or even Russia and Britain, deciding the future of the Levant on their own, France added its weight to their efforts in July 1827 by signing with them the Treaty of London. This largely reiterated the terms of the Saint Petersburg Protocol as it called for an immediate ceasefire and the creation of a Greek state under Turkish protection – very like the situation agreed for Moldavia, Wallachia and Serbia. What was new was that a naval force was gathered together to impose the proposal if Turkey refused to comply. It was again Russia that pushed along the policy which led to the British and French fleets starting a blockade of the Greek islands so as to cut the supply lines for the Egyptian force in the autumn of 1827. The terms of engagement were ambiguous. The commanders were instructed not to use force, yet they had to impose a blockade in a period of war against an enemy that had a rival fleet. The result was that the man in charge of the great powers' ships, Admiral Codrington, was provoked into attacking the Turco-Egyptian vessels when they were anchored in Navarino Bay in November 1827 and destroyed almost all of them. This made the position of the Greeks much stronger and led within a few months to the creation of a completely independent state. Nicholas was prepared to countenance this because of his anger towards Turkey and it at least conformed to the traditional Russian aim of supporting fellow Orthodox Christians.

Turkey was made very weak by the events of Navarino Bay. It gave the allied fleet instant naval supremacy and Ibrahim recognised this within a few months; he readily accepted the peaceful evacuation of his troops from Greece from August 1828. This left Sultan Mahmud in a more vulnerable position still, but his reaction to Navarino Bay was to reject the Treaty of Akkerman in November 1827 and to declare war on Russia once more over the unrelated issue of Moldavia and Wallachia. This seemed to be an emotional response, since opinions among the great powers agreed that Russia was now in a powerful position. War between Russia and Turkey began in April 1828. The other great powers were worried by this since they feared Nicholas; troops might reach Constantinople, for many years the dream of Russian tsars. Russia therefore needed to fight the war quickly so as to present the other powers with a *fait accompli* before they had time to react. Major concerns were that Britain might declare war on Russia's fleet in the Mediterranean or that Austria might send an army over land. Predictably the war went Russia's way but not as quickly as its commanders had hoped. Moldavia and Wallachia were occupied in May 1828 but the advance stalled at a number of fortresses such as those at Silistria and Varna. Only in the summer of 1829 were these obstacles passed and the Turkish capital became a realistic target for attack.

But in September 1829 Russia made peace with Turkey in the Treaty of Adrianople. This was because the war had not gone as well as Nicholas had hoped; his forces were depleted after the effects of dysentery and they did not significantly outnumber the Turks. Nor could he be confident of the other great powers remaining aloof from events. The threat to Constantinople was too great a concern to them to leave it in his hands. The Treaty of Adrianople, signed in a town just to the north of the capital, confirmed once more the status of Moldavia, Wallachia and Serbia as being semi-independent; this, after all, had been what the war had been fought over. Russia rewarded itself with some territory on the Danube delta as well as two areas taken from Turkey in Asia. Turkey was punished by having to pay an indemnity of ten million ducats and by having to keep open the River Danube and the Straits of the Dardanelles to the merchant shipping of all states. Turkey also had to allow in principle the creation of an independent Greek state. This was ratified later by Russia, Britain and France in the Treaty of London, February 1830. Russian policy was to allow the survival of the Turkish Empire in a weak state since it offered no threat to Russian security, rather than to try to annex large tracts of land which risked the wrath of the other great powers. The Greek state, for example, fell under Anglo-French influence but Tsar Nicholas was content to have made gains closer to the Russian frontiers.

The Eastern Question: Egypt

The Eastern Question was by no means resolved by the end of the Greek revolt and the changes to the principalities of Moldavia and Wallachia achieved by 1830. In fact, the precarious state of the Turkish Empire continued to trouble the great powers for the rest of the century and beyond, but in the 1830s it became an issue again because of the aftermath of the problems encountered in the 1820s. These revolved around Egypt. In the period 1831–33 it was because Mehmet Ali attacked Turkey and it then occurred again when the Sultan tried to get revenge on Egypt when he attacked it in 1839–41. This internecine fighting was of importance to the great powers because Turkey's integrity was at stake and because Russia in particular seemed very well placed to benefit from its demise.

Mehmet Ali felt short-changed by the war he had fought on the Sultan's behalf against the Greeks. During the war, he had been promised the three provinces of Syria as a reward for his help but with the return of peace had been given nothing. He therefore sent his eldest son, Ibrahim, to take Syria by conquest in November 1831. His attack succeeded and by the summer of 1832 he had advanced past Acre and Damascus and was penetrating into Anatolia by the winter. He was able to exceed the parameters of his original campaign relatively easily. By the beginning of 1833, little stood between him and Constantinople and, if he were to capture the Turkish capital, then some kind of reaction by the great powers was certain. Sultan Mahmud II tried to prevent hostile intervention by the great powers by finding friends among them first. He turned to Britain but its priority was its Reform Bill, and the problems in Belgium and Portugal; he tried Austria but Metternich could not act alone and he could find no allies; he turned to France but its sympathies lay with Mehmet Ali because of the relationship it had developed with Egypt since 1798. Thus, by default, the sultan had to rely on Russia, his traditional enemy. Nicholas was pleased to have such an opportunity but was unsure of his ability to rescue the situation. 'I lack the power to give life to a corpse', he said to the Austrian ambassador, 'and the Turkish Empire is dead'. Nevertheless, he sent a small fleet to protect Constantinople in February 1833 and followed this up with troops who began to march south through the Balkans. Realising that he could not hope to defeat the forces of a great power, Ibrahim decided on making peace and in May 1833 signed the Convention of Kutahya which gave him what he wanted – control of Syria. This ended the threat from Egypt.

Russia remained in a strong position, having sent not only a fleet but also some 14 000 troops to the Turkish capital. This gave it a strong bargaining position with Turkey's Porte and in July 1833 the Treaty of Unkiar Skelessi was signed between the two states. This put Russia into an extremely strong position for the life of the treaty, which was set at eight years, and it marked the high point of Russia's influence over Turkey in the nineteenth century. Under its terms, Russia and Turkey confirmed the terms of the Treaty of Adrianople but, chiefly, signed a mutual defence pact. This was of great concern to the western great powers because of its stipulations for the Straits of the Dardanelles. These were kept secret which added to their anxiety. What the treaty said was in fact nothing new – that in any war between other states, and in which Turkey itself was neutral, it would close the Straits to all warships. This applied to Russian vessels as much as to any other, but it had most value for Russia since it meant that its Black Sea coast could not be attacked by a maritime power such as Britain – or even by a lesser state such as France. The secrecy attached to this clause made for confusion and in the event a misunderstanding of the situation by Britain and France, each of which believed that Russia would continue to have use of the Straits in wartime whereas their own ships would not. This meant that the policies of both states were dedicated to overturning the treaty. Russia's motives were misinterpreted, as Nicholas agreed to a defensive pact and not (as the west feared) an aggressive one either towards them or to the Ottoman Empire itself. He was simply shoring up Russian defences with the help of a weak neighbour that still had control of a strategic area. This was good policy.

Without publishing the secret parts of the treaty, Nicholas tried to reassure the other states. First, he told his foreign minister, Nesselrode, to send a circular to Russian embassies which was passed on to the other great powers. This explained that no new deals had been done between Russia and Turkey. It did little to assuage the doubts of Palmerston in Britain. Next, he focused his attention on the two German great powers. In September 1833 he met the Austrian Emperor, Francis II, and Metternich to sign the Treaty of Münchengrätz in which the two states made plain their support for the maintenance of the Turkish Empire. If, however, the empire were to fall, they agreed to co-operate in any redrawing of frontiers. It was a measure of the distrust of Russia felt in Britain and France that they believed the meeting had been to plan for the partition of the empire. Their protests fell on deaf ears; they had been outmanoeuvred by Nicholas while they were dealing with foreign affairs closer to home. Their formation of the 1834 Quadruple Alliance with Spain and Portugal was meant to act as a counter-balance but was accompanied by more rhetoric than meaning. Russian relations with Britain were very poor throughout the 1830s.

In 1839–41 problems in the Near East erupted yet again. It became known as the 'second Mehmet Ali crisis' and was a renewal of the conflict between the sultan, Mahmud II, and the aforementioned ruler of Egypt. In April 1839, Turkey sent an army under Hafiz Pasha to defeat the Egyptian forces in Syria and recapture the area for the sultan. The attack failed. The sultan's army was still too weak and, far from marching south, it was beaten by Ibrahim Pasha at the Battle of Nezib. Turkey once more seemed open to attack, the more so because Mahmud died in June 1839 only to be replaced by an inexperienced boy of sixteen and then his fleet surrendered to Egypt almost straight away. Mehmet Ali demanded that he become the hereditary ruler of both Egypt and Syria. This threatened the unity of the Turkish Empire and prompted the great powers into action instantly; this time, there were no other foreign problems to distract any of them. The Russian policy was to work in conjunction with the other four great powers and this led to Egypt suspending its war efforts indefinitely. During the 1830s, Britain had worked hard to build up its commercial links with Turkey and they signed a commercial treaty in 1838. Tsar Nicholas may have decided that such rivalry was to no one's advantage in a matter as serious as this. He was also quite pleased to take an opportunity to work with Britain so as to chip away at the Anglo-French entente; whereas he rivalled Britain, he despised France under its new ruler. There was therefore a lacuna of about a year during which European diplomacy rather than warfare prevailed in the Levant. Talks between Nicholas and Britain's Palmerston dominated and they concentrated on the terms to be offered to Mehmet Ali.

From the middle of 1840 France began to take an independent line as it hoped to maximise its influence in the Near East by supporting Egypt's claims against Turkey. France had helped to develop the Egyptian economy and had trained its army in the previous decades and was trying to support its ally as best it could. However, this did little more than lead to the isolation of France as the remaining four great powers continued to collaborate. By July, they had agreed the terms they were going to give to Egypt. This led to a war-scare not in the eastern Mediterranean but in western Europe as the French government led by Thiers (backed by public opinion) stood its ground and rejected the peace terms. These were that Mehmet Ali should become hereditary ruler of Egypt and become the lifetime ruler of southern Syria. When Ali refused these terms, military and naval action by the four great powers (excluding France) began, including landings in Lebanon, and culminating in the appearance of a British fleet off Alexandria. Mehmet Ali was defeated and his hopes of building his own empire were destroyed. More importantly, the five great powers – with France now reconciled – drew up a new agreement for the Near East.

The Straits Convention was signed in July 1841. It was timed conveniently since it coincided with the lapse of the eight-year Treaty of Unkiar Skelessi which Nicholas had decided to abandon, or at least make no attempt to renew. The Convention meant the preservation of the Turkish Empire was guaranteed and the sticking point of the 1830s, the access of warships to the Straits of the Dardanelles, was made the same for all five great powers. The Straits were not open to warships of any kind (including those of Russia) while Turkey was at peace. Nothing was said of the situation in wartime, but the circumstances of a conflict – with or without Turkey – and the nature of the alliances involved was something that could never be foreseen. The convention gave Russia sufficient security but it had to maintain a fleet of warships on the Black Sea in case of an attack by Turkey or by any ally that it might have. It may well have been that Nicholas was taking a short-term view of the agreement as he seemed to have no confidence in the survival of the Turkish Empire. He had previously referred to it as 'a corpse' and in the early 1850s he described it as 'a sick man' and as a 'dying bear'. Still, Nicholas also made efforts in the 1840s to allay the other powers' fears about Russian intentions. He told Austria, in 1843, that he would 'never cross the Danube' into the Turkish Empire and felt that Austria should increase its territory in the area instead. How far he could be believed, though, was a matter for each state to decide for itself.

The Eastern Question: the Crimean War

The Eastern Question continued to bedevil European relations and, after the wave of European revolutions in 1848–49, it emerged once more as the most urgent of international issues. This time, however, diplomacy failed to prevent a war and for the first time since 1815 there was a direct conflict between some of the great powers. Russia found itself isolated and fighting on its own soil against Britain and France; more worrying still, it lost the Crimean War.

Superficially, the Crimean War was caused by a dispute over access to the holy sites of Palestine, such as those found in Jerusalem and nearby Bethlehem. France supported the rights of Catholic monks while Russia backed those of Orthodox brothers. Russia had for many years claimed the right to defend the Orthodox Church in the Turkish Empire, which it traced back to the Treaty of Kutchuk-Kainardji, 1774. How much justification there was for this slant on the treaty is dubious, but it also gave Russia leverage within the Turkish Empire and an excuse for intervention. This in turn could lead to war and aggrandiSement. In the years 1852 to 1853, the wrangles over access became more serious as the French and Russian delegations at the Porte began to see it as a measure of their relative importance in Turkish policy. When Napoleon III despatched a warship to Constantinople, Nicholas responded by mobilising troops near the border with Turkey. The question of religion was quickly transcended by that of prestige.

In practical terms, the scale of the dispute became clearer in May 1853 when Russia's envoy to Constantinople, Menshikov, was withdrawn. Russia broke off diplomatic relations with Turkey and then occupied the Principalities of Moldavia and Wallachia in July by way of a protest against the sultan's refusal to grant sufficient privileges to Orthodox monks. In order to provide a deterrent against further Russian aggression, the French and British sent fleets to the eastern Mediterranean as an act of support for

Turkey. However, this token was taken to mean rather more and the sultan felt able to declare war on Russia in October 1853. So began the Crimean War, almost by mistake and over issues that did not warrant combat. Various diplomatic efforts had been made to salvage the situation but none of them had worked; the most promising of them was a conference at Vienna in July 1853 but no Russian representative attended.

The fundamental issue over which the war was fought, was the extent of Russia's power in the Near East. By taking Bessarabia in 1812, defeating Turkey 1828–29 and then signing the Treaty of Unkiar Skelessi in 1833, Russia had shown its ability to wage war successfully against Turkey. It had emerged as the dominant regional power and had been able to coerce the sultan into giving concessions. Russian influence was reaching into the Black Sea and its coasts – to the west in the Balkans and to the east in the Caucasus. The 1841 Straits Convention had reversed the trend in Russia's aggression as far as Britain and France were concerned but to Nicholas the agreement had changed very little. Both of the western great powers' governments remained sensitive to any further Russian advances and the press and reading public in each heightened their awareness. Thus, when Russia occupied the Principalities of Moldavia and Wallachia in July 1853 there was consternation. If Russia was to gain ready access to the eastern Mediterranean for its warships, western observers believed it would soon be in a position to dominate the area with dire consequences for British trade (to India and the Far East) and for French influence (still based in Egypt). Russia therefore had to be resisted and, ideally, pushed back. If these two great powers over-reacted to the immediate circumstances it was because they were acutely aware of the risks connected with any further threat to the Turkish Empire. It was, of course, a revival of the Eastern Question just as the Greek rebellion had been in the 1820s and as the attacks from Egypt had been in the 1830s.

The war began with skirmishes between Turkey and Russia in October 1853 mostly around the River Danube but also on the east coast of the Black Sea. The main exchange took place at sea and Russia destroyed the Turkish fleet moored in the harbour at Sinope at the end of November. A joint Anglo-French fleet therefore passed through the Bosphorus into the Black Sea to cancel out the Russian advantage. At the end of March 1854 they declared war on Russia as Nicholas had refused to withdraw his troops from the Principalities. Much of the fighting then centred on the Crimean peninsula, but the war was fought elsewhere as well. While the armies of Russia and Turkey fought on land, Britain and France were able to attack any Russian coastline they chose. Attacks were launched at different times in the Baltic, the Arctic and in Asia. There was also a war fought for allies. Britain and France were eventually able to persuade the north Italian state of Piedmont to join them but only in 1856 when the war was almost over. Of far greater importance was the attitude of the other two great powers, Austria and Prussia. Nicholas expected that if he did not have military support from Austria he would have its diplomatic backing. This was because he had played such a large part in crushing the revolutions that affected Austria in 1848–49. He had sent troops in to Hungary on Austria's behalf to suppress the rebellion there, and he had given it his support in Germany in 1850 when it wanted to restore the German Confederation. Put bluntly, Austria owed Russia several favours. But Austria gave Russia no help at all and instead suggested that Russia take its troops out of the Principalities! This was perhaps to protect its trade along the Danube which the Russian advance might jeopardise. Austria also signed a treaty of neutrality with Prussia in April 1854

The Crimean War 1854–56: Siege of Sebastopol, Russians blow up remaining fortifications before evacuating the city on 19 September 1855 (Published in the *Illustrated Times* 13 October 1855. Source: Peter Newark's Military Pictures)

and a treaty with Turkey that set out the future of Moldavia and Wallachia. Tsar Nicholas had miscalculated, but for good reason, and was thus left to fight alone.

The war was fought in the Crimea because Russia did withdraw from the Principalities, at Austria's suggestion, in June 1854, but the momentum of the conflict had gone so far that this retreat did not make much impact on the combatant countries' attitudes. This may have been a reflection of Britain and France's fundamental aims over the issue of the Eastern Question. By this stage they had the opportunity to attack Sebastopol, the major Russian naval base on the Black Sea, and a victory there could ensure the reversal of Russian policies that they had wanted since at least 1833. They duly secured this victory but it took much longer than necessary and no army came out of the war with much credit. Casualties on both sides were unnecessarily high, the most infamous in Britain being the 'Charge of the Light Brigade' but the number of injured and killed on all sides totalled half a million. Western successes at Alma, Balaklava and Inkerman in September, October and November 1854 respectively were crowned by the capture of Sebastopol in September 1855. The combined forces of the British, French, Turkish and finally Piedmontese troops were able to win a foreign war hundreds of miles from home and to overcome Russia's vast reserves of troops. While some of the Russian commanders fought well, notably General Totleben (who fortified Sebastopol with great haste) and Admiral Nakhimov (who also defended the town), Russia consistently lost more men than their enemies. This was just one of the terrible failures of the Crimean campaign.

Why did Russia perform so badly? Part of the answer lay in the previous wars and successes that Russia had experienced. Having defeated no less a general than Napoleon in 1812–15, Russia thought highly of its own army. Alexander I had increased its size to one million men and it had been invincible in the wars it had fought against the Turks, even if its attacks had sometimes been held up for some time. It had also beaten the Poles and, in a separate series of wars, the Persians. The history of Russia's army looked impressive. But, it had not had to fight against a modern army (or navy) put into the field by another great power and the passage of time had left the commanders with an illusion of credibility. Russia no longer possessed the formidable army they believed it had.

There were, of course, further good reasons for these appalling statistics. The traditional Russian battle tactic was to charge at the enemy with fixed bayonets and this never failed to produce high casualties. The vast manpower available to the army meant that it undervalued its recruits and saw them as expendable. Entry to the army was typically for twenty-five years which was a life sentence, if not a death sentence, and hardly attracted men into the ranks. In fact, many men who joined the army were sent there by their landlord or community as a punishment. This meant that from the beginning to the very end of his career in the army, a Russian soldier had no reason to show any attachment or liking for the life he led. Living conditions during peacetime were grim as soldiers might be posted to one of the hated military colonies; they were also dangerous as disease was endemic and in the period 1830–55 Russia lost one million troops from non-combat situations. The training was inappropriate as, under Nicholas, the accent was on parade ground drills and the regimentation of lines of troops. This even extended to the cavalry where the horses were sustained on a diet of oats and beer which was excellent for their presentation and glossy coats but which meant that they were quite unfit. During one training exercise when Nicholas ordered everything to be performed at a gallop, seven hundred horses died from exhaustion. The level of equipment was poor as some regiments of infantry were still issued with flintlock muskets which had disappeared from service in the west the previous century.

Communications to and from the Crimea were poor as the roads were little more than tracks that turned into swathes of mud in winter and the rail network was far too small to be of any help. Reinforcements were held up in this way as they often relied on traditional horses and carts which simply got stuck. The quality and quantity of the rations distributed to the soldiers was poor too as corrupt army officers sometimes kept part of the allocated supply budget for themselves and food could have rotted in transit. Ironically, even the vast size of the Russian army was of little help since three quarters of it was pinned down elsewhere in the empire protecting the frontiers against a possible land attack from Austria, Prussia or Sweden or a sea-borne attack from Britain and France in the Baltic. There was even the danger of unrest within Russia

Table 3.4 Casualties in selected battles of the Crimean War

Battle	Date	Russian casualties	Enemy casualties	
Alma	Sep 1854	6 000	3 000+	British and French
Inkerman	Nov 1854	11 000	4 000	British, mostly
Sebastopol	Sep 1855	13 000	11 000	British and French

itself, originating from the peasants or the Poles. Often, Russia fought its battles in the Crimea with fewer men than its enemy. The extent of the problems facing the Russian army were clearly exposed by the war and its lessons were to lead to huge changes in Russia in the reign of the next tsar, Alexander II.

To be fair, the Russian experience in the Crimean War was not unremitting in its failure. There were successes by some of its commanders fighting against the Turks as well as those who defended Sebastopol. General Muravyov besieged the Caucasian town of Kars with its strong geographical position and large garrison, and eventually took control of it in November 1855, for example. Russian medical facilities were improved dramatically through the work of a pioneering surgeon, Pirogov, and thanks to the formation of a nursing corps of 250 women. The Crimean War should also be put into a broader diplomatic context. First and foremost, it was a limited war. Neither of Russia's main enemies, Britain and France, had any intention of pursuing the war beyond the Crimea and the Black Sea. They did not have the reserves of troops or the sheer size of population to mount a war against Russia even if the ratio of casualties remained the same. Their supply lines were also likely to become highly vulnerable to attack if they tried to advance very far north. There were probably not the financial resources to pay for such a war and the political will was absent. A war against the whole of Russia was therefore never envisaged and never possible. Equally, the kinds of warfare used remained limited as no attempts were made by any party to stir up local populations against their rulers, such as the Poles against the Russians or the Bulgarians against the Turks. No appeal, then, was made to nationalism. It was remarkable how gentlemanly the conduct of the war turned out to be.

However, Russia did suffer a defeat on its home soil for the first time since 1712 and it was forced to accept the peace terms laid out for it in Paris in March 1856. The main part of this was the neutralisation of the Black Sea, such that Russia's naval bases were to be completely dismantled and what remained of its fleet was to be removed. Reciprocal terms were accepted by Turkey, but it had the advantage of controlling the Straits and so could quickly reassert its naval power in time of war. The Principalities were made completely independent and the southern part of Bessarabia was added, so Russia lost some territory. Overall, the terms were not particularly harsh, although the Black Sea clauses rankled; Britain and France had set out only to check Russian advances after all. The real significance of the Crimean War as far as Russia was concerned, was that it underlined the need for urgent internal reforms. This was to be the major task facing Alexander II.

Europe in revolution in 1848

While the Eastern Question was the dominant area for foreign policy activity in Nicholas' reign as a whole, he was also heavily involved in European affairs in 1848–49 when he sent in a Russian army to suppress the unrest in Hungary on Austria's behalf. It was this phase that truly saw Nicholas as the gendarme of Europe as Russia itself suffered no rebellions and so was free to help the other autocracies. Such was the impression left by these two years that it seemed as if the balance of power created at the Congress of Vienna in 1815 was over. Russia had become too strong and the fear that Castlereagh had felt about Russia becoming overbearing due to its occupation of Poland appeared to be vindicated.

There were revolutions all over western and central Europe. France, with its revolutionary tradition in Paris, was affected first in February 1848 but it was followed by similar events in Berlin, Vienna, Frankfurt, Budapest, Rome, Naples, Milan and elsewhere. The pattern of the uprisings was that economic hardship in towns, caused by poor harvests over the previous years, led to demonstrations, riots and then political protests. Austria was unable to cope with so many crises occurring in its multinational empire simultaneously; it encountered not only a rebellion in Vienna, but also a war in northern Italy and a rival for its hegemony of Germany in the shape of Prussia. The national uprising in Hungary, led by Kossuth, was suppressed by Russian forces in cooperation with Austria's troops under the command of General Haynau in 1849. The campaign was not a difficult one as Russia lost barely a thousand men and it served the dual purpose of becalming Hungary and discouraging any rising in Poland. The effort was minimal and the effect was maximised.

Expansion in Asia

Far more effort was expended throughout the reign in the Caucasus, the mountainous area between the eastern edge of the Black Sea and the western shore of the Caspian Sea. At the beginning of the reign there were perhaps 50 000 troops stationed there but by the end the figure was over 200 000. Nicholas hoped to defeat the tribesmen of Circassia, the area closest to the Black Sea, so as to strengthen Russia's naval position there and to this end he began the construction of a series of forts. This was impeded by malaria and the hostility of both Persia and the local population, each of which fought to defend their territory. The result was a rather tenuous hold on the coastline. Raids were frequently made against the Russian outposts and, despite the best efforts of Ermolov and Paskevich to Russianise and Christianise the area in keeping with the doctrine of Official Nationality, they made little progress. In 1844 Nicholas appointed Vorontsov as viceroy of the area which marked a change in policy as he was much more conciliatory to the local peoples. Their culture was respected and their hostility subsided to an extent.

The central part of the Caucasus saw limited Russian advances through a war of 1826–28. The Persians launched a surprise attack but they were forced back such that they had to cede the zone of Armenia that they had controlled. On the western side, the sporadic attacks of tribal leaders based in Daghestan continually harassed the Russian troops and inflicted thousands of casualties in the later 1830s and early 1840s. Russia held onto the gains she had made in the past but was unable to advance at all. In order to reinforce Russia's grip on the area, Nicholas created a sixth Section in 1842 dedicated to the Caucasus.

Further east in the region between the Caspian Sea and the Aral Sea, Russia consolidated its hold over the Kazak area but only gradually and it was unable to make any inroads into Turkestan. Expeditions were mounted, especially in the 1850s, but the steppes were inhospitable and made even military ventures risky. Sustained rebellions by local leaders such as Kazymov restricted Russian action and delayed any progress towards Afghanistan or India, which was to store up trouble for later because it gave the British the chance to extend their influence into the area through northern India.

Expansion in Asia had allowed Russia to reach the north American continent and its hold on Alaska was well established. However, Nicholas had little enthusiasm for areas as far south as California, especially after the United States' declaration of the Monroe Doctrine which defied any European involvement in the Americas. Thus, the trading station at Fort Ross was sold in 1841. Good relations with the USA were nurtured from 1832 when a trade treaty was signed and in the middle years of the century there were no obvious reasons for conflict. Indeed, the Russian view was moving towards a withdrawal from north America (as the sale of Alaska demonstrated in 1867) and the exploration of new areas for trade on its own side of the Pacific Ocean with China and Japan.

The death of Nicholas I

The death of Tsar Nicholas I has already been hinted at earlier in this chapter. His demise was caused by pneumonia, contracted whilst inspecting a unit of troops in severe sub-zero temperatures. Still not sixty years of age, he was exhausted by the Crimean War's demands and Russia's failures and so his spirit was weak; he seemed unable or unwilling to fight off the illness. At the end of his reign he remarked how he was disappointed to bequeath the empire to his son, the future Alexander II, in such a state. True to form, it was in military language, 'I hand over to you my command, but unfortunately not in such order as I should wish'. He finally passed away on 2 March 1855.

The Crimean War was still in progress but the western allies were set to achieve their objective of defeating Russia in the peninsula and there was little prospect of Russia recovering from such a position. Alexander II recognised this and continued with the war for only a short time, almost out of respect for the policies of his father. However, the defeat was enormously useful for Alexander as it gave him a launch pad for a number of fundamental reforms to Russian society. The old maxim of 'Orthodoxy, Autocracy, Nationality' had to be jettisoned and Russia was forced to face new approaches to its old problems.

The problems that Nicholas had inherited from Alexander I had not seemed to be urgent in 1825. Russia was, after all, still in a very strong position in Europe because of its giant army and its two long-term allies in Austria and Prussia. Rebellions could be dealt with by using their support as had happened in Italy 1820–21 or, if the need arose, in conjunction with the other great powers so as to overcome problems with Turkey as the intervention in support of the Greek rebellion demonstrated. The peoples of the Russian Empire were largely quiet and unlikely to become restless since the army and the military colonies were continuing to operate effectively.

What was less obvious at the start of Nicholas I's reign, though, was that reform was going to be needed as the western states became increasingly industrialised. This, moreover, was happening at a time when Russia had a singularly unimaginative tsar whose ability to innovate was confined to the creation of new Sections of government that concentrated power more firmly in his own unskilled hands. The obstacles to reform were therefore increasing. In consequence, there were very few reforms either to the army or to the economy in the thirty years of Nicholas' reign. If there had been, Russia might have been saved from the ignominy of the Crimean War and the sudden need for change that Alexander II had to meet. The creation of the fifth Section in 1836 augured well for Russia's economy as it aimed to modernise the state peasants' farming practices but it was far too little. Despite introducing new crops such as potatoes and resettling many peasants, the biggest change that these reforms wrought was an increase in the state's revenues. Important economic initiatives, such as the construction of railways, were slow to develop and meant that Russia became relatively more backward. The one major area of change was in population growth and this was at a time when agricultural yields were not improving. The rising levels of unrest were something that Nicholas did not deal with adequately and bequeathed to Alexander II as a major problem.

The changes that Nicholas did make became steadily more restrictive. This was especially true of education where the fourth Section under Uvarov worked closely with the secret police of the third Section. By the start of the 1850s, the state had limited the supply of university places and graduates to a desperately low level and so deprived itself of skilled administrators as well as potential entrepreneurs or innovators. It was entirely in keeping with tsarist policies that the most successful area of policy was in administrative reform and in this case it was the work of Speransky in codifying the laws. This gave the state and the tsar more power as the system of laws and courts became more efficient. Nicholas did not appreciate that as time passed the requirements of statecraft also changed and that Russia's system of rule needed to adapt. It was not sufficient to champion the ideas of 'Orthodoxy, Autocracy, Nationality' and hope that they could solve any problems. They were applied to Poland after its failed rebellion but then they always were better suited to policies of punishment and repression. Even the main intellectual debate of the period, that conducted between Slavophiles and westernisers, did not animate him into creative activity.

The Crimean War served as a means by which Russia's decline was exposed. Yet it was in foreign affairs that Russia experienced most success under Nicholas. His prowess in dealing with the Eastern Question seemed impressive as he worked first with Britain and France in the late 1820s to allow the Greeks their independence and then in the early 1830s with Austria to underpin the gains he had made regarding Turkey. The eight year Treaty of Unkiar Skelessi gave Russia what seemed to be, at least to the other great powers, an unassailable degree of influence at the Porte. Even the Straits Convention of 1841 left Russia in a strong position as it could patrol the Black Sea with its fleet. The shock of defeat in the Crimea was felt throughout the Russian bureaucracy as it was a system failure rather than a breakdown of one part of it; the economy and the armed forces had both failed and were in need of an overhaul throughout European Russia.

Nicholas died just in time for Russia to reform. His previous policies gave no indication that he was equipped to deal with the situation that Russia was in by 1855. Large-scale reforms were needed immediately so as to avoid any repeat of the Crimean fiasco on a national scale; it was no longer the case that the tsar could rely on a holding operation as the basis of policies. A more determined and imaginative leader was needed.

Notes

1 M. Raeff, *The Decembrist Movement*, New Jersey, Englewood Cliffs, 1966.
2 J. Westwood, *Endurance and Endeavour*, Oxford, Oxford University Press, 1973.
3 J. Blum, *Lord and Peasant in Russia from the Ninth to the Nineteenth Century*, Princeton NJ, Princeton University Press, 1961.

Chapter 4

The reign of Alexander II
The Tsar Liberator?

The single most important law or decree issued by any tsar in nineteenth-century Russia was passed by Alexander II. In 1861, he published terms for the emancipation of the serfs and so set free from their forced labours approximately one half of the entire Russian population. It was for this reason that he was popularly known as the 'Tsar Liberator'. It took six years for him to negotiate this because it was such a delicate matter, risking as it did the wrath of the nobles. But it was also a fundamental issue which necessarily meant that a great many other reforms were needed in Russia to fill the void left by serfdom in the legal system, education, local government and army. What has exercised the minds of historians of this period is how far Alexander II was motivated by liberal ideals or by the absolute necessity to reform so as to perpetuate the autocratic system. Close attention has also been given to the effects of the reforms and to how far he deserves the accolade of 'liberator'.

Alexander II: biography and background

Unlike his father who had been quite unready to become tsar, Alexander II was prepared from an early age for the responsibilities that he would have to face. As Nicholas I's oldest son, he was groomed for government by joining the senior administrative committees during his father's reign. He was part of the Council of State in 1841 and joined the Committee of Ministers. He was a member of some of the secret committees that met to consider the emancipation of the serfs and he was even left in charge of the day-to-day running of Russia when his father was away from the capital. Alexander's education had prepared him well for the position too. Born in 1818, he was educated by the poet Zhukovskii between the ages of six and sixteen, with the help of General Merder, and their impact was to give him a kinder outlook on Russia than many previous tsars. He was taught to speak several foreign languages, attended lectures on law given by Speransky and, inevitably, he undertook some military training as well. He was also educated by travelling at home and abroad. He was the first Romanov to visit Siberia (in 1837) and in 1838 he toured Europe and was introduced to his future wife, Marie of Hesse-Darmstadt, whom he married in 1842. His marriage produced six sons and two daughters which secured the succession of the dynasty.

His familiarity with the ways of government and with the Russian Empire itself could not make up for Alexander's own weaknesses, though. He was not a talented pupil and understood little of what the writers of the day were really saying; for instance, his liking of Turgenev's *Sportsman's Sketches* seemed to rest on his interest in hunting rather than on any deeper appreciation of what was being said about the conditions of the serfs. Indeed, one contemporary remarked that when he spoke with intellectuals, 'he has the appearance of someone with rheumatism who is standing in a draught'. Assessments of character are difficult to gauge since it is such a subjective matter. Grenville had described him as being indolent and indecisive which might be based on his stout figure at the tender age of twenty; yet in his public role as tsar he could be tenacious and determined as the process towards the emancipation decree will show. Perhaps the observation of Kropotkin was accurate when he described Alexander as someone who had 'two different men' within him. 'He could be charming in his behaviour, and the next moment display sheer brutality.' The personality of the tsar remained as central to the events of the reign as it had under his father and uncle.

The decision for emancipation

As with the two previous reigns, the start of Alexander II's period of rule affected much of what was to follow. In March 1855, when he came to power, Russia was losing a war on its own soil in the Crimea. This was the first time that Russia had lost on its own territory since the reign of Peter the Great in the early eighteenth century and came as a heavy blow. The army had been badly organised, poorly equipped and hardly trained; the economy had barely taken the strain; the infrastructure had been inadequate and government finances had been severely stretched. The shortcomings of the Russian campaign have been picked out in detail in the previous chapter. If Russia was to engage in another war against a great power without having the advantage of fighting in familiar terrain then it was very unlikely to win. At worst, Russia appeared to be vulnerable to foreign attack and its security was not assured. The most basic task of the tsar, as of any ruler, was to ensure the defence of the state. On his accession, Alexander was not in a position to be able to do this. Fundamental changes were needed.

If the most important aim was the maintenance of security, then the most urgent areas for reform were the army and navy. These could not be modernised without the emancipation of the serfs since most rank-and-file recruits were drawn from this class which was poorly educated and difficult to train. The logic behind the decree of 1861 to free the serfs was therefore the external security of the state, which was recognised by the key decision-maker, the tsar. The problems with recruitment and training and, to an extent, the under-performance of the economy, were the result of the system of serfdom. Both of these could be solved by emancipation. If Alexander had not wanted to drive through such a reform then it was unlikely to have happened because there were major social and political obstacles in his way. The six year period in which he kept the momentum for reform turning over was a demonstration of this.

The obstacles to reform in Russia were the same as those that Nicholas encountered at the start of his reign – and indeed that Alexander I had met at the turn of the century – and need not be reiterated here. However, before considering the process that Alexander used in order to pass the emancipation decree, it is useful to outline some of the other reasons, other than military or defensive, for his decision. The different advice that Alexander received must be taken into account too.

Having worked on the secret committees of Nicholas I's reign, Alexander was aware of the problem that serfdom presented. He had read the reports by the third Section that had warned 'serfdom is a powder cellar below the state' as early as the 1830s.

While he was surrounded by political advisers, Alexander was probably persuaded by some of the Romanov family members at court. His younger brother Constantine had been a supporter of emancipation for some years and he was highly esteemed by the tsar and, like his namesake of the 1820s, he was appointed as ruler of Poland. Alexander's aunt, the Grand Duchess Elena Pavlovna, was also able to lobby him effectively. Both of these relatives were liberal in outlook and may have reassured Alexander that the option of emancipation was the only course to take.

An economic crisis?

Economic reasons also weighed heavily in the balance. How far it was responsible has been the subject of enormous debate among historians and the historiography shows no sign of the debate being resolved. The arguments that have been launched here have probably exaggerated the importance of the economy as a cause of reform. The basic contention of Soviet (Marxist) historians was that there was a 'crisis in the servile economy'. In other words, the use of serfs on farms and in factories was failing to produce the goods and the situation was becoming so desperate that reform was needed urgently. Any failure to relieve the situation was likely to cause either a mass rebellion or a collapse in the economic system. Unfortunately, this view has been based on Marxist theory which presupposed an interpretation of the past prior to any scrutiny of the evidence. Marxist historians had to find the evidence to support the interpretation, which was officially sanctioned by Soviet Russia, rather than look at the evidence and then synthesise an interpretation. Western historians have tended to read what evidence there is available first and then draw their conclusions, but they did not have the same access to Russian archives and museums. This state of affairs came about as a result of the cold war and it led to difficult East–West relations over intellectual matters. The result has been to complicate an already complex and difficult historical matter. The end of the cold war in the 1990s has meant the potential for a freer exchange of ideas and evidence but revised analyses of the past will take years to research and publish. In the meantime students of the period must use the existing work of both western and Soviet historians to unravel the relative importance of the economy in causing the emancipation of the serfs.

What both groups have agreed is that the performance of the servile economy was central to the situation since 80 per cent or more of the population was either a serf or a state peasant and so subject to the control of a landlord. What kind of condition the servile economy was in varied from region to region and from estate to estate and this diversity – the difficulty in generalising about the Russian economy – has made for more disputes. For example, some of the landlords ran very efficient and productive farms and could produce yields that left them with regular surpluses and the opportunity to export grain. These nobles, however, tended to be in the fertile black earth belt to the south and they traditionally fed the population in the northern and central reaches of European Russia. Serfdom did not operate in Siberia, the vast expanse of territory to the east of the Ural mountains, and so any discussion of the servile economy excludes the people living there. Two thirds of all serfs were concentrated in the fourteen provinces around Moscow. The statistics that try to quantify the level of serf ownership give some indication of the situation but they are not a measure of the day-to-day living conditions. Eighty per cent of Russian nobles owned one hundred serfs or less but, conversely, 80 per cent of serfs lived on estates of one hundred serfs or more. The ownership of serfs was therefore weighted towards an élite group of landowners within the nobles' own class. This group seemed to show no signs of feeling that there was a crisis. Perhaps they took a short term view and felt that, given they had a great deal of control at the local level, they could manage any unrest themselves.

At least there seems to be some common ground over how the serf economy operated and this gives insights into why the abolition of the servile economy was set to be such a fundamental change. Russia's serfs and peasants amounted to an abundant source of workers totalling 74 million in 1860. This dwarfed its nearest rival, France, with only 37 million as well as Austria's 32 and Britain's mere 29 million people. There were approximately 27 million state peasants and 23 million serfs; the latter were usually treated more harshly than the peasants on the state lands. The vast majority of them worked the land but there were about one and a half million serfs employed as domestic staff and one million who worked in industry by 1860. A further group of some 800 000 'apanage peasants' belonged to the personal estates of the royal family. What affected all of them was certain to have repercussions in every other area of Russian life. This was because they typically lived in self-contained rural communes of between one and three hundred individuals whose basic needs were met by the village community and its lord. This meant they were not only self-sufficient for food and building materials but also in their systems of law, education and justice. They also paid taxes to the tsar and dues to their landlord, and they supplied recruits to the army. Any significant change to the commune, which was based on serfdom, necessarily meant adjustments in these areas.

The farming methods that they used were based on a three field rotation in which one field was kept fallow each year while the other two produced cereal crops such as rye, wheat or oats. The peasant or serf families farmed several strips of land which were distributed in each of the fields so as to share out the most productive areas. This was wasteful of time and land as the labourers had to walk to different parts of the village to reach their strips and there was more than one-third of the cultivable land never being used in any given year. Pathways between strips left more bare soil or provided a base for weeds. In return for being able to cultivate their strips of land, the serfs were obliged to work the lord's own land each week and to spend more time on it during the harvest. All these arrangements had existed for so long that they were adopted by each generation and perpetuated by the ruling council of the mir, made up of the heads of each family. This made change and innovation extremely hard to achieve. It accounts for the peasants' resistance to the introduction of potatoes as a new crop in the 1840s and it partly explains why yields remained low. Some landlords did try to improve farming practices on their estates but they often met with stubborn, if passive, opposition from their serfs. Many landlords were absentees and simply took what surpluses were scraped together each year which also served as a disincentive to improve the methods used. The scope for the serfs and peasants to take the initiative was very limited, though, given that most of them received only very low levels of education. Their awareness of the wider world, however, was sometimes remarkable in that they knew of some major events abroad and optimistically expected their emancipation after the wars, in 1815 and 1856.

Obedience to the decision of the mir was expected and deviant behaviour could be punished by expulsion or consignment to the army or Siberia. This was something that the lord had the right to do as well since he was merely disposing of his property as he saw fit. Any minor breach of the law could be dealt with in the commune and whipping was a common punishment. Likewise, the lord could intervene in the affairs of his serfs to forbid – or to insist on – their marriage; he could buy more serfs or sell those that he had and he could decide what kind of work they did in his fields, as domestic servants or in paid employment elsewhere. Only in the most serious cases of illegal activity, such as murder or rebellion, did the state interpose between the lord and his serfs to decide their fate.

The serfs and peasants had a very strong sense of community, perhaps because of the brutality they experienced but certainly reinforced by their isolation from other villages, and this was expressed in the folk wisdom of proverbs and common sayings. Whereas the serfs have left desperately little by way of written records, their attitudes can sometimes be discerned from phrases that survive in the Russian language itself. Thus, they felt that the mir had a strength and importance that was much greater than any individual within it when they remarked 'a Russian taken alone will not get into heaven but there is no way of keeping an entire village out'. Not even God, it seemed, could resist the moral authority of the mir. Similarly, village society was patriarchal and women were not ordinarily the family members to take decisions, after all 'The hair is long but the brain is short'.

The operation of the servile economy, then, was central to many other institutions and practices in Russian society and any serious changes to it were set to have repercussions elsewhere. For this reason, successive tsars were reluctant to do anything more than tinker with serfdom and to pass reforms that enabled the landlords themselves to take action but which in no way threatened the system.

Table 4.1 Summary of the reforms for serfs and peasants, 1801–55

Tsar Alexander I		
1803	Free Cultivator's Law	Landlords could voluntarily free their serfs. There were only 47 000 freed by 1825, mostly by one noble, Golitsyn.
1816–19	Baltic serfs were freed	They were not freed with any land.
	During Alexander I's reign, 250 groups of state peasants were given away by him as gifts to nobles, and they became serfs.	
Tsar Nicholas I		
1829–48	Secret Committees	Several of these were set up to investigate the conditions of the serfs. Limited humanitarian measures followed, such as a ban on knouting.
1834	Army conscription	Period of service cut from 25 to 15 years.
1836	Fifth Section set up	Kiselev tried to modernise farming among state peasants; new crops and forced settlement of 200 000. Riots in the early 1840s.
1841	Purchases of serfs	Serfs could only be bought with the land they worked.
1842	Law on Obligated Peasants	Private contracts between landlords and serfs could be drawn up to best serve their purposes. Only six landlords did so before 1858.
1844	Household serfs	These could now buy their freedom; none did so.

The Marxists' evidence for a crisis in the servile economy rests on the low levels of performance for the Russian economy at a time when parts of western Europe were passing through a period of 'industrial take-off' that saw the output of their manufactured goods suddenly surge upwards. There is certainly good evidence of this. Iron production remained unsophisticated and labour intensive and reached just 300 000 tons in 1860, well behind Britain's four million tons and France's one million tons. Russian agriculture, in the view of Marxist historians, was also in crisis. The main evidence submitted in this case is the extent to which nobles had borrowed money from the state on the strength of their land assets. As a class, it has been argued, they were heavily indebted to the state because their farming practices were inefficient and the only way that they could maintain their standard of living was to get loans. Some estimates put the level of debt at more than half the total value of the nobles' estates but others suggest the proportion was closer to one-third. This left them largely unable to invest in their land and an on-going and deepening crisis in agriculture.

Western historians have challenged these claims. Although there is an absence of complete agreement, the basic view that they adopt is that mid-nineteenth-century Russia was going through a period of economic transition. It was shedding its reliance on a servile economy and moving towards industrial production; this shift, however, caused short-term upheaval – just as it had in the west – with protests in both the countryside and the burgeoning towns. The most comprehensive exegesis of the western view has been by Jerome Blum.[1] Writing in 1961, on the centenary of the Emancipation Decree but also in the middle of the cold war, he contended that serfdom remained profitable for both the nobles and the serfs themselves. This is not to say that the system of serfdom was expanding. Where it continued, it worked well enough but it was releasing more and more of its manpower to a free labour market as many serfs moved from farming in the mir to manufacturing or skilled trades in the towns. They had been able to convert their labour dues (barschina) to cash payments (obrok) with the lords' consent and only remained tied to the lord's estate in a technical sense. Blum found that in 1811, 58 per cent of the population could be classed as serf but by 1860 that figure had fallen to 44 per cent. It may have been that the birth rate among the serfs was declining too, but this is not certain.

His view has been augmented by subsequent studies. For instance, the study by Richard Rudolph shows how the serfs could combine both farming and cottage industry to give them access to a cash economy and the ability to buy manufactured goods.[2] This is also true of the work by Edgar Melton.[3] The creation of demand among many ordinary consumers is one of the features of an emerging industrial economy. The level of consumption by serfs and peasants in the century before emancipation increased enormously according to figures calculated by Mironov, one of the Marxists' own historians. He also stated that the tax burden fell overall during the same period and so on the eve of emancipation they were richer and buying more. New industries had been started in recent decades with a cotton industry from the 1830s and the Ukrainian sugar beet processing industry from the 1840s. Agricultural production may not have been quite so successful, with larger outputs being achieved only by bringing new land into cultivation – which was likely to be marginal, less fertile, land – and this led to problems with feeding the growing population. The situation is difficult to assess, however, because of the local variations in crop yields. Revised figures for the landlords' indebtedness indicate the level of assets mortgaged to the state was just 27 per cent.

The western historians seem to have had the better of the argument regarding industry and the dynamics of the economy but the debate over agriculture remains vexed.

The poor state of the Russian economy was also due to its acquired and natural disadvantages. The harsh climate, for instance, left enormous areas of land frozen over in winter and waterlogged in spring. Transport and communication were difficult as the rivers flowed north-south and away from population centres; the warm water ports in the Black Sea were cut off from those in the Baltic. Few canals existed and the roads were only mud tracks that often became impassable in winter. There was a historical reliance on innovation coming from the state which could be traced back to Peter the Great who had given new impetus to the economy by importing western technology. The overbearing role of the state continued in the nineteenth century, especially under Nicholas I, when the state inadvertently retarded industrialisation. The construction of railways was restricted under Kiselev and education was limited under Uvarov. Western ideas were considered dangerous especially by the Slavophiles and although the west was becoming wealthier it was also prone to riots and revolutions in the larger industrial towns. What surpluses there were in Russia tended to be taken by the state in taxes to pay for the army – or else squandered by the landowners on western luxury goods such as French wine – neither of which were productive uses of capital.

To blame the backward state of the Russian economy entirely on the use of serfs is therefore too simple an interpretation. The range and diversity of economic activity was huge and there were, despite the natural disadvantages of Russia's climate and geography, many examples of progress and modernisation. The historical debate over whether or not the economy was entering a period of 'crisis' has hinged on two problems. First, the debate has been affected by twentieth-century ideologies that have left a significant legacy. Second, and just as significantly, there is still a shortage of good evidence available due in no small part to the absence of any records left by the serfs themselves. Further research is still needed in this area.

Social unrest

The emancipation of the serfs may also have been triggered by the rising level of unrest in the countryside. This cause has been subject to debate between Marxist and western historians too since the state of the economy has been seen as the main cause of unrest.[4] It is probable that there was too little food being produced (or distributed effectively) for a population that was growing rapidly. It was a case of Malthusian economics in which the population was set to be restricted by famine and in protest against this the serfs and peasants rebelled. Their protests were not co-ordinated and the tsars were able to deal with them on a local basis so there was no threat to the autocracy in the way that there was in the eighteenth century with risings such as that of Pugachev in the 1770s. The scale of the problem is still in some doubt as several sets of revised figures have been released by a number of historians. The pattern has been the same, though, as all the statistics stress the rising level of protest. Jerome Blum's figures have been mentioned before but are worth repeating here: that between 1826 and 1834 there were 148 disturbances that had to be stopped by troops, 216 during 1835 to 1844 and 348 for 1845 to 1854.[5] Alternative figures by Marxists historians increase the level of protest. Ignatovich identified 1467 examples between 1800 and 1850 and

Okun raised this again. However, a more recent account by a Soviet historian concluded in 1989 that 'Soviet literature frequently exaggerates the part played by peasant movements in the build-up to the abolition of serfdom'.

Just as historians have disputed the extent of the problem, so the tsar and his contemporaries had problems assessing the situation. Local officials might have exaggerated the extent of the problems they faced in trying to keep law and order so as to procure more help from the tsar. There was an upswing in unrest in the aftermath of the Crimean War because of the expectation of emancipation among the peasantry but what was becoming apparent to the tsar and his advisers was that the underlying trend of unrest was rising and that short-term solutions were not going to resolve the problem. It was not going to be enough merely to call out troops and stifle the protests; the long term solution had to be to tackle the root cause. At the time, more educated Russians were beginning to recognise that changes were needed and, after the repressive final years of Nicholas I's reign, they were starting to express this attitude. Count Tolstoy, for example, spoke of a coming 'holocaust' if reforms were not implemented. In the words of Daniel Field, however, many others were 'willing to take their chances' with the peasant unrest.[6]

The peasants and serfs themselves did not have any mass movement in favour of reform; there was no co-ordination of their efforts. Protests were often provoked by hunger but periodically there were also waves of serfs who travelled great distances to try to secure their freedom, based on quite spurious rumours. Typically, this occurred after a war and that of the Crimean was no exception as many serfs went to Perekop near the Black Sea in the hope of meeting the tsar in person and asking him directly for their freedom. This fanciful hope was of course without any truth in it at all but it was supported in the minds of the serfs by the belief that the start of a new reign might signal a new beginning for them. When this occurred at the same time as a war finishing their anticipation was heightened. Indeed, during the Crimean War many serfs had volunteered for the army in the belief that in doing so those who fought would subsequently be freed. While the peasants and serfs were largely mute in the way they applied pressure, their desperate actions spoke for them.

Legal and moral arguments for reform

The case against serfdom was irrefutable. In law, it had been illegal for decades and the reforms of Speransky in the early 1830s had served to highlight this again. Serfdom had been devised in order to reassure the nobles that, while they were away from their estates serving the state (which was compulsory), their labourers would remain *in situ* to continue the work that was necessary. Once Tsar Peter III ended the requirement of the nobility to serve the state in 1762 serfdom could have been taken out of the equation too. But it remained as an anachronism because it was so convenient (if illegal) for the nobles to operate such a system. Their defence of it was usually based on the dangers inherent in any sudden end to the system; it was, in a sense, in their interests to stress the likelihood of violence because their argument rested on fear.

Strongly allied to the legal argument was that of the immorality of serfdom. On humanitarian grounds alone it was indefensible and the educated classes in Russia – and abroad – were increasingly conscious of this. Russian writers campaigned for emancipation, most famously Turgenev in his *Sportsman's Sketches* in which the serfs he describes were elevated from the soil that surrounded them onto a higher plane of existence. Opinions were turning in favour of emancipation for selfish reasons, in that the nobles and bureaucrats began to appreciate that owning serfs reflected very badly on themselves as it said little for their own morality. There was a role reversal in which the serfs were lifted from their lowly position and the nobles were cast down from theirs. One landowner, Koshelyov, expressed this succinctly in 1858 when he wrote to the tsar saying 'This measure is more necessary for the welfare of our class ... even than for the serfs'. During the war, there had been growing criticism of the continuation of serfdom from Tsar Nicholas's own closest supporters among the Slavophiles. People such as Chicherin and Aksakov no longer saw such a traditional Russian practice as worthwhile. The westernisers tended to be more critical still and could point to the abolition of serfdom in virtually every other state in Europe as sufficient evidence for Russia to modernise in a similar way. Only the United States, among the major powers, persisted in using (and trying to justify) slavery. The most vocal critic of serfdom was Alexander Herzen who published critical journals from London aimed at a Russian readership. The popularity of these took off in the late 1850s and the journal called *The Bell* was especially successful – and influential – from its foundation in 1857. By this stage, there was a long history of protest against serfdom from which writers could draw for support, going back to Radischev in the 1780s and the Decembrists of 1825. This gave their arguments further weight but perhaps not the legitimacy they needed in the eyes of the tsar since Radischev was exiled by Catherine the Great and the leaders of the Decembrists were executed. Nevertheless, the issue of servile labour remained current.

None of these wise and well informed arguments counted for much, however, unless the tsar himself could be persuaded and Pereira has asserted this view clearly.[7] As an autocrat, he could hold out against the opinions of others indefinitely or until, perhaps, he was removed from power for incompetence and aggravating the nobles. This, of course, was not an empty threat since his uncle, Tsar Alexander I, had come to power in 1801 after the murder of Tsar Paul. How far Alexander II was won over by any of these reasons for emancipation is difficult to determine.[8] Perhaps it is wisest to agree with Maureen Perrie who, in her work for the Historical Association, decided that 'Debates on the reasons for the emancipation of the serfs have ... been largely inconclusive'.[9]

The steps towards emancipation 1855–61

A further way to discover Alexander II's view, has been to study the way in which the Emancipation Decree was reached 1855–61 and in particular the participation of the tsar himself in it. The research completed on this has been informative but, once more, ambiguous. Some historians, such as Blum and Pereira, believe that Alexander intervened at crucial times so as to push the faltering process along, but others such as Field and Saunders insist that he had no deep convictions about emancipation and that the 1861 Decree was achieved despite him.[10] The stages can be narrated briefly but it is useful in doing this to take notice of when Alexander did make a contribution.

The starting point for the process is generally recognised as being a speech that Alexander made to the Moscow nobility in March 1856. Here, he seemed to be ready to take responsibility and make the decision that only he could. What he said to his

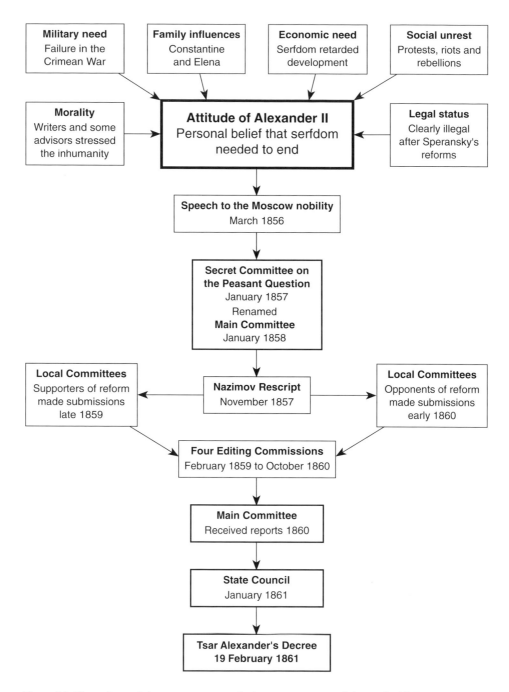

Figure 4.1 Flow chart of the progress towards the emancipation of the serfs, 1855–61

audience was meant for all of the nobles to hear not just those in front of him. The crucial part of his speech warned them that 'It is better to abolish serfdom from above than to wait until the serfs begin to liberate themselves from below'. This initiative by Alexander was significant but can be played down since it did not lead to any response from the nobles and on its own was clearly not enough.

The second step that Alexander took was almost a year later when he set up the 'Secret Committee on the Peasant Question' in January 1857. This too could be seen as merely a token gesture that need not lead anywhere since it was in keeping with the pattern of the previous reign when Nicholas had arranged for a series of secret committees and Alexander himself had sat on several of them. However, it was probably a genuine attempt to make some progress since Alexander needed to prepare the nobility gradually. He did not want to rush the process since he wanted to give the nobles every opportunity to participate in it and to have a stake in the final outcome. To allow this to go further, the existence of the Secret Committee was made public in January 1858 (and it was renamed the Main Committee) and the discussion of the idea of emancipation by the press was permitted the same month. The lifting of press censorship was a major reform in itself as journals such as *The Bell* and *The Contemporary* came out very clearly in favour of emancipation and this added to the pressure to do so. Their readership soared in a matter of weeks. Making the Main Committee's existence public was also breaking with past practice since the secrecy of previous committees had been to prevent the news leaking out to the serfs. In government circles, the fear was that if they heard of the decision they might seize the moment and try to take their freedom prematurely. This move was therefore a gamble calculated by Alexander to excite debate among the nobles who were being warned that the idea of reform was not going to go away. There was a veiled threat that if they did not become involved then emancipation, to which the tsar was now committed in principle, might take place without them. It was a dangerous balancing act, between keeping the nobles' support and ensuring progress was made.

Thirdly, Alexander issued an edict – which became known as the Nazimov Rescript after the governor to whom it was first sent – instructing the nobles in November 1857 to form local groups to discuss the idea of emancipation and to come up with some proposals for how it might be done. Whether or not he was going to listen to what they had to say is debatable but he was keen to get them involved and feel as if their views were being heard. He issued the rescript because the Secret Committee was making desperately little progress of its own. It had the desired effect and in the course of 1858 the Russian provinces began to form their local groups to discuss how best to proceed with emancipation. The debate had moved on apace since the question was now when (and how) rather than if the serfs were to be freed.

Almost all of the responses from the local committees were hostile to the idea of emancipation but the nobles who were present at these had missed the point. Alexander's own views had moved forward much more quickly and by the end of 1858 he had already given up the idea of liberating the serfs in the same way as the serfs in the Baltic states had been freed 1816–19. What had happened there was that the serfs had been freed without any land. Tsar Alexander II resolved now, however, that the Russian serfs were to be freed with land! How this change of mind occurred is not entirely clear. It was certainly true that in 1858 there was a shift within the Ministry of the Interior and the Main Committee itself towards a generous deal for the serfs, though.

Lanskoi, the aged Minister of the Interior, had become persuaded that the serfs needed land probably because those subordinates within his own department who had the expertise to deal with the issue were liberal-minded. They themselves avidly read the newly freed press and reflected on the arguments put forward by radical thinkers like Herzen. And Rostovtsev, one of the conservatives whom Alexander had appointed to the Main Committee also shifted his ground in 1858 in favour of land being included in the settlement. The net effect was that the tsar agreed to free the serfs with land and this was duly incorporated into the bureaucratic process.

It was Rostovstev, a reactionary who had conceded the need for land to be part of the settlement, who was put in charge of the Editing Commissions that Alexander created in February 1859 to collate the evidence submitted by the nobles' local committees. The personnel on these Commissions was also liberal in outlook. After a year's work, Rostovstev died and was replaced by the reactionary Panin but he made no changes to the other bureaucrats and could not materially alter the course that events were taking. When the Editing Commissions reported back to the Main Committee at the end of 1860 it was certain that their recommendation was going to be for emancipation with land and so it turned out to be. The Main Committee was hurried by Alexander to reach its decision in January 1861 and it too voted in favour of emancipation with land. The final meeting in the process was that of the Council of State. Given Alexander's determination to see the reform passed, there was no doubt about the final result and, whatever opposition might be put up at this late stage, the announcement of the emancipation of the serfs was not going to be stopped. On 19 February 1861, the Emancipation Decree was signed by Tsar Alexander II.

The Emancipation Decree, 1861

The circumstances in which the Emancipation Decree was released and the amount of time taken to produce it must also be put into context before outlining the actual terms. It is not an exaggeration to say that the measure had been awaited for decades by generations of serfs who believed that they would eventually be given the land that they considered to be rightfully theirs. Tsar Alexander was therefore hailed as a liberator for passing it in the relatively short period of just six years. It might have been passed more quickly had he not had to balance so carefully the conflicting claims of the nobles (and his position with them) against those of the serfs. Even at the very end of the process when the decree had been signed, Alexander had to be cautious because he did not want the publication of it to trigger unrest. He launched a major internal security exercise by mobilising the army on the eve of publication so as to prevent any serious rioting. To limit the scope for unrest as much as possible, he also waited for more than a fortnight between signing and actually announcing the decree. The date of publication was therefore 5 March 1861, the first day of Lent, a time when he was likely to catch the serfs in a mild temper. Finally, it is important to point out his reasons for delaying in this way. He had few qualms about publishing the fact that the serfs were to become free. What animated him was his fear of the serfs' reaction when they heard about the way in which they were to be freed. Despite the complexity of the Decree's nineteen laws and the special cases made for different areas of the empire, they were sure to see that they were not going to be given without charge the land that they felt was theirs. They were entitled to land but they were going to have to pay for it and they were not going to be able to do so immediately. There was to be further delay after the decades of waiting.

Under the terms of the Emancipation Decree, the status of serf was abolished. Those people who had been serfs were given a new status, that of 'temporarily obligated peasants' which was to last for two years. During this time, they were to continue working for the landlords in exactly the same way as before but they were also to co-operate with their landlords in drawing up legal documents that set out who owned which areas of land and what labour dues or 'obligations' were attached to the land. Land commissioners were appointed to complete this task, though they had to be drawn from the landowning class itself and this gave them a bias towards the nobles in many cases. They had to separate out just two types of land. The first type was the land on which the serfs' dwellings were built and which amounted to a garden plot. This became the property of the serfs and there was no right of appeal by the landlord. The second type, which was the bulk of the land and included the three major fields of each village, could be purchased by the serfs if the landlord consented. If the serfs chose to buy both their garden plots and the arable land, then they passed out of the transitional phase of being 'temporarily obligated peasants' and became independent farmers and small-holders. The ex-serfs were from this point on able to act as free citizens in so far as the law and their own material prosperity allowed. Thus, they could marry without any intervention by the local landlord and they could become involved in any trades they chose. They no longer owed any labour dues either in cash or in days of work. They were not subject to punishments that the landlord had decided on and they were not conscripted into the army in the same way. All of this looked like freedom and is what their emancipation amounted to.

However, this simple model of emancipation had many complexities, variations and drawbacks that left the ex-serfs in a situation that was less than ideal. Moreover, it was a situation that many of them quickly came to dislike and resent. At almost every turn, the serfs were vulnerable to decisions that went against them and to circumstances that made their plight more difficult. For instance, the two-year period that serfs were meant to spend as 'temporarily obligated peasants' could last indefinitely if the landlord did not want to sell any land to them. The process relied on the goodwill of the landlords for it to take its full course. The work of the land commissioners in drawing up legal charters of land ownership and dues favoured the landlords who therefore tended to acquire ownership to common or other land where the legal title could not be established. The most obvious problem, though, was that the serfs were not actually given the land as a gift. The Decree clearly stated that the land the serfs had worked for decades belonged entirely to the landlords. This was what made the serfs so angry and for years afterwards they still could not believe that the tsar had allowed this to be the case. By letting the nobles keep the legal ownership of the land, the tsar was hardly

Table 4.2 Simple diagram of the emancipation process

80 per cent of the land was paid for by the state giving the landlord the money and making the mir repay the loan at six per cent interest over 49 years.
Which pieces of land were offered for sale was decided by the lord.
20 per cent of the land was paid for by the mir, in cash, direct to the landlord.

liberating them. In order to become the owners of the land they worked, the serfs had to buy it; they had to purchase what they already considered to be their own property.

The method of purchase was not straightforward since the sums of money involved were enormous and quite beyond the reach of individual serfs. A landlord had to be given 20 per cent of the value of the land in cash by the serfs; the remaining 80 per cent was given to the landlord by the state in the form of a government loan. The serfs then had to repay the interest on this loan, which took the form of a bond, over a period of forty-nine years at 6 per cent per year which was quite a high rate of interest. The roubles that they paid over were called 'redemption payments'. The sale price of the land was also something that the land commissioners fixed and they tended to overvalue it so as to incorporate into it the worth of any labour services that used to be attached to it. Moreover, which areas of land the landlord offered for sale were at his discretion, and he tended to make only the least fertile pieces available. In every conceivable way, the serfs were exploited and over-charged for the land they considered theirs. Almost certainly, this was deliberately done by Alexander, or the Main Committee, so as to build in a system of compensation for the nobles and gentry which the state itself did not have to finance. This then reassured them and made Alexander's position safe.

There were innumerable clauses and allowances made for situations that could arise where one or other party was reluctant – or plainly refused – to co-operate. The lord could not refuse to sell the serfs' dwellings, but if he refused to sell any land at all then there was no way forward. If the serfs refused to buy the land the lord was offering then the lord could insist on a sale but had to forfeit the 20 per cent cash payment normally handed over by the serfs. If neither the serfs nor the lord wanted to participate in the emancipation process then that was tolerated but the serfs still had the ownership of their houses and garden plots. A landowner could hand over to the serfs, free of any payment, a set amount of land that then released both the parties from any obligations (either to buy or to sell) to each other. These plots were known as 'beggarly allotments'. The diversity of situations that the process could generate was limited, though, by clauses that required the transfer of land ownership to take place between the landlord and the entire village community of serfs; individual serfs could not negotiate their own deals and set up farms on their own. The collective life – and farming practices – of the mir was perpetuated in this way since joint decisions about what to farm, when and where, had to continue as before.

The results of the Emancipation Decree

The results of the emancipation of the serfs (and apanage peasants in 1863 and of the state peasants in 1866) can hardly be over-estimated. It was not just a change to the relationship between the landlords and their serfs; nor was it merely an attempt to modernise antiquated farming techniques. It amounted to a fundamental shift in the organisation of Russian society such that all classes of people became independent and none were subject any longer to the tyranny of the local lord. This did not mean that all Russian subjects were equal; the processes of adjustment that followed emancipation shored up the nobles' status in new institutions and provided them with compensation for the loss of their local powers. However, it did mean that ex-serfs and ex-state peasants could participate in more of Russia's public life. Not all of the consequences were foreseen. While the serfs reacted to the terms of the decree with some violence in the first few months after its publication, the more serious response came later from the intelligentsia. It became disillusioned with the tsarist system for the way that it had betrayed the serfs and, helped by the emergence of an independent body of trained legal professionals, this group began to campaign for the tsar to make more serious changes. Ultimately, they wanted the introduction of a constitution and, when this was not granted, they became revolutionary and turned to terrorism. One of these groups assassinated the tsar in 1881. His successor, Alexander III, sought refuge from such radical groups by maintaining as autocratic a system of government as he could manage. In the long term, this only encouraged more secret societies to form and was to contribute to the revolution of 1917 which overturned the entire tsarist system. The emancipation of the serfs was therefore a turning point in the reign of Alexander II and in the history of modern Russia.

The reaction of the serfs in the first few months after the Emancipation Decree demonstrated their anger and reflected fairly the way that the measure had not been devised with their interests in mind. According to figures produced by the tsar's own Ministry of Internal Affairs, there were 647 incidents of rioting between April and July 1861, the worst of which saw the use of armed troops and the deaths of dozens of 'temporarily obligated peasants' at Bezdna in Kazan province. Altogether, the army had to be used to keep order on five hundred occasions in 1861 in incidents of riot that spread across forty-two of European Russia's forty-three provinces affected by the Decree. But, thereafter, the countryside fell quiet and there was remarkably little protest at all. For the remainder of the century the rural labouring class was quiet; the Decree evidently succeeded in one of its aims, that of ending one of the root causes of social unrest.

None of the ex-serfs were completely free because they were obliged to remain within their communes and pay off their part of the debt owed by the village as a whole. To this extent, they had succeeded in swapping one landlord – the local noble or gentry – for another, their own village council. This body took over the responsibilities of the previous landlord relating to farming practices, payment of taxes (and now redemption payments), law and order and army recruitment. It could impose its will by refusing to give its members the passports that they needed in order to travel any distance even within Russia. The peasants were free only in theory; in practical terms they had to live with severe limits imposed on them by the terms of the settlement. There was little choice but to accept the situation since it was not going to be reversed and it was the best deal that they were going to get. Most landlords were prepared to sell at least some of the land so that the process could proceed and by the end of Alexander's reign 85 per cent of former serfs were in possession of the land they worked.

The way that land was redistributed and the amount that was charged for it varied considerably from region to region. In the provinces of the non-black earth belt the redemption payments were almost twice the value of the land itself but this reflected the value of the labour dues attached to it that the landlords had lost. In the black earth belt itself the charges were in excess of the land values by 25 per cent as the labour dues were valuable but not as important as elsewhere because of the fertility of the soil. By contrast, in the western provinces such as Poland the amount paid reflected very closely the monetary value of the land. This was because the tsar was prepared to see the Polish landlords receive no more than was necessary given that their serfs were often Russian. The corollary of these figures was that the amount of land the landlords were prepared to sell also varied. The figure for all of the provinces affected was that the peasants farmed 18 per cent of the land. In the black earth belt, the landowners were reluctant to part with any more of their profitable land than they had to and so the serfs were able to buy approximately 25 per cent less land than the average. In some provinces, the proportion was even less, such as in Samara and Saratov. In the western areas, serfs were able to buy a considerably higher proportion of the land that they had farmed – as much as 90 per cent in Podolia. Again, this was a deliberate effect since the tsar was confident of the support of the nobility elsewhere in the empire and did not need to treat the Polish nobles generously. However, the temporarily obligated peasants often suffered in other ways as they lost their rights to use woods and common land or else were charged for the privilege as the economy moved towards more cash transactions.

Problems remained, though, since the redemption payments were so high; when the scheme had run its course, the peasants had paid back one and a half billion roubles for land valued at one billion. Poverty persisted and productivity stayed at a low level as the payments were unrelated to current income and peasant communes did not and could not make improvements to their land. The fundamental problem of an increasing population and a limited food supply was not overcome and the danger of famine did not disappear. The Russian population grew from 76 million in 1861 to 125 million by 1897 and thence to 170 million by 1917. Famine did break out in 1891–92 and again in 1898 with the deaths of millions of people. Some relief from the debt that accumulated from failure to keep up with repayments was granted periodically but not until 1906 were the outstanding payments cancelled. In the early part of the twentieth century rural unrest emerged again and was only suppressed with some difficulty by Stolypin, 1905–07.

The nobles and gentry stood to gain, as a class, a great deal from the emancipation and land redistribution. In most cases, they were compensated for the sale of land with high prices and the opportunity to pay off the debts they owed to the state in the form of mortgaged estates. Forty-four thousand estates were in this position so when the state issued the lords with a bond to pay for 80 per cent of the sale price, the debt was deducted first. In the decade after the Emancipation Decree came into effect, 1863–72, the landowners received 770 million roubles for their land but immediately had to pay to the government 425 million roubles. The emancipation of the serfs was therefore of enormous benefit to the tsar and his treasury's reserves and met the financial need for reform head on. The landlords also had the chance to invest in their estates and make them more profitable. Some of them did just this, notably in the Ukraine, where they concentrated on grain production for export markets. Many, however, squandered the opportunity and spent their capital on good living with the result that the estates had to be sold within a few years and the families concerned had to turn to other sources of income to survive. Typically, they found employment in the army and bureaucracy but, as a class, they were increasingly divorced from the land. By 1905, one third of the land that they had owned in 1863 had been sold.

The reaction of the nobility was not as positive as Alexander might have hoped given the generous terms on which emancipation was based. One of his reasons for beginning the process of reform was the need to strengthen the political system and this meant maintaining the autocracy. When, therefore, some of the early reactions from the nobles were to call for a constitution or some way of expressing their grievances he was rightly concerned. Examples of such complaints can be found among the nobles

Table 4.3 Land-holding in Russia by *c.*1880

Social group	% of land owned
State and royal family	42
Peasants	31
Nobles	19
Cossacks and others	4
Townsmen	3

of Tula and Tver, and in Smolensk. Their protests turned out to be short lived and by April 1861 the tsar felt more secure in his position; when he visited Novgorod the following September the potentially hostile nobles were in fact quite welcoming. The danger remained, all the same, that the disruption to local communities and the loss of the nobles' power in them might still lead to calls for further political compensation. To forestall this, Alexander pressed on with his reform programme and set about reorganising the structure of local government and building into it privileged positions for the nobles.

The intelligentsia initially welcomed the prospect of the emancipation of the serfs but when the terms of the Decree were studied – in ways that were quite beyond the serfs themselves – their attitude hardened. It was clear that the serfs were to be exploited in one last final gesture. 'The people have been deceived by the tsar' wrote Ogarev in his *Analysis of the New Serfdom*. He worked closely with Herzen in London and he too was angry about the Decree and wrote to this effect in his journal *The Contemporary*. Hostile reactions were recorded by Shchapov, a lecturer in Russian history at Kazan University, and by Zaichnevskii, a student of just twenty who called for outright violence against the tsar and his ministers. Several pamphlets were published at the time calling for thorough political reform and in the early summer of 1862 Saint Petersburg suffered a series of fires that suggested a deliberate campaign of arson was taking place as an act of political defiance. In the event, the wrath of the intelligentsia subsided after these initial outbursts but there was an undercurrent of discontent that remained and which was set to re-emerge in later years.

Tsar Alexander's own concern was that reform could continue and he set about this by reshuffling his closest advisers in order to allay the fears of the nobility. Those men most closely connected with emancipation were dismissed as a short-term strategy. The biggest heads to roll were those of Lanskoi, the Minister of the Interior who had piloted much of the draft Decree though the bureaucratic process, and of his deputy, Nikolai Miliutin. The new Minister of the Interior was Valuev and there was also a new Minister of Education, Putiatin. By the start of 1862, Alexander was looking to appoint more reformers, though, and quickly substituted Putiatin with the more liberal Victor Golovnin and the Ministry of Justice was headed by Zamiatnin. Further reforms were set to take place.

Army reform

The Decree that emancipated the serfs dealt adequately with many of the original problems that had made Alexander decide that reform was needed. The social unrest declined after an initially hostile peasant reaction and the legal anomaly was ended.

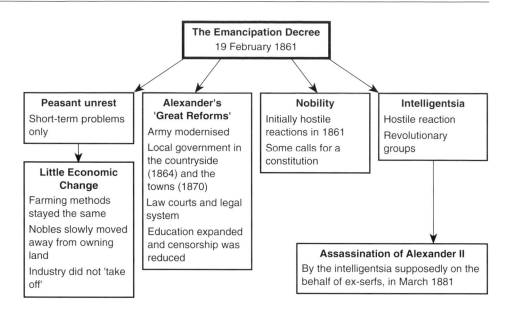

Figure 4.2 Summary of the reactions and results of the Emancipation Decree, to 1881

The moral argument for reform – supported by writers and family members alike – was met successfully. Government finances were bolstered by the redemption payments and the economy had at least some chance to modernise if the nobles were prepared to adopt new methods. But the circumstance that made plain the need for reform was the Crimean War and the army's failure to defeat a foreign army on Russian soil. The need for military reform was crucial to the defence and possible survival of Russia as a great power. It was this cause of reform that was by far the most important but it is easily obscured and overlooked by the size and complexity of the changes that took place in agriculture. The function of the army was to protect Russia from attack both from foreign powers and disruptive groups within Russia. Its position was vital. In a series of unpublished lectures, Professor Edward Acton has consistently rejected the notion of emancipation and the subsequent reforms as being for the benefit for Russian society at large.[11] The purpose of the 1861 Decree was to strengthen the autocracy and then to fill the gaps in the social order left by the decline in nobles' authority on their own estates. Military reform was, in fact, the priority. This gives the lie to the popular idea of Tsar Alexander being the 'Tsar Liberator'. The huge redemption payments and the peasants' commitment to the mir make this plain from the agricultural perspective.

After the Russian defeat in the Crimea, Alexander appointed a new Minister of War, General Sukhozanet, who began to implement a large number of minor reforms. Among the most important of these were the partial closure of military colonies and the demobilisation of large numbers of troops. However, something more fundamental was needed if the problems of the Crimean campaign were to be overcome. He was encouraged by Dmitry Miliutin, brother of Nikolai who had served under Lanskoi in the Ministry of the Interior, to make bigger changes. He lobbied for the emancipation of the serfs so as to benefit the army as soon as the war was over. By 1861, Alexander was persuaded that Miliutin's ideas were what the army needed and he appointed him to the post of Minister of War, a post which he was to retain until 1881.

There was a great deal of work to be done if Russia was to have the kind of modern army it needed to fight against the other great powers. Its internal organisation, recruitment, training and technology all needed to be improved. The first of these began to change as early as 1862 with the creation of four regional command centres which were followed by a further six in 1864 and the entire empire was subsequently divided up into fifteen of these areas. This decentralised structure made for greater speed and efficiency when troops had to be called up. A large number of regiments were kept active in peacetime which could be tripled in size if war broke out; this ended the previously chaotic system of creating entirely new regiments just as war began. A new military code was introduced which did not set about dehumanising recruits as soon as they arrived and it abolished some of the harsh punishments.

The main area of concern, however, was the system of recruitment since it traditionally relied on conscripted serfs as its raw material. These were treated like criminals (and were often sent to the army because of crimes committed in the mir) who could not be trusted. If they were not killed in action they were freed from their servile status but then confined to military colonies to prevent battle-hardened soldiers stirring up unrest among the rest of the population. With the end of serfdom, this system had to change since ex-soldiers could not be treated in this way. Tsar Nicholas I had already ended the twenty-five year period of service and cut it to fifteen years or less. Alexander formalised this and Miliutin devised a new system of frontline and reserve troops that was not only more economical to maintain but also less of a threat to law and order. He proposed that troops remain on active service for just seven or eight years and then spend a similar period of time in the reserve (available to be called up by the new command centres). As a result, the Russian army increased its reserve from 210 000 to 553 000 men who could support the 800 000 or so already in uniform. This system also cut the costs to the state significantly.

Education and training were also revitalised. Most of this focused on the officers rather than the ground level troops but at least they were subjected to better leadership. Miliutin set up military gymnasia similar to those available for civilians but from which there was access to the reformed military colleges (which replaced the old cadet corps based on privilege and family background). Competitive exams were set for entry and graduation and the tuition was by no means confined to military matters. Non-nobles could enlist in these schools and colleges so that the system of promotion was increasingly (but not exclusively) based on merit. Miliutin's aim was to foster a spirit of excellence within the army's hierarchy and to make its approach much more professional rather than gentlemanly and the exclusive preserve of the nobility. Commissions had to be earned; they were not just awarded to those from a wealthy background. At the lowest level of entry, even peasant recruits were given an elementary education and this raised literacy in the ranks such that by 1890 between two and three million ex-soldiers in civilian life could read and write.

A further impetus to change was the Prussian victory over France in the Franco-Prussian War of 1870–71. Alexander and, more acutely, Miliutin, appreciated the significance of this war and responded by imitating the Prussian army's methods. The key change was that recruitment was extended to all classes of society and was not confined to the peasants. Under the Statute on Universal Military Service, published in 1874, all males over twenty one were registered as eligible to serve and about one quarter of them were required to do so. Selection was by chance – effectively, lots were drawn –

and service was set at seven years in the front line units followed by eight in the reserve and five in the militia. There were significant dispensations from the number of years service required for those who had any form of education – a kind of sliding scale operated from university graduates to school-leavers – as recruitment became more sensitive to ability. This roused the nobles who wanted to retain their special status but they were overruled as the military reforms were deemed essential. Nor were those from richer classes able to pay for a substitute to take their place. The only exemptions allowed were based on poor health or a family's extreme economic need to keep a son. And, to drive up standards throughout the armed forces, the tsar's brother, Constantine, carried out a similar series of reforms in the Russian navy.

The impact of these reforms was important. Russia was able to mobilise more men more quickly than at the start of the reign and could rely on a higher calibre of soldier. In the next war that Russia fought, in 1877–78 against Turkey, the army performed well. However, the test was not a difficult one as Russia defeated Turkey in wars throughout the nineteenth century and the Prussian general, Moltke, dismissed the affair as 'the one-eyed beat the blind'! Prussian military efficiency was, at the time, the target for the rest of Europe. The reforms also helped to integrate Russian society a little better as different social classes could meet in the armed forces. This was by no means a thorough process, of course, as time was needed and there were deficiencies in the new arrangements. Doctors could be bribed (by nobles) to declare recruits as unfit and the officer corps remained dominated by the nobles. As a measure of the lack of progress that was made in the long term, it should be borne in mind that in 1904–05 Russia was defeated by a country it felt was no rival: Japan.

Local government

When serfs had been forced to work the estates of the nobles, there was no need for a system of local government in Russia since the serfs had so few rights that they were compelled to accept the decisions of their owners. Political decision-making in the localities was the exclusive preserve of the nobility and its members often exercised complete control on their estates. Indeed, such was the extent of their power that it was a powerful remedy to any calls from the élite for a constitution or national assembly. When the serfs were freed from this form of control, Alexander II therefore needed to forestall any demand for a parliament since his aim was to preserve his own status as an autocrat. He did this by granting the nobles control of the new local government authorities that were set up in 1864 and 1870. This was not so much an example of liberalisation and the creation of more rights for Russian citizens as an essential concession to the gentry. He set up a commission to study the matter in 1860 but its verdict on reform became urgent in 1863 when the ex-serfs became free peasants and, at length, a decree was issued in January 1864 so as to establish a structure of rural government.

Besides the emancipation of the serfs, it is this area of reform that has attracted most interest from scholars of Alexander II's reign. Partly, this reflects its importance but it also shows how many aspects of Russian life the new bodies had to deal with. Before 1861, there was very little administrative apparatus between the tsar and the nobles' estates since the maintenance of control relied on methods that went back to the eighteenth century via provincial governors. From 1864 – and until 1917 – there was a new hierarchy of representative bodies, beginning with groups of peasant communes (arranged into cantons) and progressing to district and then provincial government. The first of these included an elected committee to deal mostly with judicial matters. Above this, a more elaborately organised district government was elected by separate groups of nobles, peasants chosen by the cantons, townsmen and clergy with, respectively, 42 per cent, 38 per cent, 11 per cent and 7 per cent of the votes. The preponderance of power therefore rested with the nobles who were the least numerous group. The delegates were elected for three years. From the district governments that the electoral colleges returned, a provincial government or 'zemstvo' was selected in which the influence of nobles was even greater. The law applied to twenty-seven provinces at first and was extended to a further seven soon afterwards.

The activities with which the various zemstvos were concerned were restricted to very practical local matters. They dealt with education by founding new primary schools; public health by building small hospitals; transport by constructing roads and, occasionally, railways; and insurance schemes which included the provision of emergency supplies for when food stocks were low. Although they built jails, they were not responsible for the maintenance of law and order which remained under the control of central government. The elected assemblies met only once a year but they appointed a standing committee to implement any decisions. In this way, the zemstvos were steered away from any political aspirations and encouraged in their parochial good works. The tsar tended to see them as money-raising groups for immediate needs and in no way were they pressure groups. The fact that co-operation between zemstvos was forbidden is sufficient to underline this.

It was no coincidence that the countryside was affected first since this was where the serfs had lived. Town councils were not set up on a general basis until June 1870. Most of the powers of town councils dated back to Catherine the Great's ineffectual 1785 Charter to the Towns but Nicholas I had passed a new statute for Saint Petersburg in 1846, which was copied and applied to Moscow in 1862 and Odessa in 1863, each of which were granted further rights. The 1870 law made eight major towns equivalent to a province and many smaller towns equal to the county districts and on this basis the practices of the zemstvos were applied to urban areas – although the towns' electorates largely excluded workers. The outward appearance of towns and their amenities duly improved as street lighting was put in place and pavements were built.

Not all of the empire benefited from these reforms. Poland remained outside the system because of the rebellion of 1863 and the borderlands of Caucasia and Trans-caucasia also missed out. All of Siberia was unaffected too. Local government was a privilege granted mostly to Russians and withheld from groups who could not be trusted. No national assembly was allowed until the unrest of 1905 forced a state duma on Nicholas II by the following year.

Law courts and the legal system

As with so much else in Russian society, the law courts became subjected to a reformed hierarchy with tiers of administration. Just as local government was set up in this way in 1864, so the legal system was changed in the same year. Hitherto, the main areas of tsarist policy had been to study the problem (with Alexander I's Law Commission of 1801) and to then codify the laws (through the work of Nicholas I's minister Speransky

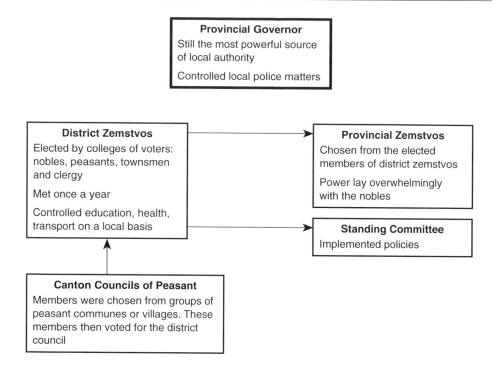

Figure 4.3 The structure of local government in Russia from 1864

in the 1830s). With the demise of serfdom and the end of justice being administered on the nobles' estates, a new platform was needed for the law.

There were serious problems with the operation of the existing system. It could be enormously slow in reaching decisions if those involved were anxious to delay any verdict and were able to exploit legal loopholes. Cases could be passed from court to court and judge to judge for years on end. This favoured the richer classes, especially the nobility, which had the financial resources to sustain such a strategy. The system was also corrupt since the police expected to be bribed in the course of their work or, if nothing was forthcoming, they could use their right to levy fines to victimise defendants. This gave credence to the popular Russian saying 'No grease, no motion'. Only written evidence was admissible in court which was bizarre given that most judges were illiterate, and certainly most of the peasants, so the richer classes again had an advantage. There were also rules that assessed the quality of evidence submitted in court based not on the circumstances or the witnesses in a case but on the social status of whoever made a statement. The testimony of the nobles was given most sway and this too gave them an unfair position in any proceedings – even to the point of them being let off for serious offences. Their claims were made stronger by the fact that the judges never met the accused and so a great deal of the courts' business was a paper exercise in which those involved never had a chance to plead their case. There were no juries and no lawyers.

The matter was subject to investigation, discussion and even dispute at government level. Alexander asked for a report on the situation in 1861 which was written jointly by the Ministry of Justice and the second Section of the Imperial Chancery. The key figure was Zarudny, who was the deputy in the second Section, and he was supported by Zamiatnin who was his counterpart at the Ministry of Justice. As reformers, they had to overcome the conservatism of their superiors, Bludov in the Section and Panin in the Ministry. A tug of war between the senior officials and their subordinates ensued in which the latter eventually prevailed because of pressure from the nobles at large. They were concerned that the existing legal system would not continue to favour them in a post-emancipation Russia and so sought extra guarantees. The investigation reported back to Alexander in 1862 with a set of Basic Principles which, after consultation with the Council of State, he adopted. A new legal system was introduced in November 1864.

The new arrangements completely overhauled the old order and created an independent judicial system that turned out to be beyond the control of the tsar. The reforms he introduced allowed a new and legitimate source of opposition to the autocracy that he had not foreseen and, although he tried to claw back some of the control, he was not able to do so fully. What the changes brought in was a west European style of law court and procedure. There were five tiers of courts created, beginning at district level with a Justice of the Peace appointed for three years by the zemstva, and dealing with petty offences. It then rose through district courts that had a panel of JPs, to provincial courts, to ten tribunals or 'Chambers of Justice' and finally to the highest court in the land, the Senate. There was therefore no change to the status of the Senate. Judges were appointed in the three higher tiers and were sufficiently well paid to be above bribery. They could not be removed from their posts unless they themselves broke the law and so they were able to reach decisions regardless of what the tsar or central government wanted to see happen. Trained lawyers were needed in order to defend both the plaintiff and the defendant in oral – rather than written – exchanges before a judge and a jury. Limits were set on the number of times that cases could be referred to more senior courts so as to speed up the process. And trials were conducted in public with seats available for interested onlookers to attend and subject the process to further scrutiny.

Not all of Russian society was subject to the new legal system, though. Just as the borderlands of the Russian Empire did not benefit from the local government reform, so those in weaker positions in society were excluded from the new system of justice. The most glaring example of this was the ex-serfs who, from 1861, joined the state peasants in having their own courts based on the cantons of communes. These had been created originally by Nicholas I in the 1830s and were designed to settle disputes only between peasants. There were further courts for the army which presided over exclusively military crimes. Church courts ran in parallel with the state courts and had full jurisdiction over divorce cases. Later the state tried to take back some of the control it felt it had lost. In 1872 a new procedure was used to try those accused of 'crimes against the state' so as to deal with political enemies more secretively and the Senate was entrusted with this role. It also allowed the state to take pre-emptive action and arrest those individuals it believed might commit crimes. This procedure was for internal security reasons and was referred to as 'administrative arrest'. The courts were bypassed and victims could be exiled without him or her having any right of appeal.

Despite these exceptions, the new system worked very well. The open nature of trials attracted public interest and the judges and juries remained impartial. Sentencing of defendants who were found guilty was intended to be prescriptive and leave the judges little choice. However, the juries found ways of showing more compassion to those individuals found guilty of committing serious crimes but for whom they felt the stipulated punishment was too severe. Thus, criminals could be convicted of crimes that were less serious than the one they had in fact committed thereby incurring a lesser sentence. Another development was the degree of free speech that the courts tolerated. As a professional class of lawyers emerged, they were often very sharp in their criticism of local officials and eloquent in their denunciation of the regime's injustices. The most famous case of this was in Saint Petersburg in 1878 when the revolutionary leader Vera Zasulich was put on trial. This was unusual because such cases were normally subject to the rule of the Senate under the amendment of 1872. However, she was put on trial in a regular court and, despite admitting to shooting at and wounding General Trepov, the Governor of Saint Petersburg, she was acquitted. The moving defence speeches and the jury's sense of natural justice prevailed. It was not only the state authorities that disliked the new courts due to the verdicts they returned. Some of the revolutionaries who were to emerge in the 1870s and 1880s – notwithstanding the result for Zasulich – believed that the nobles' influence remained too strong and they used it as a justification of their violent activities.

Education and censorship

The system of schooling and higher education in Russia had been set out by Alexander I in his 1804 Statute on Schools which formalised and extended a four tier pyramid of institutions. The merging of the ministries of Education and of Spiritual Affairs under Golitsyn in 1817 reflected the tsar's devotion to Christian ideals. Under Nicholas I further work was carried out by Uvarov and Shikmatov at the fourth Section but their dictum of 'Orthodoxy, Autocracy, Nationality' hardly furthered the cause of education and after 1850 the conditions under which university students worked were very harsh. The third Section, the secret police, worked closely with the Ministry of Education and as such applied very strict regulations on censorship to any books or printed matter. Alexander II's education and censorship policies could therefore hardly do anything but relax the rules that he inherited. For most Russians, however, education was something that affected other people.

The initial policies of Alexander's reign were very cautious and did little more than reverse the excessive restrictions imposed by Nicholas. The number of places available at the universities was increased and foreign lecturers were tolerated once more. However, student riots in 1861–62 prompted the tsar to appoint Putiatin as Minister of Education in June 1861. He proposed another round of severe measures against the universities but was opposed by so many of the professors that he had to be replaced by a liberal. In 1861, Golovnin was made Minister of Education and he brought great energy to the process of expanding the state's network of schools and ensuring more students went to university. Three new laws were passed in rapid succession, dealing with universities, secondary schools and elementary education, 1863–64, and these led to a huge amount of progress by the end of the century.

Elementary or primary school education benefited from a law of July 1864 which placed it under the control of district school boards. These were heavily influenced by the zemstvos. They provided lessons for the peasant population in 'safe' subjects such as religion, reading, writing and arithmetic and steered around the 'dangerous' subjects of history and foreign languages. Education was steadily taken away from the church since, although priests were able to teach in the new schools that were set up, the number of state schools soon overtook the church's foundations. By 1915 there were 34 000 primary schools controlled by the church compared to 81 000 under the local councils. Between five and ten million children received some form of teaching at the elementary level by the turn of the century.

Secondary schools received similar treatment the same year with a law in November 1864 which began by confirming the distinction between the technical schools and the more academic gymnasia. While both types taught a core of religion, history, geography, maths and Russian, the gymnasia also offered classical and modern languages while the technical schools gave tuition in science and drawing. In the first ten years of Alexander's reign the number of pupils at these schools doubled to 800 000.

The University Statute of June 1863 built on the U-turn of the mid 1850s and increased the numbers going to university still further. There was, after all, a backlog of likely candidates who had been deprived of a place under Nicholas and who were by the mid 1860s more mature – and more political in outlook – than before. In 1855, there were just 3000 students; by 1860 this had risen to 5000 and, as the number of universities increased as well, the total number of students by 1900 has been estimated as being close to 100 000. Universities became self-governing but accepted the curricula laid down by the Ministry of Education as well as its end of year exams. The state invested heavily in the university system as bursaries were made available to students and the salaries of lecturers were increased.

Golovnin's period as Minister of Education was short lived because, after an assassination attempt made against the tsar by an ex-student in 1866, he was dismissed and replaced by Dmitri Tolstoy. The fundamental aspects of Golovnin's work were not changed but Tolstoy made amendments at each level of education. The elementary schools were made subject to inspections from his ministry, the secondary schools' curricula were changed in favour of classics and away from science courses, and the university intake was cut back a little. As Tolstoy was also Over Procurator of the Holy

Table 4.4 Russian universities, 1801–81

Year	Changes and details
	Alexander I
1804	*Statute of Schools* increased the number of universities from 3 to 6
1817	Ministries of Education and Spiritual Affairs were merged under Golitsyn
	Nicholas I
1828–49	Uvarov dominated and demanded 'Orthodoxy, Autocracy, Nationality'
1835	Universities' autonomy was weakened
1848–49	Arts courses faced more restrictions; Shikmatov took over until 1855
	Alexander II
1855–61	Relaxation of university regulations
1863	*University Statute* led to autonomy and more academic freedom under Golovnin (1861–66) and then Tolstoy (from 1866)
	Universities and their foundation date: Moscow 1755; Vilna 1803; Dorpat 1803; Kharkov 1804; Kazan 1804; Saint Petersburg 1819; Odessa 1864; Warsaw 1816–31

Synod, there was a close link established once more between the church and education but their school systems still ran in parallel.

Censorship was also closely linked to the education system; until 1860, when the task was given to the Ministry of the Interior, it was the Ministry of Education that was responsible for most forms of censorship. In the first five years or so of the reign, the regulations affecting universities was relaxed and in line with this there was much more toleration of what periodicals and journals could publish, including of course anything to do with the emancipation of the serfs. From 1865 (and until 1905), the method of censorship was shifted from pre- to post-publication methods although the Minister of the Interior, Valuev, tempered this by issuing warning letters to editors, taking them to court and even banning *The Contemporary* for several months in 1866. Journals had to lodge funds with the Ministry which could be seized if they took too much liberty and there was even the threat of censorship operating after printing but before distribution. Censorship of any kind, however, was becoming more difficult simply because of the growing number of publications and the increasingly literate public. Evidence of this can be found in the number of new book titles published in Russia each year. In 1855 there were just over 1000; in 1864, 1800 and by 1894 there were 10 700. This tenfold increase in forty years was partly due to the more relaxed period of censorship under Alexander II and there was a corresponding rise in the combined circulation of the press. By 1894, there were almost 90 newspapers being printed.

The interest in books was also due to the outstanding authors who emerged during the reign, chief of whom were Dostoyevsky and the more famous Tolstoy. These men wrote from opposite perspectives. Dostoyevsky began at the bottom of Russian society and looked up. He spent much of his time in debt having gambled away his money and often had to beg his wife for a few coins. He seemed to write out of desperation and he

Table 4.5 Major works of Russian literature under Alexander II, 1855–81

Writer		Major works	Date
Turgenev, Ivan (1818–83)	novelist	*Fathers and Sons*	1862
		Smoke	1867
		Virgin Soil	1876
Tolstoy, Leo (1828–1910)	novelist	*Sebastopol Stories*	1855
		War and Peace	1869
		Anna Karenina	1877
		Resurrection	1889
Dostoyevsky, Fyodor (1821–81)	novelist	*Notes from the House of the Dead*	1862
		Notes from Underground	1864
		Crime and Punishment	1866
		The Idiot	1869
		The Devils	1871
		The Brothers Karamazov	1880
Leskov, Nicholas (1831–95)	novelist	*Lady Macbeth of Mtsensk*	1865
		Cathedral Folk	1872
		The Enchanted Wanderer	1874
Goncharev, Ivan (1812–91)	novelist	*Oblomov*	1859

drew on his experiences of poor living conditions for the social context of his novels. By contrast, Tolstoy wrote from the peaks of Russian society, placing his characters in a world of luxury and diplomacy. Both men were concerned with life at its most fundamental, religious level; Dostoyevsky has been seen as the man who best described the 'Russian soul' while Tolstoy struggled terribly with his Christian conscience in later years. The importance of Russian fiction to the life of the nation was apparent from the reign of Nicholas onwards, as it provided an outlet for otherwise forbidden discussion and Dostoyevsky for instance was arrested for his membership of the Petraschevsky Circle and sentenced to death. His suffering in the labour camps of Siberia provided him with material in a similar way to the gulag for the twentieth-century novelist Solzhenitsyn. What these men did was to elevate their experiences beyond parochial Russian concerns and into the realm of profound human experience. They carried forward a moral crusade that many of their contemporaries felt was their duty as writers.

The achievement of Dostoyevsky, Tolstoy and other leading writers of the time was perhaps the more remarkable because Alexander II was not entirely sure of the regime's security. In particular, the period 1860–62 was very difficult for him as a number of potential threats emerged at the same time. The process of emancipation was going through its final stages and this brought the spectre of peasant unrest – which materialised briefly in 1861 – as well as a hostile reaction from the nobles. Student unrest was rising in the early 1860s, possibly because of their heightened political awareness after having been denied university places under Nicholas, but possibly too because of their poverty (in spite of the state bursaries). There was a series of arson attacks in Saint Petersburg in May 1862 for which students were blamed. Events outside Russia also served to stir up disquiet. The unification of Italy in 1860 and above all the inspirational leadership of Garibaldi served as an example to political activists; and in Poland in 1863 there was a second nationalist uprising that urgently needed to be suppressed.

The early 1860s was a volatile period for the tsar and some Russian historians have suggested that the country was close to revolution at this time. Certainly, there were many political radicals and some of them were prepared to use violence against the tsar. One of these was Karakozov, whose assassination attempt against Alexander led to the fall of Golovnin at the Ministry of Education. He fired a pistol shot at the tsar in April 1866 but missed and was executed the following October. This event might be construed as a turning point in the reign since in the short term it made many of Russia's ordinary folk have a distaste for their better educated social superiors and in the long term there were very few further reforms. Almost all of the legislation that Alexander II effected during his reign was passed between 1861 and 1865, from the Emancipation Decree to the Press Law; only the extension of district councils from the countryside to the towns in 1870 and the on-going army reforms occurred later. However, there is also a great deal of coincidence in the timing. The work that was carried out between 1861 and 1865 did not cease to function after the assassination attempt. True, it was amended – especially in the vulnerable areas of the education and censorship – but there was no dramatic change of course. Alexander had done the work that he needed to do and was determined to stay with it.

Conclusions on the reforms

The emancipation of the serfs was a ground-breaking measure in Russia and needed to be followed by a sequence of further 'Great Reforms' immediately afterwards. Did this amount to a revolution? Whereas there was a fear of rebellion felt in government circles between 1860 and 1862, it was in fact the state that was making all the changes. Consequently, they were bureaucratic, hierarchical and centralised by nature. But what needs to be considered at this point are the common characteristics of these reforms and how much, in sum, was altered by them.

The autocracy remained in place and this was paramount. Alfred Rieber has argued that the sole purpose of the emancipation of the serfs was the strengthening of the state's military and economic position and this was almost certainly true.[12] However, the results were not a perfect match with the intentions. The 1861 Decree kept the ex-serfs in their place because they remained effectively tied to the soil they tilled through the high redemption charges, and their parochial outlook meant they remained stuck with the commune. Despite being freed, they were not treated equally; it is true that more and more of them had access to schools, especially the younger generation but in 1897 (the year of a major census) only a little over one-fifth of the population was credited with being literate. Elementary education was not universally available and only a tiny proportion of the Ministry of Education's spending was devoted to schools. It is also true to say that the peasants had representation on the district councils and they were given better terms in the army. But they had their own separate courts based in the communes and the councils were dominated by the nobles and gentry. The land that they bought was only made available to them by its owners because the landlords realised that they stood to receive a very good price. The poll tax remained in force and so the burden of taxation continued to fall mostly on the peasants since it was a flat-rate charge from which the nobles were exempt. Not until 1916 was income tax introduced. The serfs, then, had some additional opportunities after 1861 but to describe them as free is an exaggeration.

The autocracy continued most obviously because there was no national assembly or parliament. This was something that Alexander abjectly refused to contemplate since the reforms were designed, in part, to thwart calls for such a reform. The rural and town councils were the main sop to any such campaign but this did not stop periodic calls for a parliament coming from within the government; Constantine, Valuev and Golovnin all pressed the tsar for change. The most likely beneficiaries of a parliamentary system in Russia were the nobles and gentry – a mass democracy was inconceivable – and they were kept sufficiently content through the compensation package of the Emancipation Decree and the local councils. University and press freedom also grew and they were able to take advantage of this. However, the army reforms, which from 1874 made even the élite eligible for compulsory military service, were not popular and Alexander had to be careful how this was introduced. The increase in the effectiveness of the army reinforced the tsar's position at home and abroad.

What was not taken into account sufficiently by the regime was the radical change to the judicial system since this established a legitimate source of opposition to the autocracy which was extremely difficult to uproot. High profile court cases served to establish their power in the public mind and subsequent remedial action by the tsar,

Table 4.6 Timing of major reforms, 1855–75

	Government reforms	Protests and problems
1855–61	Relaxation of university regulations	
1856		
1857		
1858–59		Vodka riots
1859		
1860–62	State Bank (1860)	Student riots; fires in Saint Petersburg
1861	*Emancipation Decree*	
1862–74	Army reforms	
1863	University Statute	Polish rebellion
1864	Rural councils, law courts and schools	
1865	Press laws	
1866	State peasants were freed	Karakozov's assassination attempt
1867		
1868		
1869		
1870	Town councils	
1871		
1872		
1873		
1874	Universal military service	
1875		

for instance the use of 'administrative arrest', came too late. Nor was the autocratic structure fully thought through. The provincial governors who served the tsar via the Ministry of the Interior had less direct power over their areas and assumed a position of supervision rather than of control. The courts were part of this, but the councils and universities also played a part. Nor could the censors at the same ministry adequately cope with the burgeoning quantity of printed matter. In the long term, the tsarist autocracy was being undermined by its own attempts to safeguard its position.

Economic and financial policies

The tsar was able to control the state's economic and financial policies since the budget was not subject to outside scrutiny. The first major task was to stabilise the financial situation after the ravages of the Crimean War and the uncontolled expenditure that it had entailed. This was something that Kankrin, the elderly finance chief of Tsar Nicholas I, had worked hard to achieve before the war broke out. The early stages of recovery were set in place by Tatarinov who made government departments submit annual statements of likely expenditure and made departmental budgets become open to internal audits. In 1857 the Tariff Act cut import duties and was followed by further reductions in 1868. In 1860 a State Bank was founded although it was not given the right to be the sole source of paper money and this limited the government's ability to control the money supply and thus inflation.

In 1862, Alexander appointed a new Minister of Finance, Reutern, who was to retain the post until 1878 (when another war, again against Turkey, unpicked his years of work). He tried to make the Russian rouble convertible against gold but found within a matter of months that this was not feasible. He quickly turned to other means of financial prudence. Government accounts began to be published; the poll tax was retained after some doubts about it in 1870; and the duty paid on vodka was reduced in 1863 (partly for political reasons, as high prices had led to rioting) but still returned good revenues. In fact, it generated one-third of government income. The effect of these measures was to make Russia appear a much safer prospect in the capital markets of western Europe and inward investment grew significantly. The French Empire of Napoleon III lent funds for railway construction.

Under Nicholas I, Kankrin had retarded railway development because he did not see the need for such a form of transport and the tsar had to step in. It was therefore primarily under Alexander II that a rail network was built. In 1854 Russia had only 700km of track but by 1876 this had risen to 18 500km. The routes between major towns were planned so that there was no duplication of effort (but no competition either) since the state was constructing these lines with military needs in mind, rather than private travel. The mobilisation of troops and the movement of supplies were of prime importance. There was massive investment in railways by the state and between 1860 and 1876 it spent 1.8 billion roubles. The 1860s also saw private funding reach 700 million roubles. Foreign expertise, especially from the USA, was drafted in so as to advise on the building of rolling stock and cuttings but the work itself was carried out by Russian army engineers under contract. Until the end of the century, the state preferred to offer guarantees on investors' money put into railways rather than to build and own the lines itself even though this was not always possible. The pattern was reversed in the twentieth century.[13]

Better transport and communications had considerable benefits for the rest of the economy, as goods of all kinds could be distributed cheaply and this allowed the specialisation of production necessary for a modern and competitive economy. Grain production increased and exports rose threefold in Alexander II's reign. Extractive industries also boosted their production of coal, iron and, due to the opening up of the Baku oil fields, petrol. These commodities fuelled the expansion of the rail network and were used in the making of other goods.

These figures hide some short-term fluctuations in levels of output the most significant of which occurred immediately after the emancipation of the serfs in 1861 as the industries struggled to adjust to the loss of servile labour. Iron production in the Urals fell by nearly a third between 1860 and 1862 for example. Sudden upswings in production were possible too, the most obvious of which was the growth of the cotton industry while the American civil war (1861–65) halted exports from the southern states. The loss of US supplies of raw cotton meant unemployment and low output at first but the planting of crops in Turkestan and the building of larger factories for spinning and weaving led to long-term growth. The return of American supplies in the later 1860s saw huge increases in consumer spending on cotton clothing. The problems that

Table 4.7 Industrial expansion in the reign of Alexander II

Industry	1860	1890	Units
Coal	0.30	6.03	million tonnes
Pig iron	0.33	1.06	million tonnes
Petrol	–	3.90	million tonnes
Railways	1000	31 000	kilometres

agriculture as a whole faced – due to retention of the mir as the unit of production and the heavy redemption dues – have already been discussed.

Financial institutions flourished under Alexander II as well and these either made funds more readily available or were able to use the money more effectively. Joint stock banks, railway companies and industrial enterprises were all formed rapidly and much of the credit for this must go to Reutern who set up regulations for the formation of municipal banks (1862) and savings banks (1869). These contributed to a much greater pace of change but Russia also began to experience the cyclical booms and slumps typical of an industrial economy and these reflected the west European cycles as the international economy began to affect Russia more and more. Booms occurred in the late 1860s, late 1870s and late 1880s with slumps during the intervening years. Very good harvests in 1878 and 1879 also contributed to the middle boom.

The economic development of Russia in the second half of the nineteenth century was therefore quite impressive and certainly contrasted with some of the policies under Nicholas that were either confused (railways) or too traditional (innovation in state agriculture). Both tsars strove to maintain a stable currency but their finance ministers, Kankrin and Reutern, were undermined by the wars that Russia fought. The emancipation of the serfs allowed enormous changes to the way that Russian society was governed but its economic impact was not a complete answer to Russia's needs.

The Polish Rebellion 1863

Most of Poland had become part of the Russian Empire in 1795 after the three partitions that Catherine the Great had agreed with Austria and Prussia. It was soon conquered by Napoleon and became the Grand Duchy of Warsaw until in 1815 at the Congress of Vienna it was reconstituted as 'Congress Poland' under Russian domination once more. Prussia also had the Polish lands of Posen and Thorn, Austria annexed Galicia and Krakow was a small independent state. The Poles, however, were a nation with a distinct culture and language and the nobles were able to mount some resistance against Russian rule because they had not only a constitution but also a separate army. In 1830–31 there was a nationalist rebellion against Russia led by the army that was defeated because the Polish peasantry did not give it their support. Tsar Nicholas I imposed his idea of 'Nationality' on Poland and began to Russify it; this was so successful that when there was a wave of unrest across Europe in 1848–49, Poland remained quiet. However, Polish nationalists continued to oppose Russian rule, not least because Russia claimed a large area of land – Lithuania – to the east as its own, and in 1863 a second major rebellion broke out.

The early measures that Alexander II passed with respect to Poland were conciliatory. A new viceroy was appointed in the figure of Mikhail Gorchakov who replaced Nicholas I's choice of General Paskevich. Warsaw was allowed to have a new medical school (as a substitute for the University of Warsaw that had been closed down after the last rebellion) and a new archbishop was appointed. Yet these gestures did not assuage the hostility of Polish nationalists to Russian rule and the new Agricultural Society was turned into a clandestine parliament. Alexander hoped that Wielopolski could lead the moderate elements in the Polish nobility to a new understanding with Russia and he became Prime Minister in 1862 as the deputy to the second new viceroy, Grand Duke Constantine. Wielopolski wanted to set up national governmental institutions, even if they fell short of the idea of independence, and he wanted to reform the system of land holding. Neither of these programmes got very far.

Unrest began to develop mostly in Warsaw, in commemoration of past victories and patriotic moments, in the course of 1861. In February, the battle of Grochow from 1831 was marked with a demonstration; in April, a protest march was held in defiance of the Agricultural Society being disbanded; in October, the deaths of the Archbishop of Warsaw and of Kosciusko more than half a century before prompted marches. Tension was mounting and the hatred of foreign rule was intensified by the ham-fisted methods of crowd control that Russian troops used so as to keep order. Martial law was declared. Wielopolski persevered but by now the radical elements were determined to force some kind of confrontation and made a number of assassination attempts against Constantine, the viceroy, and against Wielopolski himself. None of them succeeded but these two men responded with new measures which included the conscription of all young Polish men. It was this that brought the tension to the point of crisis and in January 1863 the rebellion broke out.

The uprising did not have any major battles, unlike in 1830–31, and there was no clear-cut pattern to the events of the rebellion. It lasted until the middle of 1864 because the Russian army of 80 000 had difficulty finding and engaging the 10 000 rebel Poles. The attitude of the Polish peasantry was equivocal, sometimes helping the Poles but sometimes siding with the Russians. Overall, however, there were more that joined the rising than in 1830–31. Landowners' views were also variable. The Poles in the Prussian and Austrian territories did not rise up in sympathy because there were German armies moved into position there, but Lithuania did experience some unrest. Britain and especially France gave vocal support to the rebels and criticised Russia for the severity with which it crushed the insurrection, but they could do nothing practical to help. The Russian generals resorted to public hangings, for example, as part of their repression. The last rebel leader was hanged in August 1864.

Alexander had to decide how next to deal with Poland; his father's policy of Russification had hardly brought the country closer to the bosom of the greater Russian family. This time, generous terms for land reform were introduced by the man who had organised the emancipation of the serfs to Russia. In 1864, Miliutin ensured that some 700 000 Polish peasants became farmers of freehold land for which they had to pay no redemption dues (which served as a punishment of the Polish nobles). This attempt to isolate the peasantry from their former landlords did not succeed, though, and Russia was left with a permanently hostile province. A Russian university was set up in Warsaw and education in Polish secondary schools had to be carried out in Russian from 1866. This rule was applied to primary schools in 1885. The property of the Catholic Church was confiscated and sold off. And the Lithuanian lands were dealt with more harshly as the use of the Polish language was forbidden and the property of the Catholic Church was confiscated.

Foreign policy

After the defeat of Russia in the Crimea in 1856, Alexander II wanted to make reforms to the country beginning with the emancipation of the serfs. While external security remained the overall priority, he was prepared to give more time to internal matters and as a result Russia was relatively passive in European affairs between 1856 and

1870. The end of this period was marked by Alexander unilaterally ending the Black Sea clauses of the Treaty of Paris, something that he had wanted to end from the very start of his reign. Russia was still able, though, to continue to expand in Asia.

From 1856 and until the end of Alexander II's reign in 1881, Russia's foreign secretary was Alexander Gorchakov. He was confronted with a difficult situation because of Russia's defeat, which meant a loss of prestige and confidence within the country; and he found Russia largely isolated as a result. His first response was to issue a rather defensive circular in which he explained that in the coming years Russia's allies could not necessarily rely on it for support since it 'was thinking'. Britain remained adamantly suspicious of Russia and most unwilling to co-operate with it when, for instance, it tried to make some minor changes to the 1856 treaty. Austria was no longer seen as an ally because of its failure to come to Russia's aid during the war and therefore its failure to repay the diplomatic debt that Russia felt it was owed after rescuing Austria from revolution in 1849. In fact, Russia was quite ready to work against Austrian interests in the late 1850s by way of revenge. By far the best prospect of friendship that Russia had in Europe was to be found in France with its new leader Napoleon III. Despite being one of the two countries that had defeated Russia in the Crimea, France was keen to see some territorial changes in Europe – so as to alter the frontiers laid down in 1815 – and was interested in working with any state that could help this process. Alexander II and Gorchakov wanted to end the Black Sea clauses and were willing to contemplate changes elsewhere in order to achieve this, so the two countries were able to work together from 1856 to 1863.

Russia supported Napoleon III's foreign policy in two major areas in this period. The first of these was in the Near East where they agreed that the principalities of Moldavia and Wallachia could unite to form a single state which was called Romania. This policy had to be carried out in conjunction with Britain since its vital interests in trade – as well as the wider concern it felt for the balance of power and stability of the Ottoman Empire – were affected. Significantly, Austria was opposed to any such unification since it feared the possible impact in its lands in the Balkans. Any encouragement of nationalism was likely to provoke its own national minorities in the area, such as the neighbouring Romanians in Transylvania. After an international conference in the summer of 1858 had been held in Paris, the new state of Romania duly came into being early in 1859. The second area of co-operation between Russia and France was in Italy where Austria had kept hegemony since 1815 and consequently it could only lose as a result of any changes. In March 1859 they signed a treaty in which Russia promised to remain neutral (and not to help Austria) in any conflict between France and Austria in Italy. This was no vague contingency but part of a carefully constructed plan on Napoleon III's part. He agreed war terms with Piedmont in 1858 as well, in order to enlarge the army that he used to attack Austria during the following summer. His aim was to 'free Italy to the Adriatic' – that is, to seize Lombardy and Venetia from Austrian control – and to give the conquered lands to Piedmont in return for it giving Nice and Savoy to France. Russia refused to give Austria any help, of course, and so it soon lost Lombardy but was able to hang on to Venetia by retreating into the mighty Quadrilateral fortresses. The contrast with 1849, when Russia saved Austria from the rebels in Hungary and freed it to use troops in Italy, was very plain.

The period of co-operation came to an end in 1863, however, when the Polish rebellion occurred. As has been seen, Russia crushed the nationalist uprising brutally and then developed its policy of Russification even further than before. Napoleon III, who claimed to champion nationalism (as in Romania and to an extent in northern Italy) could do nothing but denounce the Russian policies. Partly, this was to satisfy public opinion at home which included a large contingent of exiled Poles in Paris. Nevertheless, the effect of this was to alienate France from Russia as it considered that it was dealing with an internal affair of no concern to any foreign state, including France. Austria, for what it was worth, also joined in the chorus of criticism despite its fears of Poles in its Galician lands rising in sympathy; no better relationship was built between Russia and Austria as a result. Prussia made serious gains from the position as it offered what help it could to Russia through its emissary General von Alvensleben. He negotiated a convention that provided for the joint pursuit of rebels across the Russo-Prussian frontier. While Alexander was surprised (and mildly irritated) by a power such as Prussia offering help to Russia, the message of friendship that was conveyed by Prussia was what counted in the long run.

With Austria still estranged from Russia and Prussia now viewed more kindly by the tsar, changes in Germany were much more likely to occur. And, as Tim Blanning has pointed out on numerous occasions, the most important changes that have happened in Germany over the past two centuries have taken place when Russia has been absent from international affairs.[14] This was the case in 1917–18 when the Russian Revolution took it out of the Great War and the peace settlement at Versailles; it was also true in 1989–91 when Germany reunified as a result of Russia deliberately withdrawing from intervention in eastern Europe. And, by contrast, when Russia was fully engaged in European affairs, as in 1848–49, it prevented any changes in Germany by defeating the Hungarian rebels under Kossuth and supporting Austria at Olmütz. This treaty, known as the 'humiliation of Olmütz' in Prussia meant that Prussia had to give up its own plans for Germany and accept the return of the German Confederation as created in 1815. The 1860s was another period of Russian absence and it allowed Prussia's Chancellor, Bismarck, to co-ordinate the unification of Germany around his own state. Russia simply watched as Prussia defeated first Austria in 1866 and then France in 1870, the two states that had previously been its allies. The real importance of the two wars was not their defeat but the victory of Russia and its creation, by 1871, of the German Empire. It meant the end of the old Congress of Vienna balance of power, something that had been in jeopardy since 1856, as Prussia was a new great power of the first rank; militant, powerful and ambitious.

The defeat of France also gave Gorchakov the opportunity he had been waiting for in order to publicly reject the Black Sea clauses. The other great powers could do little but accept this declaration. Prussia was broadly sympathetic but in any case preoccupied with the final defeat of France; France was distracted for similar reasons; Austria and Britain were sour about the situation but could do nothing about it. In 1871 Gladstone, Britain's Prime Minister, opened a conference in London to discuss the matter although the verdict was agreed in advance. The meeting merely confirmed that Russia could remilitarise the Black Sea (as could Turkey) and that in principle no state should unilaterally abrogate an international agreement. How this was to be enforced was a moot point. Russia was suitably pleased with the result since its security was shored up once more and it meant that it could entertain ambitions in the eastern Mediterranean again. Russia also began to become more involved in European affairs. The Holy Alliance of Russia, Austria and Prussia was resurrected by Bismarck in 1873, with the German

Empire replacing Prussia, in an attempt to maintain the status quo. This was in Germany's interests since it had achieved what it wanted to do and feared French aggression in particular. Alexander II was ready to join this league since it made no definite commitments, a feature that was demonstrated in 1875 when a Franco-Prussian war scare occurred; Gorchakov was able to warn Bismarck off any aggressive moves whether they were intended or not.

The Eastern Question also required a serious amount of attention from Alexander, just as it had in the reigns of the two previous tsars. The traditional Russian policy was to try to preserve the Turkish Empire as a weak neighbour on its frontier since it was unlikely to present any threat. This allowed Russia to exert a certain amount of influence over the sultan, a policy that had been most effective under Tsar Nicholas I in the 1830s. Such an approach was periodically jettisoned in favour of expansionist wars against Turkey which Russia invariably won, as in 1806–12 and 1828–29; the only aspect of these wars that changed was the period of time taken to force Turkey to agree some peace terms. Since the future of the Turkish Empire was a matter of grave concern to the other great powers as well, their attitudes had to be taken into account but Russia remained the dominant force in the region. This remained true even after the defeat in the Crimea and the demilitarisation of the Black Sea. And once these terms had been overturned in 1870, Russia was able to plan a more aggressive policy towards Turkey, beginning with the reconstruction of its Black Sea fleet.

What was changing by the 1870s, however, was that some of the peoples of south east Europe who still lived under Turkish rule were becoming increasingly aware not just of their separate national status (something that had been causing unrest for decades) but also of their wider identity as Slavs. This movement became known as pan-Slavism. It had begun among the élites of the Balkan states in the first half of the nineteenth century but became more broadly based both socially and geographically as it encompassed ordinary men and women as well as the various Slav peoples living elsewhere. These included Poles, Ukrainians, Czechs, Slovaks, Slovenes, Serbs, Croats and Bulgars. In Russia, it was a movement that attracted many ex-slavophiles and patriots partly because it gave Russia a new opportunity to provide leadership abroad. The Slavs living beyond Russia's frontiers were less enthusiastic about the idea of Russian domination but had little choice other than to turn to it for leadership. In terms of practical foreign policy decisions, pan-Slavism worked in Russia's favour since it acquired more leverage in the European parts of the Turkish Empire. There was the potential to stir up – or to threaten to stir up – nationalist revolts in areas such as Bulgaria and this could be used as a device early in the development of the pan-Slav movement against the Porte. Turkey realised this and made at least some effort to placate the Bulgars when it allowed an independent Bulgarian Orthodox Church to be established in 1870.

Tensions between the Slavs (who were Christian) and the Turks (who were Moslem) began to erupt when in 1875 an uprising broke out in Herzegovina and soon afterwards in Bosnia. The immediate cause of rebellion was harsh taxation. These two areas were at the most north-western edge of the Ottoman Empire which made them difficult to control and they had the support of the semi-independent Balkan state of Serbia which was also Slavic. A rising soon broke out in Bulgaria and all of the great powers quickly became animated in their concern that the Eastern Question was about to fulfil the many predictions of Turkey's catastrophic collapse. They tried to mediate between the warring parties by submitting ideas for reforms and regional changes to each side, first

Europe. There was an awareness of the shortcomings of the tsarist system. This stream of thought was maintained in the 1850s primarily by Alexander Herzen who edited a journal called *The Bell* from his exile in England. Sufficient copies of this periodical were smuggled into Russia for it to have an effect on the young student minds. Initially, he welcomed the news of the 1861 Emancipation Decree as it seemed as if the tsar was beginning to act in the interests of his people. However, when Herzen read the terms carefully he was compelled to condemn Alexander for the mean and narrow view he had taken of the serfs' plight and made plain his contempt for the Decree in *The Bell*.

But by the 1860s, Herzen was not the only writer to be publishing critical and inflammatory tracts. The growing number of radical-thinking students were confirmed and encouraged in their attitudes by Chernyshevsky's *What Is To Be Done?* a novel printed in 1863. In it, he told the story of how an ordinary Russian woman was able to take control of her own life and lift herself out of poverty so as to become free. Chernyshevsky contributed to and sometimes helped to edit *The Contemporary* which became the leading journal among radicals. Dobroliubov also contributed to *The Contemporary* as a literary critic who highlighted a number of utilitarian ideas. Further reading material was provided by Mikhailovskii's *What Is Progress?* (1869), Lavrov's *Historical Letters* (1870), and Bakunin's *Statism And Anarchy* (1873). From their efforts emerged two groups of radicals and potential revolutionaries by the early 1870s. The followers of Lavrov tended to believe that the best way in which to reform and improve Russian society was by propaganda and the dissemination of information. By contrast, the 'Bakuninists' put forward a more violent programme of anarchy and rebellion and found in Nechaev a committed revolutionary who collaborated with Bakunin on yet another subversive tract entitled *Catechism Of A Revolutionary*. He attracted a substantial student following in Moscow before murdering one of his closest supporters and being forced to flee abroad in 1869. The dilemma over which route to pursue for the best results was akin to the debate between the Slavophiles and westernisers of the students' intellectual 'fathers'.

Despite Nechaev, it was the Lavrovists who prevailed at first. Leading members of this following included the 'Chaikovsky Circle' composed of a handful of Saint Petersburg intellectuals such as Mark and Olga Natanson, Sofia Perovskaya and Nikolai Chaikovsky himself. They numbered just thirty or so and began by founding a student bookshop that carried radical titles. Their efforts increased as they set up a printing press and began to publish books that the regime had banned. However, their efforts had a limited impact and some of its members became restless – Kropotkin in particular began to urge more direct action. The exchange of ideas during this period was necessarily rapid and the attitudes of many of those involved were quite fluid. Allegiance to particular groups could be transitory and sometimes only fleeting as radical individuals tested the ideas of groups such as the 'Union of Workers of Southern Russia'. Despite the name of the latter group, the entire movement lacked any practical experience of transferring their radical and revolutionary creeds to the people at large since most of the debate had been confined to intellectual student circles.

This changed in the summers of 1873 and 1874 when hundreds of students answered the call made originally by Herzen to go 'To the people'. In part this was triggered by the government ordering the Russian students in Switzerland to return home during 1873 and 1874 thereby ending a relatively liberal period of study for them. The move was also inspired by members of the Chaikovsky Circle who had begun to go out into the countryside to meet the peasants and try to persuade them of the need for changes in Russian society. Altogether, perhaps as many as 21 500 individuals went into villages as teachers, doctors, nurses and even storekeepers so as to pass on their messages of political change. Typically, they dressed as peasants and workers. It was because of their belief in the readiness of everyday Russian people to listen to them that the students who went out proselytising became known as the 'Populists' or 'narodniks'. Many of the most conspicuous students who tried to preach to the peasants – some of whom listened politely before going about their daily business once more – were soon rounded up by the police. Information was frequently passed to the authorities by the peasants themselves. In short, the 'To the people' movement was a failure. The penetration they had into the popular mind was minimal.

As a result the government put large numbers of the Populists they had just arrested on trial. Two famous court battles were fought in the 'Trial of the 50' and subsequently the 'Trial of the 193'. These trials took place in full public view, in keeping with the tsar's own reforms of the legal system and they were widely reported in the press. Far from demonstrating the dangerous and deluded nature of the accused, the prosecution was humiliated by the impassioned defence speeches which won over public opinion. Sympathy for those on trial was reinforced by the long sentences that were imposed on the small number who were found guilty. A great many of those who were put on trial were actually freed without further charge; in the Trial of the 193, as many as 153 were acquitted. Worse still, from the government's point of view, the trials served to strengthen the students' resolve and it made many of them become revolutionary in outlook as they decided that the peaceful methods espoused by Lavrov were too slow. It made an increasing number of activists turn towards violence for a quick solution to Russia's problems, regardless of what the peasants thought. Changes were to be sought without first persuading the people of the need and without gaining their consent.

There was an instant and largely spontaneous example of this within a day of the Trial of the 193 ending. On 24 January 1878 Vera Zasulich attempted to shoot dead General Trepov, the governor of Saint Petersburg. She did this in revenge for his brutality towards a political prisoner called Bogoliubov. Zasulich was arrested and duly put on trial but she was found not guilty despite admitting her crime. She also avoided re-arrest immediately after her trial as the crowd outside the courthouse prevented the secret police from reaching her. The mood in Saint Petersburg was clearly in favour of the revolutionaries and hostile to the government at this time. In part, this was due to the setback of the Congress of Berlin held in 1878 in which the tsar seemed to show little support for fellow Slavs. A further assassination attempt was launched in August 1878 by Kravchinskii who this time succeeded in killing the head of the secret police (Third Section). The government was finding the situation more and more difficult to control.

The situation did not become any easier for the authorities as the revolutionaries began to step up their efforts. Perhaps the key development after the Trial of the 193 was the support that a new group known as 'Land and Liberty' began to attract. It was founded in 1876 and sought just two key reforms, as its name suggested. It wanted land to be given to the peasants so that the over-inflated redemption payments would be abolished and the peasants might then become free. Second, it hoped to dismantle the autocratic system of rule and the machinery of the state. Its methods combined the ideas of Lavrov with those of Bakunin; it possessed a printing press and began to distribute its own propaganda, and it included a number of dedicated revolutionaries who were prepared to kill (or execute) its enemies. Both Zasulich and Kravchinskii were members of Land and Liberty, for example, although they were not among the group's leadership. The leaders included Marl and Olga Natanson from the Chaikovsky Circle, Mikhailov, Deutsch and Stefanovich. They formed a strong, central committee that decided policy and issued instructions to members. This was in sharp contrast to the peaceful Populists who had generally been opposed to any formal hierarchy because of their anarchist beliefs. Beneath the central committee were five departments each with a specific task, whether it was administration, recruiting from particular sections of society or special activities such as murders and jailbreaks.

It adopted some very practical approaches to its tasks. A second wave of revolutionaries went out 'to the people' in 1876 having learnt from the failure of 1873–74 and this time they tried to spend time with the peasants so as to win their confidence before trying to persuade them of the need for revolution. This succeeded in at least one case when a peasant rebellion broke out in Kiev in 1877. Urban workers were also targeted and in 1876 Land and Liberty helped to organise a demonstration in Saint Petersburg. The debate about methods, whether they should be peaceful or violent, soon surfaced within the organisation, though, and in 1878–79 the question began to dominate Land and Liberty's agenda.

The People's Will

In July 1879 Land and Liberty split into two groups. The Black Partition group led by Plekhanov and Akselrod was peaceful and wanted to work with the peasants while the People's Will was committed to violent change and within weeks of its formation had passed a death sentence on the tsar. Led by Mikhailov and Zhelyabov, it was determined to assassinate Alexander for his failure to grant freedom to the ordinary subjects of Russia. They believed that such acts of terrorism could force the regime into submission and they set about a series of assassination attempts. These were feasible because the membership was quite large at 500 or so with a following of several thousand others who were sympathetic but passive. Mostly, these were drawn from the middle classes

Table 4.8 Development of unrest after the emancipation of the serfs

1860s	Disillusionment with the Emancipation Decree was expressed in literature such as Chernyshevsky's *What Is To Be Done?* (1863) and was sustained in journals
1870s	Students took more political action, most clearly the 'To the people' campaign of 1873–74, which was repeated in 1876
6 Dec. 1876	Demonstration in Saint Petersburg by workers led by Land and Liberty
Feb. 1877–March 1877	Trial of the 50
Summer 1877	Peasant rebellion in Kiev province organised by Land and Liberty
Oct. 1877–Jan. 1878	Trial of the 193
24 Jan. 1878	Attempted assassination of General Trepov by Zasulich
May 1878	Stefanovich and Deutsch rescued from jail by Land and Liberty
4 Aug. 1878	Assassination of General Mezentsev by Kravchinskii
July 1879	Land and Liberty split into the Black Partition Group and The People's Will

and included both men and women. A hard core of twenty members directed the policies which aimed at the transfer of power to the Russian people. National government was to wither away and be replaced by locally run communes; likewise, the national army was to be replaced by a popular militia. Peasants were to be given the land they farmed and workers were to have control of their factories.

The threat posed by the People's Will was taken seriously by Alexander's government since an assassination attempt made in April 1879 by Solovyov had almost succeeded just three months before the People's Will had formed as a separate entity. Several further near misses occurred between 1879 and 1880 which served to reinforce the tsar's precarious position. Mines were placed on the tracks of the royal train but they failed to detonate and a bomb was left by Khalturin in the dining room of the Winter Palace itself in February 1880 but failed to affect its target. The timing of these events was especially difficult for the tsar who was becoming less popular personally after his affair with Catherine Dolgoruky became public knowledge. Having a mistress was not the issue so much as the fact that he had known her since she was just ten and continued to see her regularly even though the Empress was close to death. Alexander appointed Mikhail Loris-Melikov as the chief government man responsible for countering and capturing the terrorists. He was made Minister of Internal Affairs in August 1880 and then director of a new police department as well. One of his first acts was to dissolve the secret police group set up by Tsar Nicholas I called the third Section and replace it with a new group within his Ministry. He had some success with the measures that he used. Mikhailov was arrested in November 1879 and Zhelyabov was apprehended too in February 1881. The use of spies helped the government in its work and some of them infiltrated the People's Will for a while. Its leadership, now dominated by Sofia Perovskaya, consequently became more desperate in the early months of 1881 and the need to assassinate the tsar became urgent.

The government response was not confined to counterterrorism. It also tried to win over public opinion by passing a series of reforms and appointing a number of new ministers. At the Ministry of Education, Tolstoy was replaced by the more liberal Saburov and Abaza became the new Minister of Finance. The most significant proposal for reform came from Loris-Melikov in 1880 when he suggested to Alexander that some kind of constitutional framework should be established so as to include the nobles and gentry in the legislative process. His plans were very limited since they only allowed for fifteen elected representatives to be added to the Senate, the existing members of which were hand-picked by the tsar. Alexander considered the ideas and, after consulting his advisers, agreed to the change in March 1881.

Death of Alexander II

However, it was too late. Tsar Alexander II was assassinated on 1 March 1881 by the People's Will. A group of its members drawn from its special activities section and led by Sofia Perovskaya managed to throw a bomb at the royal carriage as he returned from a military inspection. Although he survived this, he got out of the carriage to inspect the damage that had been done and a second device was then thrown. Land and Liberty's greatest act of violence failed to spark the upheaval in Russian society that it had hoped to see. The assassination was swiftly followed by a series of arrests as one of the assassins made a full confession; a series of executions then took place.

It was ironic that Alexander II was assassinated after having done more to modernise and reform Russia during the first half of his reign – mostly in the decade of the 1860s – than the two previous tsars put together spanning half a century. Both Alexander I and Nicholas I lived out their reigns until the end of their natural lives and neither of them had made anything more than minor changes to the autocracy and Russian society by comparison.

The threats to the autocracy that existed in the course of the nineteenth century were much the same for all three tsars. The greatest danger was from beyond Russia's frontiers and was manifested most obviously by Napoleon. It fell to Alexander I to rescue Holy Russia from mass invasion in 1812 and he only just managed it as Russia's manpower and resources became seriously depleted; however, the vast expanses of Russia's terrain offered the greatest security and Napoleon could not prevent the constant retreats that the Russians made. The only other invasion of Russian soil during this period was in the Crimean War but this was a strictly limited war never intended by Britain or France to extend beyond the Black Sea peninsula. While Nicholas I failed to repel the attack, despite his love of military matters, Alexander II had the wisdom to conclude peace terms as quickly as possible and start to repair the damage.

Internal unrest could spring from several quarters but all three tsars at least had the steadfast support of the Orthodox Church which taught complete obedience to the 'little father' among the general population. It was the army in conjunction with the nobles who posed the greatest threat to both Alexander I and Nicholas I. Tsar Paul had been assassinated by this partnership in 1801 and so his son was acutely conscious of the danger, not least because of his own complicity. Nicholas encountered the same combination at the start of his reign when the Decembrists stood their ground in Senate Square in Saint Petersburg and had to be forced to back down by cannon volleys. Both tsars were prepared to use firm, if not brutal, methods to keep control by first creating and then maintaining the network of military colonies on Russia's frontiers. It was under Alexander II that the last of them were dismantled and he soon began to work with the armed forces so as to strengthen them. The army schools, conscription, new army code and shorter period of service kept the army's support. The nobles, most of whom were civilians, were less likely to agree to the emancipation of the serfs and so he had to prepare the way much more carefully and build into the process substantial compensation for serf owners. This took the form of the redemption dues and the generous allowances made for land redistribution. He achieved a considerable feat in passing the Emancipation Decree with so little hostility.

There was very little adverse reaction from the ex-serfs or state peasants when the terms of their release were published. After the initial shock and unrest had subsided in 1861, the ex-serfs seemed ready to settle down and pay off their debts for the next forty-nine years. Their compliance was remarkable. The Decree ended the growing number of riots that troops had had to suppress during Nicholas I's reign and the countryside fell quiet. The tinkering with the system of serfdom that had taken place under Alexander I and Nicholas I was borne of nervousness at the nobles' and also the peasants' reactions. The possibility of a repeat of the Pugachev rebellion was always recalled by senior advisers and this accounted for the large number of secret committees set up to investigate (but not act on) the serf question, mostly in the 1830s and 1840s. Internal threats were also dealt with by sharpening the instruments of the autocracy. The secret police reached its zenith under Nicholas as the third Section co-operated with the Ministry of Education to supervise and censor the educated élite, while the codification of laws made for a more efficient system of justice – or punishment.

What was new to Russian society from the 1880s was the burgeoning intelligentsia based on a class of educated lawyers and former students who despised the tsar for having passed such a dishonest measure as the Emancipation Decree. This group had existed for decades, of course, but in small numbers and its leading members such as Herzen were often forced to live abroad or were silenced by internal exile. The relatively free universities and newspapers of Alexander II's reign produced articulate individuals who were able to challenge the state in the independent courts of law. The treatment of the 193 and the 50 at the end of their trials exposed how far this had gone. Sufficient numbers of revolutionaries decided that the need for direct action had become overwhelming by 1880, at which point the state realised too late the size of the threat. It was something with which no previous tsar had had to deal and Alexander II was unable to react quickly enough. The People's Will, the heir to the Decembrists, remained one step ahead of the tsar's internal security organisations with fatal results.

Russian society was becoming more complex by the late nineteenth century. It was significant that several key members of the revolutionary groups were women; Vera Zasulich, Olga Natanson and Sofia Perovskaya were merely three of the most prominent. Research since the 1980s in particular has highlighted their role and has contrasted it with the more traditional role of women in Russian society within the home.[15] There is still scope for more research to be done in this respect but the limited number of written sources by women from lower classes is likely to make any conclusions tentative. At the level of the mir, there remained a very strong folk tradition of reconciling any opposing attitudes as those who were in the minority usually let themselves be persuaded of the majority view so that decisions taken by its council could be unanimous. To this extent, the views that were held by millions of men and women in Russian villages are likely to remain obscure. Probably, most remained obedient to the tsar and parochial in their outlook and were therefore quite detached from the activities carried out – apparently on their behalf – by the revolutionaries.

Notes

1 J. Blum, *Lord and Peasant in Russia from the Ninth to the Nineteenth Century*, Princeton, 1961.
2 R. Rudolph, *Agricultural Structure and Proto-Industrialisation in Russia*, Journal of Economic History, 1985, Vol 25.
3 E. Melton, *Proto-Industrialisation in Nineteenth Century Russia*, Past and Present, 1987, Vol 115.
4 D. Field, *The End of Serfdom: Nobility and Bureaucracy in Russia 1855–61*, Cambridge Ma, 1976.
5 J. Blum, op. cit.
6 D. Field, op. cit.
7 N. Pereira, *Alexander II and the Decision to Emancipate the Russian Serfs 1855–61*, Canadian Slavonic Papers, 1980.
8 A. Rieber, *The Politics of Autocracy*, Paris, 1966.
9 M. Perrie, *Alexander II, Emancipation and Reform in Russia*, London, Historical Association, 1989.
10 D. Saunders, *Russia in the Age of Reaction and Reform 1801–1881*, London, Longman, 1992.

11 E. Acton, *A Liberal Tsar?*, London, 1993–99.
12 A. Rieber, op. cit.
13 M. Falkus, *The Industrialisation of Russia 1700–1914*, London, Macmillan, 1972.
14 T. Blanning, *The Reunification of Germany*, London, 1995–99.
15 M. Maxwell, *Narodniki Women: Russian Women who Sacrificed themselves for the Dream of Freedom*, New York, 1990.

Chapter 5

The reign of Alexander III
Relying on divine providence

Tsar Alexander III was the second son of Alexander II. Like many of his forebears, he came to the throne in difficult circumstances and had to decide quickly on the direction of his policies. Despite his father's interest in granting limited constitutional rights, the new tsar chose to reject liberalism since he believed it was too dangerous and could be seen as rewarding the revolutionaries. Consequently, his thirteen-year reign was a rejection – and in some cases a reversal – of the reforms of the previous years and a return to the traditional repression of the Romanovs. Where Alexander III did make progress was in economic and foreign affairs. With the help of Bunge and Witte, who were highly capable ministers, the economy expanded significantly in the final years of the century. Abroad, Russia managed to avoid any wars.

Alexander III: biography and background

The accession of Alexander III to the throne was anticipated since his older brother, Nicholas, had died in 1865. The new tsar had therefore been able to become involved in government but was not well equipped to deal with its requirements. Born in 1845, he grew to be physically strong – and was sometimes compared with his giant ancestor Peter the Great – but his mental abilities were not as impressive. He was educated by Solovyev and Pobedonostsev in history and law respectively and although the latter had an impact, his interests did not lie in intellectual discussion. Military affairs were of greater importance to him and he played his part in commanding army units totalling 70 000 men in the war against Turkey 1877–78. His experience of this left him with a dislike of war, though his liking for the trappings of militarism continued. He followed the activities of several government departments in the 1860s and 1870s but with little enthusiasm and, despite the advantages of his position, he was unable to offer much advice to his father in the difficult final years of his reign.

He was, then, an unimaginative man who as the heir apparent dutifully played his part. In 1866 he married the Danish princess, Dagmar, who had been intended for his older brother and the marriage was a success. As tsar, he gave strong support to his ministers once he had adopted their policies and won their admiration for his loyalty. Yet, this was a kind of role reversal since his ministers led with ideas which he followed without necessarily understanding their implications and he did not win their loyalty to the same extent. Many commented on his stubbornness and his lack of insight. While he championed the autocracy, he seemed to have a limited view of what its purpose was; he tended to identify it with his own petty whims rather than with the greater needs of the state. Lacking ideas or inspiration, Alexander III kept to those aspects of Russian life that he knew and understood; autocracy, nationalism and dislike of non-Russian peoples.

Initial policies

Alexander III faced a number of pressing tasks at his accession. The revolutionaries had to be dealt with swiftly and the tone of his reign needed to be established firmly so as to impress upon Russia his own authority; to this end he needed to ensure that he was advised by his ministers rather than those of his predecessor. In all of this, he was closely advised by his former tutor, Pobedonostsev. His highly conservative attitudes were largely adopted by Alexander at the start of his reign. Leading members of The People's Will were arrested and hanged and those of its rank and file who were not detained consequently went into hiding. It managed one last gesture of defiance at the start of the new reign when it called on the tsar to pass a constitution and issue a general political amnesty to its members but this was futile. A set of temporary regulations were passed that allowed government officials in certain areas to arrest, search, jail and exile suspects at will. These draconian measures were designed to reinforce the security of the state during an unstable period but they remained in force into the next century, far beyond the three years for which they were initially passed.

A change of personnel among the senior advisers also occurred quickly. Directing Alexander's attitudes in this matter was Pobedonostsev who had a much more personal battle against the previous tsar's liberal-minded ministers. Pobedonostsev had sympathised with progressive views in the 1860s when, as a professor of law, he had helped to draft the 1864 reforms to the legal and judicial systems. In 1880 he had become Over Procurator of the Holy Synod and had used this position solely to advance the Orthodox Church's status. Since the church had a direct line of communication with the ordinary Russian people, Pobedonostsev felt that he was in close contact with them, a feature that further endeared him to Alexander. His contempt for representative institutions and constitutions was equally adamant, dismissing them as 'the biggest lie of our time'. The clash between Pobedonostsev and reformers such as Loris-Melikov, Miliutin and Abaza could not be avoided and was caused by their discussions over the limited constitutional changes approved by Alexander II on the day he was assassinated. At first, the new tsar seemed to be in favour of passing them but Pobedonostsev was determined to resist this and in April 1881 he submitted a memo that warned him of the impact of the reforms. He also gave Alexander a manifesto that proclaimed the tsar's right to rule by 'relying on Divine Providence' rather than the majority views of committees. The tsar liked what he read, published it without further discussion and thereby precipitated the resignation of the reformers by May. Pobedonostsev had won. He assumed a position akin to Arakcheyev under Tsar Alexander I, except that Pobedonostsev was to maintain a role as chief adviser to the next tsar, Nicholas II, as well. The period of reaction in Russia was therefore sustained into the early years of the twentieth century.

The new ministers who were appointed were therefore reactionary in their outlook. Ignatiev replaced Loris-Melikov at the Ministry of the Interior but he too soon fell from favour when he proposed a further limited scheme of constitutional reform in 1882 and was succeeded by Dmitri Tolstoy, the former Minister of Education. Before his fall, Ignatiev did manage to pass some minor reforms such as the reduction of the redemption payments that ex-serfs had to make. The new Minister of Education from October 1881 was Ivan Delianov who set about creating restrictions in the education system as never before. A further adviser was Katkov who had distinguished himself in the 1860s and 1870s as a journalist who opposed the liberal reforms of Alexander II, especially those relating to the legal system. This was a formidable array of reactionary talent. However, one reformer did survive the initial ministerial purge; Bunge was Minister of Finance until 1886 and managed to strengthen the Russian economy – despite Pobedonostsev's hostility even to industrial change – and went on to become chairman of the Committee of Ministers in the second half of the reign.

Political control and Russification

Limited though Alexander III's political vision was, he saw the need to strengthen the autocracy as best he could and that meant restoring to central control many of the functions that had been given to local institutions under his predecessor. A series of 'counter reforms' were passed that weakened the powers of both the rural and urban councils Alexander II had created in 1864 and 1870. The first step in this direction was taken at the start of the reign when a commission was appointed under Kakhanov to investigate the structure of government at the local village level. When it eventually reported in 1884 its recommendations were disregarded as they suggested an extension of the jurisdiction of locally appointed ruling councils. The commission was dissolved in 1885 and replaced by a single adviser, Pazhukin, whose view was that the status of the nobility needed to be elevated. This was entirely in keeping with Alexander III's attitude and, significantly, that of Pobedonostsev too. They believed that by making reforms that were popular with the nobility, the autocracy could be strengthened almost surreptitiously too.

The restructuring of the system of internal control and government was carried out by Tolstoy's Ministry of the Interior from 1889, using Pazukhin as an expert adviser. In order to reassert control over ordinary Russians, the tsar abolished the position of Justice of the Peace in almost every area of European Russia. The task of the JPs – who had been elected – had been to liaise between the zemstvos and dumas on behalf of the peasants and workers. By taking away this kind of work, the tsar weakened the effective rights that the labouring classes had been given. In place of the JPs, he created a new official known in the countryside as a land captain (while in the towns the job was taken on by judges) who was selected by and responsible to the Ministry of the Interior and who was therefore bound to act on its behalf rather than in the interests of peasants or workers. The position was a powerful one because in practice it meant that the individual who was appointed supervised all peasant activities. Judicial and administrative tasks were combined in the post too. The land captain had to meet certain educational and social qualifications that made the position one reserved for the nobility; thus, the status of the gentry was enhanced while the state secured more control for itself. This shift in the hierarchy also made local administration more efficient.

Further measures were taken that directly attacked the powers of ordinary Russians in the rural and town councils. In 1890, under the direction of Durnovo the new Minister of the Interior, the representation of the gentry in the zemstvos was increased while that of the peasants was limited; they were also prevented from voting directly for the district councils. Just as the idea of a constitution for the entire state was opposed by Alexander III, so he was hostile to any form of democracy at the local level and tried to cut it back. A similar principle was applied to the towns' dumas in 1892 which had the effect of reducing the electorate quite severely; in the case of Saint Petersburg, the number of voters fell by two-thirds to just over 7000 men. Local councils did survive, however, and were able to continue with those activities that had become their forte. In particular, they were successful in organising street lighting, paving and sanitation – at least in the very centre of major towns – sometimes reaching out towards the edge of towns as well. This pattern of repression of local councils and centralisation at their expense was sustained under Nicholas II after 1894 as well.

Russians therefore suffered under their own government but their experiences of late nineteenth-century government were quite mild compared to those members of the empire who were not Russian. A systematic policy of Russification was pursued by Alexander III and he deliberately persecuted some minorities such as the Jews. Previous tsars had been ready to Russify areas of their territory for strategic reasons and as a punishment for disloyalty, most obviously in the case of Poland after its nationalist rebellions in 1831 and 1863. Tsar Nicholas I had been most conspicuous in his support for such an approach as he endorsed it in his doctrine of 'Official Nationality', this being summarised as 'Orthodoxy, Autocracy, Nationality'. Under Alexander III intolerance was taken to a new level by trying to Russify all non-Russian peoples, whether they had been loyal to the empire or not.

The reasons for Russification being imposed so widely lay in the core areas of concern to the state. It was seen as a valuable strategic exercise since many of the non-Russian peoples lived in border areas such as Poland, Scandinavia and Caucasia that were vulnerable to foreign attack. It was argued by some of the bureaucrats and nobles that the more closely their culture could be made to resemble that of Russia proper the more reliable would be their support. This idea was flawed. By trying to make these groups conform, the Russian state managed to alienate many of its members which was quite the reverse effect. A second reason for Russification might be found in the demographic trends of the empire by the late nineteenth century. The non-Russian populations were beginning to overtake the true, or 'Great', Russians in terms of their numbers. The truth of this was made clear by the 1897 census that counted the non-Russian peoples as being 55 per cent of the empire's total. It may be that the Great Russians were becoming aware of this as early as the 1880s and that they tried to bolster their own position by using their positions of power. The policy was certainly supported by the Russian Orthodox Church that had for many years hoped to convert to its own beliefs those people who were Moslem or Buddhist, as well as Catholic and Protestant Christians. Practical considerations may have played a part, too, as the civil servants of Saint Petersburg were relatively remote from the provinces that they administered and this may have led to a bureaucratic drive for standardisation and simplification. The intellectual arguments of the Slavophiles also served to justify Russification since they moved on from merely asserting the superiority of the Slavs to feeling able to impose their ways to other nationalities. This was cultural imperialism. Yet again, however, the ultimate decision rested with the tsar since Russia was still an autocracy and he was its leader. If he had not consented to the policies then they could not have been carried out. Possibly, he was influenced by the policies of Bismarck, the effective leader of Germany, who was imposing German culture on the new empire in the 1870s and 1880s.

The Ukraine was populated by 'Little Russians' who were already Orthodox in their religious beliefs. Its nationalist movement was weak and confined to the intelligentsia, not least because of the suppression of the movement by Nicholas II when it first appeared in the 1840s. Not withstanding this the Ukrainians – fellow Slavs – had their cultural identity stifled and were targeted for Russification. Ukrainian was not recognised as being a separate language in Russia and books of almost any kind that were printed in Ukrainian continued to be suppressed. Intellectuals who wrote about the Ukraine's culture and past, such as the historian Hrushevsky, were typically forced into exile beyond the Russian Empire's frontiers.

Poland had been subjected to a steady process of Russification. After the 1831 rebellion, it had lost its status as a semi-independent kingdom with its own parliament and army and was subsequently renamed as the Vistula district. Tsar Alexander II had tried to win over the support of the peasantry after the 1863 rebellion by granting relatively generous terms for the redistribution of land away from the noble landowners but this failed as the Poles remained resolutely separatist. The University of Warsaw was closed down in 1869 and Russian became the language for all official business, even in secondary schools. A Russian governor was appointed to preside over the Polish lands. Under Alexander III, this policy was stepped up as Russian was imposed in primary schools from 1885 and plans were drawn up for the construction of an Orthodox cathedral in the middle of Warsaw – although work was not started on it until 1894. Russian troops continued to garrison all the major Polish towns and the most senior posts in the Vistula district were reserved for Russians. What all of this engendered was a new nationalist reaction against Russia. It was by no means as aggressive as in 1831 or 1863 but it was still seen as dangerous by the Russian state. When the radical group 'Proletariat' was discovered by the police in 1885, its four leaders were executed. The socialist leader Pilsudski was exiled to Siberia in 1887. In the 1890s, some Poles adopted a more co-operative approach to the Russian domination and sought to prosper from the trade with Russia (since there were no customs barriers). This was given political direction from 1897 by the National Democratic Party led by Dmowski.

In the Baltic provinces of Estonia, Latvia and Lithuania there was a similar pattern of attacking educational, administrative and religious institutions. The Russian language was imposed on schools in the late 1880s as well as on the judicial system from 1889. Another Orthodox cathedral was built, this time in Riga, and funds were made available for the construction of smaller churches of a similar kind. By contrast, restrictions were placed on the building of new Lutheran churches which affected the ruling German class in particular. Likewise, the University of Dorpat was renamed as the University of Yuriev and when it opened in 1894 became a Russian rather than German institution since its intake of students was mostly Russian. However, some non-German and non-Russian students were admitted and they subsequently formed the nucleus of a nationalist movement that was anti-Russian rather than (as in previous years) anti-German. Across the Baltic Sea, the Finns had remained loyal to the Russian tsars since their absorption into the empire in 1808. Under Alexander III, policies began to be introduced that penalised Finnish businesses since they – like Poland – were beginning to penetrate the vast Russian market. As Finland began to industrialise rapidly in the final quarter of the nineteenth century, its timber and textile exports began to undermine the Russian producers with the result that a less favourable customs agreement had to be arranged first in 1885 and then again in 1897. Later, Russian weights and measures were imposed and the Finnish postal and railway systems were integrated into those of Russia.

The group that suffered most during the reign of Alexander III was the Jews. Given the assertiveness of the Russian Orthodox Church during this period, and the support that was given to it by Pobedonostsev, this was hardly surprising. There were some five million Jews in Russia but they were concentrated in just a few areas where their impact was that much greater. They were allowed to live in a Pale of settlement limited to Poland, Lithuania, the Ukraine and White Russia and even in these areas they were often confined to urban sites. Attitudes among the non-Jewish populations were often prejudiced; there was a historic dislike of the race that killed Christ and there was resentment towards a community that so frequently profited from businesses. They were treated as scapegoats and were blamed by some for the 1863 rebellion in Poland as well as for the assassination of Alexander II in 1881. This irrational approach smacked of the blame they were given in the middle ages for the plague epidemics. There was already a well-established antipathy towards Jews by the time Alexander III became tsar.

What emerged from the very beginning of the new reign was an outbreak of pogroms directed against Jews. In 1881 the first of these attacks occurred, seemingly with the tacit consent of the regime, in Kiev, Odessa and Warsaw. Mobs gathered in the Jewish quarters of these towns and set about destroying their property, smashing and burning houses, shops and synagogues; the violence could turn against individuals who were beaten, raped and even killed. Such campaigns were probably orchestrated with at least some help from the state since mobs were transported in by train and the authorities were often aware of where the next attacks were going to take place. Neither the police nor any local troops were used to stop the pogroms. Ignatiev at the Ministry of the Interior sympathised with what was happening but the tsar was not comfortable with it and this in part accounts for his dismissal of Ignatiev and the appointment of his replacement, Tolstoy. He was determined to keep law and order for all Russian citizens, including Jews, though he did not particularly care for them. In the meantime, Pobedonostsev remained Alexander's closest adviser and he was anti-Semitic.

Numerous measures were taken so as to limit the influence the Jews had in the empire. Ignatiev introduced the 'Temporary Regulations' in 1882 so that Jews were, for instance, forbidden from owning land or buildings outside the Pale and were banned from trading on Christian holidays. The effect of this was to close many Jewish businesses in rural areas. It was followed by an Edict of Expulsion in 1886 that applied only to Kiev and then another one that was only for Moscow in 1891. All Jews in these towns were forced to leave and faced the humiliation of selling their goods and businesses at desperately low prices. More systematic measures were taken in education and the professions where limits were set on the number of Jews who were admitted. From 1887, a maximum of 10 per cent of students and pupils at universities and secondary schools were accepted in the Pale with smaller quotas elsewhere. The proportion of Jewish doctors working in the army was not allowed to exceed 5 per cent, while any Jewish lawyer who wished to become a barrister needed the express consent of the Minister of Justice. And at the end of the reign the right of Jews to sell alcohol was revoked.

Jewish responses to this level of persecution took various forms. Some turned to revolutionary politics and could be counted among the ranks of the Populists in the 1870s; others relied on more conventional political practices and by the end of the century had begun a social democratic organisation. A further and very large group began to emigrate to the USA, South America and to Palestine where they founded agricultural settlements and aspired to a Zionist homeland. The policy was continued under Tsar Nicholas II from 1894 with the result that in the three decades before World War One, two million Jews left Russia. The damage done to the Russian economy cannot easily be measured but the standing of Russia within the international community certainly fell significantly.

Economic and social policies

The economic development of Russia under Alexander III was a mixed experience as agriculture stagnated but the industrial sectors expanded rapidly and prepared the way for much more growth under Nicholas II. The main economic problem that Russia had faced in the 1840s and 1850s was that the increase in population was outstripping the rate at which it could produce food and this had led to growing levels of protest. The emancipation of the serfs in 1861 had stopped the riots but the failings of Russian farming persisted. The reliance on a three field rotation and communal decisions made by the mir that prevented innovation and necessarily led to low investment, each retarded agriculture. Land-holdings became fragmented and much less efficiently farmed. By the late nineteenth century, the situation was becoming critical again because population growth had begun to accelerate. Between 1870 and 1900 the total population rose from 86 to 130 million, up by more than 50 per cent in just three decades.

The government did little to ease this situation and many of its policies made it worse. Industrial development was the priority under Alexander III and it was facilitated by taxing and exploiting the peasants. Thus, even though the redemption dues (dating from the 1861 Emancipation Decree) were reduced by Ignatiev, payments still had to be made until 1905. Indirect taxes had to be paid on everyday goods such as cotton, tea, sugar, iron and tobacco as Russian products were surcharged and cheap foreign goods were made expensive by high import duties. The level of these taxes was hiked up enormously; in the case of matches by more than 100 per cent and on kerosene by 50 per cent. This was a harsh policy to adopt since many of the items were essential to the peasant households. During Alexander's reign there were three Ministers of Finance, Bunge, 1881–86, Vyshnegradsky, 1887–92 and Witte, 1892–1903 and each of them directed their policies towards industrialisation. Bunge appreciated that there was unlikely to be any prosperity in Russia while the bulk of its population, the peasants, remained impoverished so he did take some remedial measures. The poll tax (or 'head tax') was ended in 1886 and a Peasants' Land Bank was created in 1883 which could provide loans either to communes or individuals. To try to preserve the land-holding of the nobles, the Ministry of Finance then created the Nobles' Land Bank in 1885 which made loans at preferential interest rates. The tax base was widened by introducing an inheritance tax – that affected the gentry and nobles above all – and the salt tax was abolished. Legislation was passed, however, not for the benefit of the peasants but for the emerging class of industrial workers so that their hours of work were regulated. Despite all of this, the peasants still paid 90 per cent of all taxes and one of the reforms that might have made a serious difference, the introduction of an income tax, was avoided until 1916.

Vyshnegradsky took over the Ministry of Finance in 1886 and increased the pressure on the peasants immediately. Land taxes rose, arrears were collected more promptly and in 1891 duties were imposed on farm implements in a measure that could only harm the peasantry. He also compelled the peasants to sell their grain just after each harvest when supplies were abundant and prices were low; this meant that the government could cash in on selling the corn for export at good prices later in the year. The policy was taken to such an extreme that the peasants themselves were often left with too little on which to live by the following spring. This directly contributed to the famine of 1891–92 which led to his dismissal. Tens of thousands of peasants died of starvation as a result of government policies and a prolonged drought. Attempts were made to relieve the situation by the government and by private individuals such that grain exports were halted and funds were made available for immediate poor relief but another famine occurred only six years later. Witte became Minister of Finance in 1892, in the last years of Alexander's reign, but most of his work was done in the first half of Nicholas II's reign. He instantly began to reinforce the tax system's reliance on the peasants for most of its revenue by imposing a state monopoly on alcohol (which was mostly vodka) in 1894. This generated an income in excess of 300 million roubles per year. One measure in favour of the peasants, though, was to equalise the interest rates charged by the Peasants' and the Nobles' Land Bank.

The effect of the Finance Ministers' policies was to return the peasants almost to the level of serfdom. Burgeoning families did their best to scrape a living from the soil using quite inefficient methods and more land was brought into cultivation but there was a limit to the amount of change that could be achieved while the practice of communal farming by the mir continued to dominate. The emancipation of the serfs in 1861 had ensured a period of peace in the peasant villages but it had also stored up problems in that the redemption dues were very high and the land was redistributed unfairly. The nobles were reassured of their status by being given the right to choose the best land for themselves and to take any land of uncertain legal ownership for themselves. The peasants did not receive the land that they farmed and were typically left with the least fertile areas. What proportion of the land they received varied from province to province but by 1880 they owned 31 per cent of it. In the following years the peasants' share grew as the nobles were forced to sell more and more of their estates due to poor land management; it was in order to try to prevent this that the Nobles' Land Bank had been set up. By 1905, the amount of new land brought into cultivation by the peasants accounted for 20–25 per cent of their share and they had also been able to buy a substantial proportion of what the nobles had sold.

Table 5.1 Land-holding in Russia by 1905

Social group	% of land owned
State and royal family	39
Peasants	35
Nobles	13
Cossacks and others	8
Townsmen	5

The shift in land ownership away from the nobles to the peasants speeded up after 1894 as the world price of grain began to drop and forced more nobles to sell up. The Peasants' Land Bank cut its interest rate and made loans on easier terms, requiring less security for a loan and being prepared to lend over longer periods of time. Peasant society became a little more diverse during Alexander III's reign and this continued to happen into the early years of the twentieth century. By 1900, a richer peasant class of kulaks had emerged who represented something less than 20 per cent of the total. The characteristics of this group were that they owned some of their own land, operated some machinery and might own some livestock. At the other end of the scale were those who resembled the serfs; they neither owned nor farmed any of their own land and lived in poverty. Approximately 10 per cent of the peasants were in this position. The remaining 70 per cent of the rural workforce could be placed somewhere between the two extremes.

Radical solutions had to be found for the on-going problem of population growth and limited food supplies. To an extent, famine played its part in limiting the natural rate of increase and the death rate was usually at 30–33 per thousand per year – twice that of Britain – so that even in years of relatively good harvests there were many who died from malnutrition. Migration eased the situation a little. Jews fled abroad due to the programs and many peasants tried to escape to Siberia, although the authorities tried to deter this by passing a law in 1889 that made the application process for documents very slow. There was also a drift towards the towns as peasants began to look for work in Russia's new factories. The countryside remained over-populated though by some millions of people and the land-holdings thus became further fragmented and less efficient. The government did consider making changes to the system of communal land-holding but no action was taken during the reign of Alexander III. At the Ministry of the Interior, Tolstoy in particular defended the mir as a precious Russian asset and he was supported by those among the public who might still be considered Populist. The Ministry of Finance saw more need for reform but made no progress, perhaps because they found themselves supported by the emergent, and much more extreme, Marxist group.

Despite the decline of the nobles as a class, their presence and importance in the Russian economy (quite apart from their role in the government and administration) should not be underestimated. At the turn of the century, there were about 1 200 000 hereditary nobles and a further 600 000 lifetime nobles. They possessed more than half of the privately owned land which amounted to some 107 000 estates. Within the gentry class there was a wide range of wealth from such families as the Lusupovs to those whose meagre incomes could barely sustain both a town and a country house. As a class, it had not maintained its lands well since 1861 and by 1905 had lost about half of what it had begun with. Incomes could be earned from service to the state in the civil and military fields but their domination of these professions was also declining since hereditary nobles occupied only 50 per cent of the army officers' posts in 1900 and 30 per cent of the civil positions such as provincial governors or land captains. Despite the educational advantages they enjoyed, they were slow to innovate and purchased for example only a handful of tractors before the Great War. What did help them significantly was the Nobles' Land Bank which from 1885 to 1904 lent over 700 million roubles.

Industrial progress was much more successful in the 1880s and 1890s due, of course, to the support it received from the agricultural sector. It was the deliberate policy of Alexander III to boost Russia's manufacturing base because he saw it as a way of maintaining his country's great power status. The concerns of the population were therefore subordinated again to the needs of the autocracy. Output in all areas rocketed as the various statistical measures demonstrate. Production often took place in very large factories of several thousand workers and was concentrated in a few towns. Textiles were based in Moscow and Lodz, while extractive industries for coal and oil were based in the southern Ukraine and Baku (Georgia) respectively. The government did all it could to foster this industrial growth by exporting large amounts of grain – some of which was really needed for domestic consumption – so as to earn foreign currencies. Foreign trade deficits became surpluses in the 1890s and this meant that by 1897 Russia had sufficient reserves to go onto the gold standard and this engendered more confidence among foreign investors. In crude terms, the level of foreign investment in Russia might be put at 100 million roubles in 1880, 200 million by 1890 and 900 million by 1900. The gold standard also meant that the rouble was pitched at a low value, against which imports were expensive and exports were cheap. This situation suited the Ministry of Finance's existing protectionist policies which were designed to keep out foreign competition while infant industries were nurtured. Import duties were raised in 1887 and 1891. The result was that the Russian economy grew at the rate of about 8 per cent per year during the 1890s, according to figures from Gerschenkron.[1]

All sectors of the economy were helped by the development of a rail network which until 1880 had been left to the work of private individuals. Under Alexander III the government became involved on a huge scale so that each of the key industrial regions were connected. Between 1895 and 1905 the length of track laid in Russia doubled. Since it was difficult to export some Russian goods to the west, new markets were developed in central Asia and China for which specialist banks were set up and, of course, the Trans-Siberian railway was built from 1891–1903. The number of industrial workers grew in line with the changing pattern of economic activity and by 1900 there were between two and three million industrial workers employed in factories, mines and transport. There were still far more working in craft industries, though, numbering perhaps eight million.

Industrial unrest affected Russia just as it had the west. Strikes broke out in Saint Petersburg in 1878–79, Moscow in 1885 and then again in Saint Petersburg in 1896. In order to regulate the working conditions for the workers, who were often migrant peasants, Bunge and Witte passed factory legislation. In 1882 a law banned the employment of children under twelve years and set limits for those aged between twelve and fifteen. Further laws were added in 1884 and 1885 although they did not become enforced effectively until the 1890s. Witte passed a further measure that limited the

Table 5.2 The expansion of trade in the reign of Alexander III

	1880	1890	1900	Units
Exports	499	692	716	million roubles
Imports	623	407	626	million roubles
Surplus/(Deficit)	(124)	285	90	million roubles

hours of all workers in factories employing more than twenty people – regardless of age, class or sex – to a maximum of eleven and a half per day, or ten per night. The miserable working conditions were not overcome by any of this and the industrial workers, or proletariat, became politicised as a result. It was hostile to the regime and demonstrated this in the revolutions of 1905 and 1917. The exploitation of both the industrial and agricultural workers seemed, at the time, a price worth paying for the advancement of the state's strength with regard to the other great powers.

Foreign policy

Russia managed to avoid fighting any wars in the reign of Alexander III which was remarkable given that the main focus of its foreign policy was in the highly volatile Balkan region. Russia had for decades had designs on the Turkish Empire and had taken advantage of its weakness so as to acquire influence or territory by successive wars in 1806–12, 1828–29 and 1877–78. The only exception to this pattern was in 1854–56 when Britain and France defeated Russia in the Crimean War and imposed terms that neutralised the Black Sea. This demonstrated that the uncertain future of the Turkish Empire, which was at the crux of the Eastern Question, was a matter for all of the great powers and not just Russia. In addition to Russia's traditional interest in expansion into the Balkans – with the ultimate target of reaching Constantinople – there emerged in the 1870s a pan-Slav movement. This focused attention on Russia, as the leading Slav state, to provide leadership for local Slav populations such as the Serbs. However, the situation was complicated by nascent nationalism among the Balkan states that wanted to break away from Turkish rule and by a growing rivalry for influence with Austria.

After the Congress of Berlin in 1878, an agreement was reached by the great powers in which Russia asserted a dominant position in the eastern area of the Balkans based on a relatively small Bulgarian state. Austria-Hungary dominated the western area as it administered Bosnia and Herzegovina and was closely linked with Serbia. The Berlin Treaty had been brokered by Bismarck and it was he who organised a three way alliance between Germany, Russia and Austria-Hungary in 1881 in an attempt to revive the Holy Alliance that had operated earlier in the century. The new alliance was called the Dreikaiserbund, or Three Emperors' League, and its purpose was to preserve peace between the eastern great powers. It was only a temporary arrangement and it expired in 1884 but was then renewed for a further three years. The terms of the alliance were that if one of its members became involved in a war, then the other two would remain neutral unless the war was against Turkey. This suited Bismarck who was nervous of a war between the two most eastern great powers but it could not hold them together because the tensions in the Balkans proved to be too much.

The next crisis in that area exposed the strained relationship between Russia and Austria-Hungary. In September 1885 Bulgarian nationalists seized Plovdiv, the capital of Eastern Rumelia, a large area of territory that lay to the south. They immediately announced that it was now part of the Kingdom of Bulgaria. This antagonised Russia because, although Bulgaria was meant to be an area of its influence, Alexander III did not trust its ruler Alexander of Battenberg, despite him being the nephew of the tsar. Russia therefore resisted any expansion of the Bulgarian state by the annexation of Eastern Rumelia and in order to prevent any such scenario the tsar recalled from Bulgaria all of the Russian military personnel who were serving in the Bulgarian army. The local Balkan rivalries surfaced at this point as Serbia declared war on Bulgaria on the grounds that it was becoming stronger while Serbia was not. In the war that followed Bulgaria defeated Serbia despite the absence of the Russian generals. It fell to Austria-Hungary to warn off a triumphant Bulgaria from trying to take any further territory and the war was soon curtailed. In April 1886 a diplomatic compromise was reached in which Alexander of Battenberg became the governor of Eastern Rumelia without actually becoming its ruler.

However, the crisis was by no means over. In August 1886 Russian agents kidnapped Battenberg and took him back to Russia with the intention of persuading him of the Russian point of view, but this move only exacerbated relations between Russia and Bulgaria. Battenberg abdicated and the Bulgarian nationalist leader Stambolov organised the election of a new ruler, Ferdinand of Saxe-Coburg, who had served in the Austrian army and was still pro-Austrian. Russia broke off diplomatic relations with Bulgaria and considered an invasion. The 1878 division of the Balkans between Russia in the east and Austria in the west was clearly a failed policy and tension between the two countries was very high.

Germany now had to choose between its squabbling allies in the Dreikaiserbund since Alexander III refused to have anything to do with Austria-Hungary. Bismarck, however, was very reluctant to have to give up both states' friendship. He therefore maintained a close link with Austria-Hungary, something that had begun in 1879 with their Dual Alliance, and – after the Three Emperors' League had lapsed in 1887 – he signed a separate treaty with Russia. This has become known as the Reinsurance Treaty and it said that Russia and Germany were to remain neutral if the other fought a war unless that war was launched by Germany against France or by Russia against Austria-Hungary. This situation hardly seemed tenable given that Russia and Austria-Hungary were already so closely allied. In a European war between the great powers, Germany would have had to choose between Austria-Hungary and Russia, and probably it would have chosen the former. Evidence of this was a further diplomatic effort by Bismarck which led to the Mediterranean Agreement of 1887 between Britain, Austria and Italy. This stated that the three powers would maintain the status quo in the Mediterranean. The ultimate goal of Bismarck's multiple alliances, treaties and agreements was to prevent any kind of understanding being made between Russia and France since this could lead to Germany being surrounded by enemy states to the east and west. Encirclement was the great fear.

All of this left Alexander III in a very difficult position since Russia was virtually isolated by 1887. It was reassured of Germany's friendship but could not rely on its support in wartime; it had lost its area of influence in the Balkans as Bulgaria was now pro-Austrian; and relations with Britain were also becoming uneasy since their interests in Asia were beginning to clash. Britain's control of India and its advance into Afghanistan meant a potential point of contact or conflict with Russia which continued to expand into Asia. In 1885 the first danger signs appeared when Russian troops encountered an Afghan force at Penjdeh. Bismarck managed to placate both sides after a number of angry exchanges but the 1885 frontier agreement was not certain to last.

An alliance between Russia and France thus became a real possibility. This was something that Alexander had never wanted to discuss with his ministers and he had always hoped to avoid any formal agreement with a republican state. By 1890 the prospect of this alliance had become more likely as Bismarck was removed from power in that year and so the supreme skill with which he had orchestrated German and European affairs was lost. The Reinsurance Treaty was not renewed in 1890 and this freed Russia from any German connection. France was itself isolated and looking for an ally and it could provide the foreign investment capital that Russia wanted in the late nineteenth century. Alexander was advised by his cautious foreign minister, Giers, and so the diplomatic convergence of the two states was quite slow. Diplomatic agreements were made in 1891 but it was not until 1894 that a full military treaty was signed. There was also scope for co-operation in areas of mutual interest such as the Suez Canal which was completed in 1869 and through which a great deal of Russian shipping passed in order to reach the Far East. France, as a joint shareholder with Britain, was in a position to safeguard Russian concerns there. Likewise, and more importantly, the Franco-Russian alliance was vital to the defence of each state in any war that Germany launched against either of them. The terms of the alliance made this absolutely clear; if Russia was attacked by Germany then France would declare war on it and use all of its available troops to do so – some 1 300 000 men. In return, Russia agreed to defend France against a German attack with 7–800 000 soldiers. War on a massive scale was something for which both countries had to prepare and plans were laid for a rapid mobilisation using railways.

The foreign policy of Russia in Asia was not as important to Alexander III as that in Europe. Nevertheless, he made what progress he could to extend Russian power in the Far East and its control over its existing possessions. Since the new port of Vladivostok was – like many of Russia's European ports – subject to freezing up in winter attempts were made to find more coastal territory. The main area that Russia considered was Korea and it gained the trading stations it desired in a treaty of 1884. This, though, hardly gave it exclusive rights of access as Korea signed similar agreements with the USA, Britain, Germany and France in the same decade. The Russian impact on the Far East was set to increase after Alexander's decision in 1891 to build a Trans-Siberian railway. In part, this was prompted by the famine of 1891–92 and the realisation that food stuffs needed to be made more easily available within Russia so as to overcome localised shortages. Laying the track was a mammoth engineering project and was not completed until 1903 but when the work was completed it cut the journey times across the continent of Asia enormously. It gave Russia the chance to develop its Far Eastern markets and territories more vigorously but it was the pursuit of these by Tsar Nicholas II that led to war with Japan in 1904–05 and Russia's defeat.

Domestic policies took precedence over Russia's foreign policy under Alexander III as he sought to strengthen the autocracy at home above all else. This meant the reversal of some of his predecessor's reforms and a renewed interest in Russification. Certainly, Russia achieved a great deal in terms of its industrial, rather than agricultural, development as a result and the tsar believed that this was the wisest course to take. However, he was storing up major problems for the regime which began to emerge in the early years of the twentieth century and which were not overcome by the time war broke out in 1914. Because of this, the Romanov dynasty was eventually overthrown in the revolution of 1917.

Death of Alexander III

Alexander III died in 1894 aged 49 and was succeeded by his son who became Tsar Nicholas II who was to be the last tsar of Russia. Unusually for a Romanov, there were no suspicious circumstances at the death of Alexander III. Whereas Paul, Alexander II and Nicholas II were all assassinated and Alexander I was rumoured to have faked his death so as to become a wandering monk, Alexander III merely passed away peacefully. Perhaps he was fortunate to miss the turmoil into which Russia was about to enter.

His political views were comparable to those of Nicholas I in that he hoped to stem the tide of change simply by bolstering the autocracy and using its weight to crush opposition. If such a policy was unwise in the middle decades of the century then it was increasingly foolish to pursue it in the last years of the century. The policy of Russification that Nicholas I had applied as a punishment to Poland after its rebellion 1830–31 was reinvigorated by Alexander II after 1863; Alexander III, however, enforced this nationalistic approach as widely as he could on hitherto loyal provinces. Finland, the Ukraine and the Baltic coastlands were all treated in this way. There was also discrimination between classes as the tsar elevated the role of nobles at the expense of ordinary Russians. This was in an attempt to make up for their economic decline as a class and to keep their support as the core of Russian society. At the other extreme, the anti-Jewish pogroms gave vent to a long held prejudice.

While Alexander seemed ready to try to homogenise Russian society, so his economic policies encouraged a diversification of groups. In agriculture, the kulak class of successful farmers emerged with more wealth behind them and the least able peasants reverted to a position like that of the serfs a third of a century earlier. Industrial growth was impressive and was partly at the expense of farming. Foreign investment played a major part and the construction of the Trans-Siberian railway functioned as a showpiece project as well as eventually allowing the rapid transport of goods across the whole width of the empire for the first time. The work of Bunge and Witte deserves recognition for the progress made under Alexander III since it enabled Russia to enter the twentieth century with a semi-industrialised economy and a better (but not adequate) base from which to prepare itself for the future. The nineteenth century had seen Russia engaged in conflicts primarily in Europe and the Near East but the twentieth century was to see it become involved in global conflicts. The Alliance with France and, later, the war against Japan were signs of what was to come.

Note

1 A. Gerschenkron, *Economic Backwardness in Historical Perspective*, Harvard University Press, Cambridge MA, 1962.

Chapter 6

Epilogue
Russia 1894–1917

The reign of Nicholas II which lasted from 1894 to 1917 turned out to be the last under the Romanovs. It picked up many of the themes and policies of Alexander III not least because of the continued dominance of his ministers and consequently took with it many of its failings too. With the maintenance of severe repression, it was hardly surprising that unrest erupted once more. Revolution broke out in 1905 and again in 1917; on both occasions it was triggered by foreign policy failures set against a backdrop of economic and social unrest.

Russia under a new tsar

Despite the accession of Tsar Nicholas II, Pobedonostsev continued as the chief adviser and Witte remained as Russia's Minister of Finance. Their positions seemed to be strengthened by the new ruler since he was by most accounts a weak and indecisive leader. He was not lacking in intelligence, though, and had been given some preparation by his father for the time when he would rule Russia. He had travelled quite widely, visiting the Far East and becoming the director of the Trans-Siberian Railway in the 1890s. Yet when he became tsar there was uncertainty as to what his policies were going to be. Many hoped that the demise of his father would signal a more liberal period – but they were quickly disappointed when he received a delegation of nobles from local governments in January 1895. He said to them plainly that he intended to continue the policies of Alexander.

   This determined attitude hardly fits the image of a man who vacillated in his decisions. However, he had fixed views on a limited number of matters and seemed ready to let others govern on his behalf for much of the rest of the time. Above all, he stubbornly believed in the autocratic system and the domination of the Orthodox Church. Because of this he allowed the pogroms against the Jews to continue and in the early years of the twentieth century they reached a new peak. In April 1903 the Kishinev outbreak left fifty or so dead; the attacks that occurred later were worse, with more than one hundred killed in October 1905 at Odessa. His belief in the autocratic system also meant that he neglected the growing calls for political reform within Russia. He saw no need to introduce a constitution and instead upheld the degree of censorship and control that he had inherited. The 'Temporary Regulations' were extended and local governments were restricted even further in their ability to raise taxes, which meant that the central administration accrued more power to itself. Likewise, the process of Russification was unabated and Finland in particular suffered as its laws were brought

Tsar Nicholas II and Tsarina Alexandra (Source: David King Collection, London)

into line with those of Russia and a new system of military service was imposed from 1899. The governor general, Bobrikov, was widely detested as he pushed for more changes; he acquired the right to dismiss non-Finnish officials and in 1903 tightened up the surveillance of the secret police. These policies were foolish since they immediately alienated an otherwise loyal and compliant part of the Russian empire.

New political movements and new signs of unrest were emerging in the 1890s that by the turn of the century were beginning to present a serious challenge to the tsarist system. Industrial strikes became more common as the huge factories allowed large numbers of workers to combine together and to come under the influence of political agitators. Marxism was beginning to win more supporters through the work of Plekhanov and especially Lenin. They led the Social Democratic Party which formed in 1898 and attracted, for instance, a significant number of Jews. It soon split into the Bolshevik (majority) and Menshevik (minority) groups with Lenin leading the former and calling for a programme of violent revolution. An alternative way forward was put forward by the Social Revolutionary Party which was founded in 1901, the roots of which lay in Populism's call for an alliance with the peasantry. However, they too were ready to use violence to achieve their ends – and sometimes co-operated with the Bolsheviks because of this – including the use of assassins. In 1902 one of the 'SR's', Balmashev, murdered the Minister of the Interior called Sipyagin. Nicholas' secret police did manage to arrest a number of activists. A third political group to develop during these years was from the liberals to be found among students, professional classes and local government leaders and who founded the Union of Liberation in 1903. Their agenda was less dangerous than the previous two groups in that they did not agree with the use of violence (even though one liberal, Karpovich, killed the Minister of Education called Bogolepov in 1903). Its aims were for Russia to adopt a constitution with a wide franchise; thus, in 1905 the liberals formed a new party called the Constitutional Democratic Party or 'Cadets' for short.

The 1905 Revolution

With this much hostility among educated public opinion and the restless nature of industrial workers whose living conditions were very poor, there were all the ingredients needed for a serious threat to the regime. What triggered it was the war against Japan that Russia had begun to fight in 1904. The conflict had been started by a surprise attack by the Japanese against the Russian fleet at Port Arthur and what lay behind it was the two countries' growing rivalry for influence in the Far East, especially in China. The run of the battles soon turned against Russia which felt humiliated by such a small and distant neighbour. In 1905 a new Russian fleet – but one composed of ageing ships – under Rozhdestvensky was sunk. Public opinion turned against the tsar and demanded reform; the sequence of events was to look eerily like that of 1917.

In January 1905 a huge demonstration by workers in Saint Petersburg tried to present to the tsar a list of grievances. Some 400 000 or so turned out onto the streets only to be met by troops who were under orders to maintain control. In the tense circumstances, they began to shoot at the crowds and eventually killed several hundred people. The massacre became known as 'Bloody Sunday' and destroyed the image of the tsar as a benevolent figure who cared for his subjects. A general strike ensued in the capital which then spread to the provinces and began to attract the support of peasants as well. There was sympathy for the protests among Russia's professional classes too. Lacking reliable troops – many of which were still in the Far East – Tsar Nicholas II granted the 'October Manifesto' which incorporated basic rights for subjects and an outline constitution. The freedom of the press and of association were allowed and a state duma was to be elected. These measures gave the tsar more time to organise his troops and resources.

The Fundamental Laws of April 1906 reaffirmed the idea of autocracy but also provided for a parliament elected by workers, peasants and nobles with the latter having most impact. A State Council was chosen by the tsar and by the duma's representatives but he retained the right to rule by decree if necessary and he could veto any legislation passed by the duma. The tsar tried to win over the peasants by abolishing the remaining redemption payments in 1905 and allowing them to leave the mir at any point from 1906. He also passed some measures designed to crush the unrest with military courts appointed to try suspects; almost 1000 executions followed. This was surpassed, however, by the 1500 assassinations in 1906 and another 3000 in 1907 carried out by the SRs. Russia remained in crisis and the tsar's problems were compounded by the resignation of Witte in 1905. A desperate end to the tsarist system seemed to be possible.

Recovery of the regime

Witte was succeeded by Peter Stolypin who set about reversing the political defeats that Nicholas had suffered. While the First Duma (May–July 1906) was dominated by the Cadets they were quite peaceable compared to the SRs and Social Democrats. The Second Duma (February–June 1907) fell under the influence of these more extreme groups and so firm measures were taken against them. The assembly was dissolved and the opposition leaders were arrested on spurious grounds so as to try to silence them. The result was that the Third Duma (1907–1912) was much more moderate again – primarily because of the changes to electoral qualifications – and its debates were devoted to educational and budgetary issues. Neither of these were revolutionary and it seemed as if the duma had become tamed. The press was censored and more than 200 newspapers were closed down completely; a police state was created with the Okhrana secret police. Stolypin combined the management of the dumas with reforms elsewhere to try to win support for the tsar and deprive the revolutionary groups of their support. The industrial policies continued so as to strengthen the regime but there were government reforms for agriculture too. These had been conspicuously lacking in the 1880s and 1890s. The Peasant Bank became more active in providing loans to kulaks and several million peasants were thereby able to leave the communal system of farming. More land was taken into cultivation and output rose over the next decade; in the period just before the outbreak of the Great War (1910–13), Russia's grain production increased from 74 to 90 million tons. This was the sort of agricultural growth that Russia had needed decades before but which neither Alexander II nor Alexander III had been prepared to bring about.

The fall of the empire

On the eve of war in 1914, the Romanov dynasty seemed to be poised to recover from the setbacks it had suffered ten years before. It was true that there was a renewal of industrial protest with another wave of strikes; and it was also true that Stolypin's assassination in 1911 had allowed the maverick monk Rasputin to gain more influence at the court. But its economic position was improving rapidly and the parliamentary opposition seemed to have been contained. What altered the direction of events was of course the war. Russia was drawn into the Great War by its support for Slavs in the Balkan states, specifically Serbia, and its alliance with France ensured that the network of agreements and military plans devised over the preceding years came into effect immediately. The pressures that this placed on the economy and the deficient military preparations led to disasters for the tsar. Defeats in eastern Europe by Germany, massive casualties and desperate shortages for the civilians in the major towns sparked off more strikes and, finally, mutinies among troops in the capital. Nicholas II was personally blamed for the war defeats once he had left for the frontline and the dynasty as a whole lost any remaining public support when the tsarina took charge. She was rumoured to be a German spy and the lover of Rasputin. When the tsar tried to return to the court in Saint Petersburg, he was stopped from doing so by railwaymen and the telegraph sent to him by the leader of the duma, Rodzianko, said all that it had to: 'Too late'. The February Revolution of 1917 removed the tsar from power and substituted it with a provisional government that was itself toppled by the Bolsheviks in October.

What had gone wrong? Russia's persistent failure to modernise in the nineteenth century had left it with an economy that was still relatively backward but one which had developed sufficiently for a hostile intelligentsia and then an aggressive working class to emerge. The reforms of Alexander II were not enough to ensure a gradual transition from a servile to an industrial economy and the political concessions wrung from Nicholas II were too limited. Russia consequently lurched between reaction and reform. The Crimean War had exposed the need for the latter in the 1850s and the defeat by Japan in 1905 had underlined it again. The German victories of 1914–17 rammed home the point once more and contributed to the severe economic shortages of winter 1916. This explosive mix finally flung Imperial Russia into its last crisis.

In the violent aftermath of the February and October revolutions, the Romanov family was shot dead *en masse* by Bolsheviks. One of the grandest of Europe's dynasties was annihilated in a basement and one of the continent's oldest empires was plunged into further chaos.

Glossary

absolutism   when total control is exercised by the ruler.

Alliance Solidaire   Tsar Alexander I's revised proposal dating from 1818 for a Christian brotherhood of monarchs based on the Holy Alliance of 1815.

Arakcheyevschina   the period from 1815 to 1825 when Alexander I allowed one man, Arakcheyev, almost complete control of Russia's domestic affairs.

Armed Neutrality of the North   an alliance of Baltic states that was revived by Russia during the Napoleonic Wars.

assignats   a form of paper money.

autocracy   a system of rule in which the ruler takes all the decisions his or herself.

black clergy   village priests. *See also* white clergy.

Charter to the Towns   a list of rights granted to towns by Catherine the Great in 1785, including the formation of representative institutions.

Charter to the Nobility   a list of rights and privileges granted to the nobles by Catherine the Great in 1785 in which it was confirmed that they were free from compulsory service to the state. They were also exempt from taxation and corporal punishment.

citizen   member of a city or state in which the individual has rights. *See also* subject.

Coalitions   four of these were formed by some of the great powers in the revolutionary and Napoleonic wars to fight against France.

colleges   bureaucratic eighteenth-century government ministries.

Congress Poland   the Russian-dominated Polish state created at the Congress of Vienna.

Continental System   an economic blockade of Britain by Napoleon begun in 1806.

Cossack   a semi-independent fighting force based within Russia but loyal to the tsar.

Decembrist   a member of the army rebellion that took place in December 1825 against the new tsar, Nicholas I.

Dual Ministry   the combined Ministry of Education and Ministry of Ecclesiastical Affairs, formed in 1817.

Duma   Russian term for an assembly or council at either national or local level.

empire   a political structure in which one state rules over other territories.

Grande Armée   the multinational army of 600 000 men that Napoleon took to fight against Russia in 1812.

Holy Alliance   Tsar Alexander I's scheme for a Christian brotherhood of monarchs to govern Europe, devised in 1815.

Kremlin   Moscow's government buildings.

military colonies   frontier settlements composed of soldiers on active service and peasant farmers.

mir   Russian word for village or commune.

Official Nationality   the policy of Nicholas I's reign summed up as 'Orthodoxy, Autocracy, Nationality'.

Over Procurator of the Holy Synod   the leader of the Orthodox Church in Russia. The post was always given to a layman.

Permanent Council   a short-lived advisory body to Alexander I, 1801–10.

pogrom   an organised attack by a mob against a minority group. In Russia this was typically the Jews.

pood   a unit of weight, equal to 36 lbs or 16.3 kg.

Procurator-General   the leader of the Senate.

redemption payments   money paid by ex-serfs to buy their land from the nobles. It was repaid at 6 per cent interest over 49 years.

rescript   an imperial decree.

Russians   a generic name used to describe the Great Russians based around Moscow, the Little Russians of the Ukraine and the White Russians of Belarus. The dominant group in the Russian Empire as a whole was that of the Great Russians.

Russification   the process or policy of making non-Russian populations adopt the Russian culture and language.

scorched earth policy   a military tactic used, for example in 1812, in which a defending army destroys all sources of food and shelter to slow down the advance of an enemy.

Secret Expedition   the secret police.

Sections   departments within Nicholas I's own Personal Chancery.

Sejm   the Polish lower house of parliament.

Senate   an advisory body for tsars from 1711, led by the Procurator-General, and responsible in the eighteenth century for the government of Russia while the tsar was abroad. From 1802 it supervised other government bodies and maintained Russian laws.

Senatorial Party   a pressure group based within the Senate during Alexander I's reign, leading figures in which were the Vorontsovs.

serf   agricultural workers that were the property of noble landowners. *See also* state peasant.

Slavophiles   an intellectual group that emerged in the 1830s and who promoted a Russian (Slav) solution to any problems the tsar encountered. They championed the role of the mir. *See also* westernisers.

state peasant   agricultural workers that were the property of the Russian state. *See also* serfs.

subject   member of a state who has no guaranteed rights but is subordinate to the rule of, for instance, a monarch.

Unofficial Committee   a group of four advisers to Alexander I who held sway to *c.*1803, composed of Czartoryski, Stroganov, Kochubei and Novosiltsov.

westernisers   an intellectual group that emerged in the 1830s and who promoted a west European solution to Russia's problems, including capitalism and a constitution. *See also* Slavophiles.

white clergy   monks. *See also* black clergy.

zemstvo   a rural council (plural zemstvos or zemstva).

Further reading

General texts and chapter I

There are several general texts on Russia that are widely available. The most thorough for the nineteenth and early twentieth century is still Hugh Seton-Watson's *The Russian Empire 1801–1917* which forms part of the Oxford History of Modern Europe series. A lighter touch and easier read is provided by J.N. Westwood in *Endurance and Endeavour, Russian History 1812–1992* although its treatment of the nineteenth century is not as detailed as for the twentieth. It also provides a helpful critical bibliography. A major American text is Nicholas Riasonovsky's *A History of Russia* which traces the country's development from prehistoric times to the present day yet still offers clear overviews of each tsar's reign. Two books in the same series explain the recent interpretations and historiography of the period. David Saunders' *Russia in the Age of Reaction and Reform 1801–1881* is structured very clearly and includes several chapters on each of the tsars. It is followed by Hans Rogger's *Russia in the Age of Modernisation and Revolution 1881–1917* which is organised in a more complex way. A combination of social themes and then political analysis is available in *Russia: People and Empire 1552–1917* by Geoffrey Hosking which offers some long-term perspectives.

The economic development of Russia does not fit into the convenient pattern of reigns that the political histories have, but M.E. Falkus' *The Industrialisation of Russia 1700–1914* is a useful if slightly dated summary. Agriculture, which dominated the Russian economy throughout the period has been analysed best by Jerome Blum in his *Lord and Peasant in Russia*. The two economic sectors have been studied by Alexander Gershenkron in *Agrarian Policies and Industrialisation: Russia 1861–1917* although each of the last two books cited are major works of historical research.

The Eastern Question dominated Russian foreign policy in the European sphere and two books tackle it well; A.L. Macfie's *The Eastern Question 1774–1923* includes a document section while M.S. Anderson's *The Eastern Question* commentates on the diplomatic aspects above all.

The sources already listed provide some information on Russia in the eighteenth century though none of them give a snapshot of Russia in 1800.

Chapter 2: Alexander I

Undoubtedly the best modern biography of Alexander I is by Janet Hartley in her recent work entitled simply *Alexander I* which is a political study. However, her more recent publication on the Russian people which includes some of the most up-to-date research, *A Social History of the Russian Empire 1650–1825* underlines where her strengths lie. The lives of leading ministers have also been written up by Marc Raeff in *Michael Speransky* and by Michael Jenkins in the case of *Arakcheyev* although the latter is rather superficial.

Chapter 3: Nicholas I

This reign has been neglected by historians, perhaps because of the lacklustre character of the tsar but one biography stands out by Nicholas Riasonovsky *Nicholas I and Official Nationality in Russia*. Much more recently Derek Offord has written a short book on the emergence of Russia's intellectual currents in the reign in *Nineteenth Century Russia: Opposition to Autocracy*. The thoughts of some of the tsar's opponents have been published in their own right, the most obvious case being that of Alexander Herzen's *Childhood, Youth and Exile* which covers the period up to 1838.

Chapter 4: Alexander II

By far the biggest area of debate has been over the emancipation of the serfs in 1861. Major contributions have been made by Daniel Field with *The End of Serfdom* which looks at the causes. The previously mentioned work by Blum is also relevant. An accessible guide to the Emancipation Decree is contained in *Alexander II: Emancipation and Reform in Russia 1855–1881* by Maureen Perrie. Also important to the debate has been *The Politics of Autocracy 1857–64* by Alfred Rieber. The Great Reforms have been tackled very well by Hugh Seton-Watson in his general text listed above.

Chapter 5: Alexander III

This reign also suffers from a general lack of material for the general reader, perhaps because it is seen as a mere forerunner to the dramatic and revolutionary events of the next reign. Alexander III does not have a modern biographer, although his first minister does in R.F. Byrnes' *Pobedonostsev*.

Chapter 6: Epilogue, Russia 1894–1917

The literature on this period is voluminous because of the outbreak of the Bolshevik Revolution and the creation of the Soviet Union in the place of the Russian Empire. Among the more readable accounts of the period are Dominic Lieven's *Russia and the Origins of the First World War* and of course John Reed's *Ten Days that Shook the World*. As a reference book *The Blackwell Encyclopaedia of the Russian Revolution* edited by Shukman is invaluable, while a detailed narrative account of the convulsions in Russia in 1917 and immediately afterwards have been written up at length by E.H. Carr.

Index

DATE DUE			ISSCW 947
			.07
			C466
	CHAPMAN, TIM		
	IMPERIAL RUSSIA,		
	1801-1905 PAPER		

ISSCW   947
         .07
         C466

HOUSTON PUBLIC LIBRARY
CENTRAL LIBRARY